ART: The Way It Is

JOHN ADKINS RICHARDSON

Professor of Art and Design, Southern Illinois University at Edwardsville

Second Edition

PRENTICE-HALL, INC., Englewood Cliffs, N.J.   **HARRY N. ABRAMS, INC.**, New York

I am grateful to the University of Illinois Press for
permission to use brief passages from my book *Modern
Art and Scientific Thought*.

Second Edition 1980

Fifth Printing 1984

LIBRARY OF CONGRESS CATALOGING IN PUBLICATION DATA

Richardson, John Adkins.
Art: the way it is.
Bibliography: p.
Includes index.
1. Art. I. Title.
N7425.R48 1979   701'.1   79-89046
ISBN 0-13-049148-9

Library of Congress Catalog Card Number: 79-89046

Contents

1

Who's Putting on Whom? 11

2

Image Creation and Convention 32

3

Line and Form 56

Preface and Acknowledgments

This is a different kind of book. On leafing through it, you will find not only the customary masterpieces and diagrams but also cartoons, comic strips, popular illustrations, and other things rarely encountered in an art appreciation book. Normally, only masterworks appear. And usually the writer spends his time demonstrating why serious painting is more complex and genuine, more sincere and more profound, than the kinds of pictures most people like when they're not pretending to be "cultured."

But it does not necessarily follow that one *should* always prefer what is more complex, genuine, sincere, and profound. Those of us who spend our lives concerned with the arts usually do not like what is commonplace or simple, and that is natural. The true sports fan is bored by routine performance; he is fascinated by the exceptional. The professional mathematician would go mad had he nothing to do but routine applications of the calculus. The more we know of a thing the less concerned we are with its ordinary manifestations.

Similarly, when one knows very little about a subject one is apt to like what is most familiar and to be impressed with what seems difficult. As it happens, what is most familiar is quite often mediocre, and what a layman considers remarkable a professional would look upon as routine. College and high school art teachers wage eternal war against the hackneyed nature of most cartooning and illustration and dutifully oppose the shallowness of "dime-store" reproductions.

This book, however, accepts common taste as valid. But it is motivated by a genuinely serious concern for civilized values. The professional art historian or critic who reads it will realize that it takes its lead from the work of men like E. H. Gombrich, who recognize that a good deal of what appeals to people in popular art is not what is simpleminded so much as what is fundamental, and that what appears in Michelangelo in elevated form may be present in another fashion in the work of the cartoonist. And, since people unfamiliar with art are more likely, as a rule, to grasp the significance of "Tarzan" than they are to appreciate the subtleties of either Rembrandt or Picasso, it seems a good idea to begin with Tarzan rather than Rembrandt. This is not to argue that a Tarzan cartoon is equal to a Rembrandt painting; I contend only that one can learn a great deal about the latter by way of the former. In other words, this volume is based on the assumptions that it is possible to talk sensibly about art without demeaning it, to convey its values without preaching, and to do this in a book of rather modest cost.

We should not presume that one art book can do *everything*. Lectures, discussions, supplementary reading, and exposure to actual works in museums, galleries, and studios are also necessary. Yet, learning is not dependent on any of that. To help in moving beyond this volume, a bibliography and a glossary are provided. The index contains the names of all the artists mentioned. And, because many of the names are foreign, a pronunciation guide has been supplied.

Several of the reproductions are repeated over and over again. The purpose of doing this is threefold: (1) It enables the reader to grow familiar with a number of great works and to appreciate the fullness and richness of some exemplary ones; (2) it assists the reader's understanding by limiting the sheer mass of factual material to be digested; and (3) it makes it easy to refer to a picture without turning back fifty pages to where it first appeared.

Surely this book has faults. But it has some virtues too, and I cannot take credit for all that may be good within these pages. Much of that should go to others. Among these are the following: Dr. Harry Hilberry, who suggested by example the application to art appreciation of Heinrich Wölfflin's theory of style. Velta Inglis, who did yeo-person work in tracing down obscure photographic sources and securing addresses. Walter Welch of Prentice-Hall and his assistant, Marilyn Brauer, who have given more advice, support, and time than any author has a right to expect. And Paul Anbinder and Patricia Gilchrest of Harry N. Abrams, Inc., must be credited for editorial suggestions and, still more, for the exercise of superhuman restraint. My gratitude also goes to Barbara Lyons at Abrams for help in obtaining photographs. Of course, without the assistance of artists, museums, galleries, publishers, and photographic services, a book of this kind could never be produced. Although they are recognized elsewhere in the captions and the photographic credits, I offer them here my special thanks.

My colleagues at Southern Illinois University in Edwardsville have helped me by giving me altogether undeserved ego-reinforcement and have actively hindered me by election to the most time-consuming offices and committees. Perhaps in part because of the latter, the administration has been graciously tolerant of my essays into the fields of cartooning and commercial illustration. The students at SIUE have proved invaluable as resources, critics, and good friends. But more than to anyone else this book owes its existence to Dr. Betty Richardson, without whose friendship it would not have been begun.

JOHN ADKINS RICHARDSON

Preface to the Second Edition

What was said of the individuals and institutions in the Preface to the first edition of *Art: The Way It Is* can be said as well of the second edition. But, of course, there are others who have made recommendations and submitted ideas in response to the first version of this book. In particular, university and college faculty and students have been immensely helpful to me in my attempt to make *Art: The Way It Is* a work of continuing relevance. While the present edition surely contains the kinds of flaws from which no human production is entirely free, it is a more polished and comprehensive work than it was upon its first appearance.

The section devoted to architecture has been substantially enlarged, and modern architecture has been given more detailed treatment than was possible before. Too, I have added discussions of Minimalism, earth sculpture, Conceptual Art, fiber art, and jewelry, and have included additional artists and works from the past and the present. Virtually all the diagrams from the first edition have been completely redone, much to the benefit of both clarity and graphic appeal. Colorplates have been increased by 50 percent, and there are also more black-and-white illustrations. In the course of several reprintings the text has been purged of minor errors and printer's faux pas. A few clarifications from specialists in optics, physics, and the use of the pitchfork have caused the author to shift emphases slightly in a few places. We have tried to limit the use of vernacular expressions that might "date" too easily. Discriminatory pronouns which, in English, conventionally impose masculinity upon anonymous subjects such as "the artist" have proved somewhat more resistant to change than might be expected, but the editors and I have done our cautious best.

At Prentice-Hall, my editor and friend, Norwell Therien, Jr., and his assistant, Nancy Joseph, have taken care of innumerable pesky details and business matters in connection with the production of this volume. At Harry N. Abrams, I am pleased to acknowledge the help of the entire staff. Once again, Barbara Lyons produced photographs when no museum, gallery, or individual artist could. Joanne Greenspun, who edited this edition, contributed invaluable assistance and a truly remarkable efficiency to the production. The design is the work of Judith Michael and is, as you can see, a stunning format.

Locally, apart from the university personnel mentioned above, I must thank the following individuals for their support and help: Charles Cox and SIUE Photographic Services, for the quality of anything they undertake is always first-rate and highly professional. Dr. Floyd Coleman for continuing support and occasional badgering; and, to him and Professor Michael J. Smith and Dr. Pamela Decoteau, collectively, my gratitude for an integrity and fairmindedness that ameliorate the tensions of the present in academe. Amy Conger for intellectual stimulation and advice acerbic. Rick and Barbara Luster for assistance with the tiresome business of photographing fast-moving cars. And, finally, Dr. Glenda M. Lawhorn, a human touchstone to "reality," whose endeavors on my behalf go beyond what words can tell.

J.A.R.
July, 1979

1

Who's Putting on Whom?

You and I, reader, might as well level with each other straight off. For it is important that we understand each other's position.

What you have in your hands is a book on what is commonly called art appreciation, that is, on the understanding and enjoyment of pictures, statues, and the like. To many it seems odd that anyone wishes to be instructed in such activity. An acquaintance with art has no direct bearing on earning a livelihood. Nor is it necessary to a happy and fruitful life; one can get along quite nicely without knowing a Picasso from a put-on.

Still, there is a peculiar universality about books on art appreciation; they are to be encountered everywhere. And such prevalence suggests a need.

Frequently, the need is connected with one's social life. Some readers may hope to gain a bit of confidence regarding home decor. Single men must realize that it's hard to be attractive if their principal topics of conversation are injection systems, the World Series, and how many times they were intoxicated over the weekend. Too, there is real utility in knowing a little about the arts if one wishes to advance in a corporate structure from the lower to the executive levels. Yet, art is a puzzle to many people, even when they know what they like, and you may be hoping to find its key within these pages.

Such self-interested views are not altogether foreign to the writer who wishes to

1
Drawing made with a pen held in the teeth

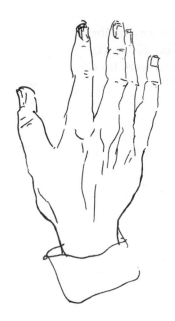

2
Left-handed drawing of the author's right hand

overcome what I call "creeping meatball-ism," that is, the increasing number of people whose idea of aesthetic progress is the paving over of all that is natural or happens to be old. What most laymen are apt to want is just a bit of polish. And that is the most an author dares hope to achieve. True, the attempt to apply a bit of polish often leads to something that is not so superficial. But I cannot promise to do more than gloss surfaces, for there are basic difficulties in dealing with a thing so all-encompassing as art.

A famous art historian, Erwin Panofsky, once raised against the idea of art appreciation the objection that it is doomed to mislead the very people it is supposed to serve. He wrote that "He who teaches innocent people to understand art without bothering about classical languages, boresome historical methods and dusty old documents, deprives naiveté of its charm without correcting its errors."[1] There is much to be said for this way of looking at the matter, but it fails to recognize that many other forces operate to deprive naiveté of any charm whatever. At least this is true in contemporary industrial society. It may not be true in other societies. A peasant rustic's enthusiasm for the folk crafts of his people is charming, and frequently the objects themselves are very appealing. But what passes for good taste in suburbia, the garish distractions that surround the urban dweller and the billboards afflicting the rural landscape, are all invitations to depravity. Perhaps art appreciation books can do little against these influences, but they can scarcely do more harm. The visual clutter that assails us all is, if you wish, a form of pollution as damaging to the sensibilities of the unwary as fertilizers are to a stream. As a matter of fact, the situation is quite similar. For, just as excessive nitrogen fed into a pond produces overgrowth that chokes out animal life, so the plethora of images in our culture tends to stifle the quality of perception.

But there is also something to be said on behalf of our excess. The dullest living layman is much better educated about pictures than were any of the generations that preceded him. He is exposed to more imagery by far than were his counterparts during the Italian Renaissance or the Golden Age of Greece. In Leonardo da Vinci's day his *Mona Lisa* was seen by but a few hundred of the elite. Today color reproductions reveal her smile to everyone. René Huyghe has said that all modern men are "importuned, and obsessed, by the visual."[2] When one considers the degree to which our lives are dominated by motion pictures and television, by diagrams and news photos, by maps, advertising illustrations, and comic strips, one sees how aptly the description *visual* fits our everyday existence. Throughout most of history a picture of any but the rudest kind has been a thing of magic and delight, but today everyone takes "living color" pretty much for granted.

We are, all of us, experts at looking. What few of us can do is *see*. If all of us knew how to see, then all of us could draw. I know that sounds outrageous, absurd on the face of it, but I assure you it is true.

Figure 1 is a drawing of a man's head that I have done with a felt pen held in my teeth. Figure 2 is a similarly shaky rendering of my right hand done by my left, the one that rarely holds a pen. No claim of quality is made for either case. I do insist, however, that neither rendering looks amateurish. Manual dexterity has very little to do with art, even in drawing; what drawing has to do with is understanding the visual. I am not particularly dextrous, but I have learned to see in terms of two-dimensional representation. Knowing how to draw is, for the most part, a question of knowing what to look for. Some will say that it is, in any case, a matter of something called "talent." Well, of course, some people have greater talent for grasping the visual facts than do others—just as some have a superior ability in mathematical reasoning, and others a gift for sleight of

hand.[3] But art appreciation requires no special aptitude. On the contrary, it is my conviction that the inadvertent education all of us received from magazines and comic strips can be the basis of real insight.

The premise of this book is that what is appealing in the popular arts is not what is naive so much as what is basic. From this it follows that the best way to understand art for those with no special interest in it is by way of its baser side.

What Is Art?

It is customary in art appreciation books to define the term *art* early on. In doing so authors hope to distinguish between what is worthy of attention and what is not. Curiously, it almost invariably occurs that—regardless of the definition—what is *really* art comprises a group of works such as those in figure 3 and excludes from consideration the kinds of things we find in figure 4. The reaction of the reader to this description is all too frequently "I guess I just don't like art," in which case he remains a sullen slob, or "I had better pretend to like only what Professor Smudgebottom, B.A., M.F.A., Ph.D., likes or I will seem a fool," in which case he becomes a phony, pure and very simple. I hope to avoid these consequences by a special strategem. But before I reveal my ploy I wish to turn some of yours aside.

It may be helpful to look at what many readers consider art. One of the most common presumptions is that art is an imitation of reality. And few of us would dispute that the amazing still lifes (fig. 5) of William Harnett (1814–1892) are art. *After the Hunt* seems so like the things it mimics that one might believe the rabbit could be taken up and cooked. Only an uncommon fool would deny that such illusion has artistic merit merely because the thrill it produces appeals to common tastes. But consider figure 6, a photograph of a tableau by Edward Kienholz

3
Types of images that
are unquestionably
"art" in the opinion
of most authorities

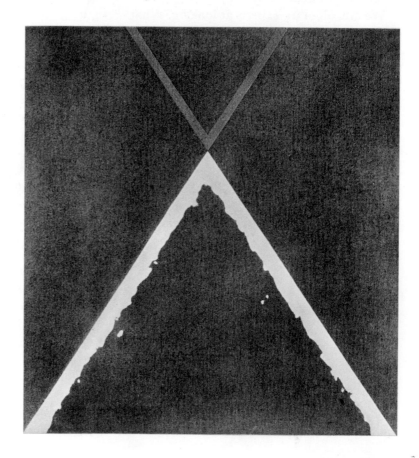

4
Types of images that are not considered "art"
by most authorities

5

WILLIAM HARNETT. *After the Hunt.* 1885. Oil on canvas, 71 × 48". The Fine Arts Museums of San Francisco. Gift of H.K.S. Williams to the Mildred Anna Williams Collection

6

EDWARD KIENHOLZ.
Back Seat, Dodge—38. 1964. Mixed media,
height 66″. Collection Lyn Kienholz, Los Angeles

7

Model airplane

8

ROY LICHTENSTEIN.
Brattata. 1962.
Oil on canvas, 42 × 42″.
Courtesy of Greenberg Gallery of
Contemporary Art, St. Louis

(born 1927) entitled *Back Seat, Dodge—38.* The Kienholz is as realistic as you can get; it *is* real. This actually is a 1938 Dodge sedan, although it is so truncated that the rear seat is up against the fire wall. Probably most people would respond that it isn't realistic, it's just real; it's junk, trash.[4]

Very well, the obvious response to Kienholz is, "I don't mean a duplication of reality when I say 'imitation of reality'; I mean something that involves more apparent skill, more artifice . . . like the Harnett." Fine. Is figure 7 a work of art? It is exact and to scale, a perfect physical model of an old airplane.

I built it and I don't consider it art. It's a trivial exercise in painstaking small-scale construction. It's worthwhile, you understand. And I got a kick out of doing it. But the fact is that I created it only to use as a model for part of a painting that I do consider art.

And how about this painting (fig. 8)? Roy Lichtenstein (born 1923) gives one the impression of imitating a comic-strip panel right down to the Benday dots that printers use to give color to the pictures (see page 289). I imagine that most readers would concede the possibility that the cartoonist on whose work this is based is some sort of artist but would think less of the man who copied the original.

Of course, you might respond to all these examples by using another presumption, saying that art has to be beautiful and that this stuff "isn't even pretty." Possibly it is true that art has to be beautiful in some fashion or other. A good deal of it is, clearly. For example, *Le Moulin de la Galette* (fig. 9) by Auguste Renoir (1841–1919) is actually pretty. There is no better way of describing it. But, then, pinup girls, apple pies, mint juleps, and gardenias are also pretty. Usually we don't consider those things artistic in and of

themselves. And a lot of what might be called art by many is not attractive in any sense normally connoted by the term.

If beauty is the measure of artistry, what is one to make of such a work as the *Crucifixion* from the famous *Isenheim Altarpiece* (fig. 10) by Matthias Grünewald (active c. 1503–1528)? It is an image of absolute ghastliness. This Christ does not suffer a purely spiritual pain; he suffers for all mankind in a horrible, perfectly physical way. The crown of thorns bites into his forehead and draws blood; his flesh, of a greenish pallor, is marked by the putrescent sores and scars of brutal treatment. His lips are blue, spotted by the foam-

9
PIERRE AUGUSTE RENOIR. *Le Moulin de la Galette*. 1876.
Oil on canvas, 51½ × 69″. The Louvre, Paris

10

MATTHIAS GRÜNEWALD. *Crucifixion,*
center panel of *Isenheim Altarpiece* (closed). c. 1510–15. Oil on panel,
8′10″ × 10′1″. Unterlinden Museum, Colmar, France

flecked vomit of approaching death. The picture inspires disgust, even revulsion. And yet it is a powerfully moving image of sacrifice, a conception that brings home the meaning of Christ's passion through an extremely naturalistic treatment. It is perhaps the outstanding example of ugliness put in service of devotion. Is it not art?

I could continue in this fashion, challenging commonplace conceptions of art with obvious exceptions, but I think the point is clear. No simple definition is sufficient to describe everything that comes under the heading of art. For that matter, I do not believe that any definition, whether commonplace or esoteric, could be true and also useful. My belief may be debatable. But that doesn't really matter. Fortunately, we don't need to define art in order to talk about it.

It may seem preposterous to assert that we can discuss a thing without knowing precisely what we are talking about, but we all do it constantly without troubling ourselves at all. The everyday speech of the most fastidious and lucid speakers is filled with inexactitude. A very important thinker, philosopher Ludwig Wittgenstein, once used the example of the term *game* to make this clear. He says that we can look at all sorts of games—board games, card games, ball games, Olympic games, and so on. We call each a "game," and yet they have very little in common. For example, compare a board game such as chess with contract bridge. There are many correspondences, but the element of chance is completely absent in chess. In most respects of actual play, the game of baseball is quite unlike either the board or card games. Moreover, some card games—solitaire for instance—are not competitive in the normal sense. Similarly, crapshooters are really playing against the odds, not against the other shooters. Likewise, a child playing a game of ball by himself, throwing the ball against a wall and catching it, is competing only with himself and gravity. Finally, think of ring-around-a-rosie, where almost all the features we associate with a game have disappeared; only the constant of amusement remains. Still, not everything amusing is called a game.

As Wittgenstein points out, what we see summed up by the word *game* is a series of *family resemblances*, like those of a real family. One can say that games form a family of activities. We are not stopped from using the word *game* because the network of similarities is so complicated.

When one deals with things in this way, he is using what logicians call an *ostensive definition*. That is, the term is defined by citing a

11

REMBRANDT VAN RIJN.
Christ at Emmaus. 1628–30.
Oil on paper, mounted on panel,
$15\frac{3}{8} \times 16\frac{1}{2}''$.
Musée Jacquemart-André, Paris

number of examples. This is precisely the way one might distinguish between a "board" and a "stick" for a child. There are arenas in which we may not, amongst ourselves, agree. Thus, I may call boxing a game and you may not. Or your notion of "stick" might include mine of "log." But for the most part we will concur. In the same way we can deal with art while not defining it precisely.

I look upon art as another family of relationships. Some members are black sheep, some are elite. A Rembrandt such as *Christ at Emmaus* (fig. 11) is surely art, and belly-button lint or metronomes are not. Of course, given so broad a description, it will be necessary for me to assume that art can be bad or indifferent in quality as well as fine. (This view is anathema to many art critics, but that is not my fault.)

Even my liberality does not allow me to evade every problem. Thus, figure 12 shows us a purported work of art, *Indestructible Object* by Man Ray (1890–1976). It is nothing but a metronome with a photograph of an eye paper-clipped to the arm. Has the metronome become an art object because of its new acquisition? I should say yes, it is an art object of a very minor sort, although, as it happens, this object is of historical moment —largely because it represents an art movement which poked fun at the silliness of men concerning themselves with just such troublesome but inconsequential questions as "What is art?"

Artists themselves rarely worry about the matter; for them, art is simply what they do. If pressed, they may come up with elaborate verbal statements to justify their works. But if it could be shown that their art was inconsistent with their creeds, they'd revise the statements rather than the work. The art generates rules and definitions; the rules don't create art.

All this may seem to leave us quite at sea. Many people feel very unconfident and frustrated without some sort of guideline

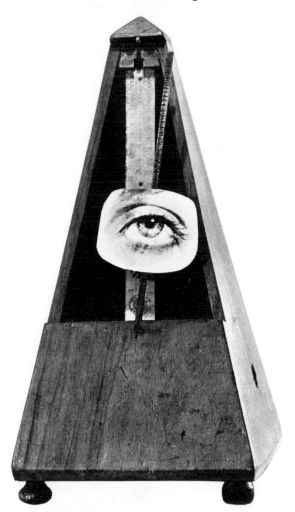

12
MAN RAY. *Indestructible Object*
(Object to be destroyed)
(1923 replica of destroyed original).
Metronome with cutout photograph
of eye on pendulum, 8⅞ × 4⅜ × 4⅝".
The Museum of Modern Art, New York.
James Thrall Soby Fund

whereby they can evaluate specific works of art. Even very sophisticated men and women are apt to respond to my attitudes with this old bugaboo: "If there are no absolute standards—if we can't even be sure whether a thing *is* art or not—how do you know whether a painting or sculpture is good or bad?"

13
PABLO PICASSO.
Ma Jolie. 1911–12.
Oil on canvas, 39⅜ × 25¾″.
The Museum of Modern Art,
New York.
Lillie P. Bliss Bequest

Granted, we do make judgments about individual works of art. Obviously, I have some kind of measure when I review art exhibits, teach painting and art history, or write art criticism. But it's rather loose and flexible. Like other standards in life. Do you know what a well-cooked steak is? Of course. Probably, you'll think I don't—I like mine cremated. No accounting for tastes, right?

Right, it is just a matter of personal preference. But in gaining knowledge of a subject, people also acquire judgment.

The Incompetent Artist Theory of Style in Art

You are not, most of you, professional musicians. This does not prevent you from making decisions of a very definite kind about popular music. By what rules do you operate when you decide that one group or artist is better than another? You make such evaluations as "This is good," "This is odd," "This is a fraud." But you don't demand rules. Again, this doesn't mean that you have no standards at all or no insight into popular music. Indeed, in this regard you almost surely have the advantage of me. And if you were going to explain popular music to me, you wouldn't begin by laying down a lot of rules and definitions for understanding it, would you? No, you would merely expose me to a lot of it, to try to show me what the performers are trying to convey—what they do convey to you. And, if you were clever, you'd begin by using something I already appreciate—like Bessie Smith's blues or Cole Porter and Duke Ellington. Well, this is almost precisely what I propose to do with you in the general field of art.

There are other parallels between rejection of popular music and misunderstanding art. Among the things that older people say about the music young people like is that it's "just a beat" or that it's "just noise" or that the performers and their audiences are so disoriented that rotten music sounds good to them. The tacit assumption is that the performers play and sing as they do because they cannot do otherwise—that, in other words, they have devised a style which passes off blaring incoherence as expression. In much the same way the layman is apt to think that Pablo Picasso (1881–1973), for example, began painting things like *Ma Jolie* (fig. 13) because he could not draw. And when an art professor like myself says that such work is very profound, really, the skeptic is ready to assume that the professor's defense is also a revelation of incompetence, that the professor is in the position of the pretentious fools in Hans Christian Andersen's famous story "The Emperor's New Clothes."[5] Fortunately, it is easy to prove that Picasso was not

just a fraud and that I am not gullible.

First, my own work tends to be rather conservative. Figure 14 gives you a random sampling. I do not believe that these pieces are outstanding works of art; they are not. But they are at least routinely competent. And I do know how to draw. So did Picasso.

Pablo Picasso, even as a child, drew with incredible facility. At the age of twelve he was already expert in drawing from Classical statuary (fig. 15). And his so-called Blue Period pictures, done between the ages of twenty and twenty-three, are very popular evocations of wistfulness and poverty (fig. 16). Most of the really important modern masters were gifted representationalists. The work of Wassily Kandinsky (1866–1944) may look sloppy and chaotic to the average layman (see fig. 17). It is easy to assume that he's just smearing paint on canvas. "My three-year-old can paint better than that!" is a common reaction, the imputation being that the artist cannot draw. But look at another picture by Kandinsky (fig. 18). From a conventional point of view it is really quite impressive. It is representational, charming, and very intricate. Well, then, is it the case that he finally learned how to paint after doing *Improvisation Number 30*? No, the picture of Russia was done in 1904 and *Improvisation Number 30* in 1913. Ah! Did he, then, degenerate? Not at all. It's just that he was trying to do something different in the later work, something that does not have to do with representations of objects. Just what he *was* getting at we'll leave until later. My only point is that it is misleading to assume that people become abstractionists because of incompetence.

The Incompetent Artist Theory of Style has another, slightly more sophisticated version. This one frequently crops up among physicians who have some interest in art but no very firm grasp of what painting is all about. In this version it is assumed that radical distortions in pictures can be traced

14
Works by the author

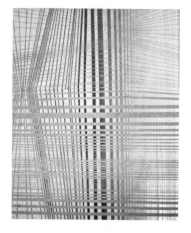

15
PABLO PICASSO.
Drawing from a cast. 1893–94.
Conté crayon, 18¼ × 25¼″.
Whereabouts unknown.
Reproduced from *Cahiers d'Art*,
courtesy of the publishers

16
PABLO PICASSO.
The Frugal Repast. 1904.
Etching, 18¼ × 14¼″.
The Museum of Modern Art,
New York.
Gift of Abby Aldrich Rockefeller

17
WASSILY KANDINSKY.
Improvisation Number 30. 1913.
Oil on canvas, 43¼ × 43¾″.
The Art Institute of Chicago.
Arthur Jerome Eddy
Memorial Collection

18
WASSILY KANDINSKY.
Sunday (Old Russia). 1904.
Oil on canvas, 17¾ × 37⅜″.
Museum Boymans Van
Beuningen, Rotterdam

19
EL GRECO. *Resurrection.*
C. 1597–1604.
Oil on canvas, 9'¼″ × 4'2″.
The Prado, Madrid

to some defect of vision in the artist. For instance, it is sometimes argued that the Spanish artist El Greco (1541–1614) drew men and women as he did (fig. 19) because he was afflicted with astigmatism. Astigmatism arises from an irregularity of the cornea in which light rays from a single point of an object fail to meet in a single focal point (as they do in normal vision), thus causing the image of a point to be drawn out into a line. Astigmatic lenses produce images such as the one in figure 20. When contrasted with the normal image (fig. 21), it is easy to see that El Greco's elongated figures are somewhat similar to the astigmatic distortion. It might follow then that the artist's style was the result of astigmatism. At least it sounds plausible. But a little thought will reveal just how muddle-headed the notion really is.

The cartoon (fig. 22) shows us what is supposed to happen. El Greco's models are fat, but because of his astigmatism he sees them as thin. Rendering them passively, just as he sees them, the plump Spanish girls appear wraithlike on his canvas. But this view of El Greco does not take into account the full experience of the astigmatic. For to an astigmatic eye the canvas, too, would appear elongated, and the image on it would look elongated. Besides, the astigmatic distortion is of such a nature that the reclining girl would not appear lean but would appear even fatter, as in figure 23. El Greco may or may not have had astigmatism, but his style does not depend upon it.

Explaining El Greco's work by referring to imperfectly formed eyes, scorning unrealistic-looking art as fraudulent, and putting down popular musicians as tone-deaf drug freaks are all alike. They are examples of prejudice. Usually prejudices are based on *some* sort of common-sense experience. After all, no one likes to think of himself as a pig-headed bigot. Yet prejudice can lead one far astray, even in things where the emotions do not play a role. Study the following columns of figures:

20
Astigmatic image

21
Normal image of the same subject

A	B	C	D
0	0	5	8
1	2	5	5
2	4	7	4
3	6	3	9
4	8	6	1
5	1	4	7
6	3	9	6
7	5	1	3
8	7	0	2
9	9	10	0

Column *A* is obvious in its order; the numerals are arranged in their conventional sequence. How about *B*? Yes, they are divided among even and odd. And *C*? A few moments of reflection should suggest the answer; they are so arranged that each successive pair of numbers add up to ten. What about *D*? Can you divine the order of that arrangement? It is no more complicated than any of the other patterns. No unusual mathematical ability is required to solve it. But if you can solve the puzzle of its order, you are in a real minority. Work on it a few minutes. If you get it, you'll understand the point I'm making. If you do not, you can find the solution on page 339.[6] There you can also find the solution to a related puzzle: On what basis have the letters OTTFFSSENT been ordered?

Our experience with numbers leads us to suppose, quite reasonably, that the order of column *D* will be arithmetical. And I reinforced this bias by giving three instances in which the prejudgment was borne out. The fourth instance did not play to your prejudice —that is, your prejudgment—and so you failed to solve the puzzle. (Yes, I know. Most of you didn't even try to figure it out. But if you had, you'd have blown it anyhow. Right? Right.) Your expectations played you false. And column *D* doesn't make any sense arithmetically. But if we wanted to index these numbers in an arithmetic book, it would make perfect sense to employ the arrangement that occurs in *D*. In the same

22
Cartoon of El Greco in his studio with models

23
Cartoon of El Greco revealing his work

way, you were probably misled into imagining that the arrangement of the letters OTTFFSSENT was numerologically determined.

The history of art since the end of the Middle Ages and the emergence of photography has led most of us to expect pictures to be more or less realistic. And Kandinsky's *Improvisation Number 30* just doesn't make sense in those terms. The best you could say for it is that it's an incredibly clumsy portrayal of cannon firing at a city. But that is not what the artist was after. He once said: "The observer must learn to look at the picture as a graphic representation of a mood and not as a representation of objects." What Kandinsky was trying to do was make of painting an art like that of music, in which feelings are evoked by the art itself. That is, you do not expect music to sound like something else—birdsong, babbling brooks, or wind through trees—you respond to it in terms of melody, rhythm, harmony and so on. We all know, however, that music, although not at all representational, can convey moods. Kandinsky, who had studied music as seriously as he had art, envied the composer. He wrote:

A painter who finds no satisfaction in mere representation, however artistic, in his longing to express his internal life, cannot but envy the ease with which music, the least material of the arts today, achieves this end. He naturally seeks to apply the means of music to his own art. And from this results that modern desire for rhythm in painting, for mathematical, abstract construction, for repeated notes of color, for setting color in motion, and so on.[7]

Whether Kandinsky accomplished his objectives is, of course, another matter. That is a problem we shall take up elsewhere in this book. I'm not sure he did achieve his goals. I do think that he painted a very good picture. You may not agree. That's all right. But at least we'll be arguing about something that is relevant to the artist's interests and not attacking him for something he never intended to do.

2

Image Creation and Convention

When someone says that he likes only pictures or statues that look "real," we know pretty much what he means. At any rate, it is not hard to predict what he probably *won't* like. But the term *reality* is one that has worried philosophers since very ancient times. It may mean very different things to different people, and may even mean many different things to a given individual. For instance, which of my drawings of President Abraham Lincoln is the most realistic? Is it the precise outline (fig. 24), the one reducing all light and shade to either black or white (fig. 25), or the one made up of little dots of ink (fig. 26)? Obviously, none of these pictures shows the way Lincoln actually looked to someone encountering him

in the flesh. Consider figure 27. It resembles nonrepresentational art until it is held up about fifteen feet away from you; then the units resolve themselves into another image of Lincoln. The image was "drawn" by a computer as part of a Bell Laboratories experiment to determine how little of an image had to be retained to preserve its identity.

What all this shows is that the creation of images does not have as much to do with the direct copying of details of reality as one might think. It has to do with highly selective choices about what to include and what to leave out. Moreover, this is two-way communication; the viewer is as much involved in creating the image as the artist is. The artist knows what marks to put into the picture and where to put them; the onlooker

24
Outline drawing

25
High contrast drawing

26
Stipple drawing

27
Computer drawing, an experiment by
Leon D. Harmon. Courtesy Leon D. Harmon
and Bell Laboratories

28
BILL BRANDT. *Nude.* 1953.
Photograph

must understand what those marks mean. To people brought up surrounded by photographs this may seem to be a relatively simple matter. It is not.

Even the most familiar and convincing of all realistic images, the reflection in the mirror, is not quite what it seems. You are almost surely mistaken about how you appear in your looking glass. I am not talking about the fact that the image is reversed or that most of us see ourselves as being far more attractive than we appear to other people. In the mirror, your face isn't even the same size you think it is. Try this: take a piece of soap and trace the silhouette of your head as it is reflected in your bathroom mirror. You will be astonished by the small size of the traced shape.[1] The psychological reality of the reflection is not at all like the reality of measurement. And if this most perfect of all realistic images does not correspond to our conceptions of visual reality, it is easy to see that a picture made of ink and paper or paint and canvas or emulsion on film will not match visual reality.

So-called photographic distortion, such as the effect in figure 28, is not a visual distortion at all; it is a psychological one. Possibly you have noticed in snapshots of your home that the rooms tend to look more spacious than they really are. This is because an object ten feet away doesn't really seem smaller; it just looks farther away. But if you hold a ruler out at arm's length and measure off heights of objects (as in figure 29), you will

29
Measuring visual scale of things
with a ruler

see that *in terms of measurements and magnitudes* the photograph is relatively accurate. You see in these terms only when you make a deliberate effort to do so, whereas the camera "sees" in terms of geometric relationships at all times. Thus, with regard to your living room, you are struck by the reduction of moderately distant objects in much the same way that the reduction of the girl's head strikes you in figure 28. Normally we sense such scale relationships only when things are very, very far off, when we speak of people looking like ants or toy soldiers.

If the relation between images and reality is so opaque, how then do artists accomplish their ends? It is a matter of organizing elements. Figure 30 does not resemble anything very much, but when the elements are re-arranged (fig. 31) we are confronted by "good ol' Charlie Brown," familiar to us from Charles Schulz's (born 1922) comic strip *Peanuts*. Charlie doesn't look human, of course. Yet cartoonists are able to convey all sorts of subtleties of human feeling through simple modifications of a few basic elements (fig. 32). We accept such marks as represen-tative of living creatures in much the same way we accept letters on paper as represen-tative of sounds. And the same thing is true when the drawing of the children seems somewhat more true to life.

One of *Peanuts'* forerunners was *Skippy* (fig. 33), a comic strip by Percy Crosby (1891–1964). In this strip the kids are more like real children, less like adult egos. But all the same, the strip is quite sophisticated. And the image is equally obscure insofar as copy-ing reality is concerned. The marks on the ground, the balloons, even the sketchiness of the figures, are all utterly beyond the ex-perience of normal visual encounters. Are the two boys sitting on a curb? A stoop? Where? We can't really determine the setting.

What about strips done in what is often called the "illustrators' style," pioneered by Alex Raymond (1909–1956) and Harold

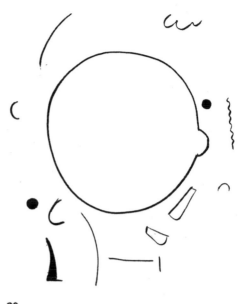

30
Some lines and marks

31
Cartoon image

32
A number of faces

33
PERCY CROSBY. *Skippy.*
© 1934, King Features Syndicate, Inc.

DALE'S LOVE FOR FLASH
IS TOO UNSELFISH---
"DON'T GO ON THIS EXPEDITION WITH
ZARKOV AND KORRO," SHE BEGS, "I
KNOW IT'S FAR MORE DANGEROUS
THAN THEY SAY!"

34

ALEX RAYMOND. Panel from *Flash Gordon*.
© 1939, King Features Syndicate, Inc.

"CONTENTMENT IS A GIFT BEYOND PRICE. AGAIN I READ
YOUR FUTURE. TOO BAD! FOR AGAIN I SEE ADVENTURE,
WEALTH, MUCH TURMOIL, BUT NOWHERE ANY CONTENT-
MENT," AND HORRIT CACKLES GLEEFULLY.

35

HAROLD FOSTER. Panel from *Prince Valiant*.
© 1943, King Features Syndicate, Inc.

Foster (born 1892)? *Flash Gordon* (fig. 34), Raymond's comic strip of the thirties, seems pretty realistic, doesn't it? And Foster's *Prince Valiant* (fig. 35) is certainly convincing. Or is it? When did you last see someone whose face was dead white and whose clean cheek contained thin black marks? That is shading, you say? True, that is what the marks represent. Still, you must admit that shadows look nothing at all like that. Moreover, all pen-and-ink renderings, all etchings, and all engravings are subject to the same analysis. The *Self-Portrait* (fig. 36) by Edgar Degas (1834–1917) is much more refined than any comic-strip image, but it is nonetheless made up of little black marks. Similarly, the sketch of an angel (fig. 37) by Michelangelo (1475–1564) is bounded by

dark lines and shaded with inky blots that stand for edges and shadows but do not appear in any real figure. This is obvious, surely. But the obviousness is wrapped in complexity. Let us consider the matter from a different angle—the appearance of movement.

Michelangelo is one of the finest artists of all time, and his angel seems to be moving through space because of the way the torso twists on its axis and the foot shrinks into the distance. What if we wished to really emphasize the notion of movement; what if we wanted to give it tremendous stress? A cartoonist might do just what we see Sal Buscema doing in *The Defenders* (fig. 38). The opponents flash back and forth with superhuman speed. We know exactly what is happening

36

EDGAR DEGAS. *Self-Portrait*. 1855.
Etching, 9 × 5⅝". National Gallery of
Art, Washington, D.C. Lessing
Rosenwald Collection

37

MICHELANGELO. *Avenging Angel*,
study for *The Last Judgment*.
Ink drawing, 9¾ × 8". Casa Buonarroti,
Florence

because the lines indicating motion are always to the rear of the objects and describe
their paths. This is not at all like the blurriness of rapidly moving objects as the eye
perceives them. But we know how to read
the symbol. Likewise, the use of lines to convey shadows is a symbol, a *convention;* that is,
an agreed-upon method of indicating darkness. It is very systematic: the more dense
the lines in the Degas etching, the more
shadowy the region.

It is important to understand that I am not
saying that only drawings are conventional
in this way. The reference to speeding objects

is worth exploring a bit. In figure 39 we have
another superbeing, The Flash, who is supposed to be the fastest thing alive. We can see
this because we are shown how terribly great
his momentum is. Again a mass of lines is
used to suggest speed. This is a conventional
cartoonists' symbol and we all understand
what it means. What would a photograph of
something moving at high speed look like?
Figure 40 gives us an example. The car is not
moving as fast as The Flash, but it's not standing still either. We gather that the car is moving because the image is blurred. But this is
also a conventional reaction. We know this

kind of blur means movement because of our experience with photography. Without such experience one might imagine that what he is seeing is the dissolution of some vaporous object. Foreknowledge tells us that blur equals motion. But all we can be really sure of is that movement occurred when the picture was snapped. In this case it could have been the camera that moved rather than the car. In figure 41 it *was* the camera. The camera was also moving in figure 42, but, because the automobile is clear and the background fuzzy, it is understood by the viewer that the car is the moving object. In figure 43 we see the result of higher-speed film and a faster shutter; it is not possible to be sure whether the vehicle is moving or stationary.

Long before the invention of photography, a Spanish painter named Diego Velázquez (1599–1660) captured the same effects in his large oil painting, *The Spinners* (fig. 44). In this picture he may be said to have devised a technique for representing motion. The spinning wheel, its spokes lost in motion, has a supporting strut whose vibration Velázquez suggested by means of an afterimage (fig. 45). This is the sort of thing the eye sees. You have only to riffle the pages of this book to observe that your eye retains briefly the image of a thing you have just seen if movement is sufficiently rapid. This characteristic of the eye is the ultimate source of the blurriness of fast-moving objects. But seeing the afterimage in the blur is one thing, and devising a way of representing it in a picture is quite another. *The Spinners* and the photographs symbolize actual visual phenomena in a way approximating ordinary vision. The cartoonists give us a schematic representation that is less like what one sees.

Sometimes the artist wishes to convey by visual means something that has never been seen and is not even presumed to exist as a visual phenomenon. Then the employment of convention is much more evident. As an

38

SAL BUSCEMA. Panel from *The Defenders*.

39

CARMINE INFANTINO AND JOE GIELLA.
Panel from *The Flash*.

40
Photograph of a moving car with both
car and background blurred

41
Parked car photographed as camera moved

42
Photograph of moving car with car
clear and background blurred

43
Photograph of moving car taken with
fast shutter speed

example, let us take the Christian art of an age gone by.

Religious Belief and Artistic Convention

During the Middle Ages—from, say, 400 to 1300—the civilization of the Western world was dominated by an ascetic ideal. We associate the term *ascetic* with monks, nuns, priests, and other people who have given up worldly pleasures for the joys of the spirit. Medieval man saw life as merely a passing moment in an eternity, most of which would be taken up by an afterlife. Worldly pleasures were seen as snares of Satan, and those who abstained from them were more highly regarded than those who did not. These people dwelt in a world where the trees growing in paradise, the angels in heaven, and the demons of hell were more real to them than anything or anyone a man beheld during his lifetime. From a contemporary point of view they spent their lives in a jungle of the imagination where the abnormal was routine and the fabulous commonplace. They believed. And, since what they believed in most fervently of all was supernatural, the art they created looks *un*natural. To them the meaning of a work of art was more important than its appearance. This is quite consistent with the Bible itself. In the Greek epics by Homer, in Vergil's *Aeneid*, and in the *Satyricon* of Petronius there are many descriptive passages; the world is observed in some detail even when the land concerned is only mythological. But the Bible contains hardly any description; we do not know what kind of landscape the characters inhabit, or what clothing they wear, or whether they have long noses or short ones. Moreover, every meaning seems to have another one behind it. Everything is, as it were, fraught with significance. Thus, in the book of Genesis, where God demands of Abraham that he sacrifice his only son,

44
DIEGO VELÁZQUEZ.
The Spinners. 1656.
Oil on canvas, 7'3⅜" × 9'5¾".
The Prado, Madrid

45
DIEGO VELÁZQUEZ. Detail
of *The Spinners*

46
S. Vitale, Ravenna.
526–547 A.D.

Isaac, we are told that Abraham and his followers rose "early in the morning and went unto the place of which God had told him." As Erich Auerbach points out in his *Mimesis*, the true significance of "early in the morning" is not that it specifies the time of day but that it makes an ethical observation. It is intended primarily to express the quality of Abraham's resolution to do God's will. The author of the story is lauding the punctuality of the sorely tried father in obeying the divine command to kill his only son. These concealed meanings of the stories in the Old and New Testaments have inspired much great art and literature. (They have also provided texts for innumerable tedious and boring sermons, but that is neither here nor there.) Like the Bible, a great deal of this art is similarly indifferent to description and full of meanings that lie beneath the surface.

Consider the church of San Vitale in Ravenna, Italy (fig. 46) built 526–547. Externally drab, it has interior decorations of an extreme richness (fig. 47). Such contrast is typical; it corresponds to the notion of the banality of ordinary mundane existence as contrasted with the richness of internal spiritual life. Thus, while the interior is extravagantly decorated, the purpose is not to delight the viewer's senses so much as to remind him of the beauty of an eternal paradise.

In the apse of San Vitale are a number of works in the mosaic medium (see glossary). One of them (fig. 48) is of particular pertinence. It portrays the Byzantine emperor Justinian and his retinue.[2] Justinian is centrally located. The figures to his left are clergy, and those to his right are members of the court. An honor guard stands far over to one side. At this time in history Justinian's military geniuses, the generals Belisarius and Narses, had rewon most of the old Roman Empire from the Vandals and Ostrogoths. The administrative outpost of Byzantine power in Italy was Ravenna, and San Vitale owed its existence to imperial support. The gift Justinian holds in his hands, a golden paten, used for holding the communion

47

Interior, S. Vitale, Ravenna

48
Justinian and Attendants. c. 547 A.D.
Mosaic. S. Vitale, Ravenna

bread, is symbolic of the munificence of the ruler in providing this house of worship.

The august figures portrayed in the mosaic look rather stiff and a bit choleric. One is apt to attribute much of this to the medium and overlook just how thoroughly conventionalized the work is. If, however, one examines many images from Byzantium, he will soon become aware of the predominance of very strict rules and firm guidelines. For instance, what is depicted here is not a group of people posing for their portraits. What we are supposed to understand is that this is a procession, part of the dedicatory ritual of the

church. Now, did processionals in those days progress by side step? No, but there is a convention of representing important figures full face, no matter what the circumstances. This kind of frontality is frequently encountered in highly authoritarian, hierarchical societies; figures are routinely presented as imperious, indomitable, superior to the observer. Judas and Satan, however, are consistently shown in profile in Byzantine art because of the fear of the Evil Eye, a very old superstition pervading many different tribes and civilizations.

Strict convention also determines the arrangement of the personages. The positions of the figures express their precedence and rank. Justinian is on center and overlaps everyone else. That is, if the figures are conceived of as cards, the emperor is on top of the pile. Bishop Maximianus to Justinian's immediate left is labeled. He was of signal importance in the creation of the Byzantine ecclesiastical-civil structure and was also responsible for the completion and consecration of San Vitale. He overlaps the other clergymen. And so it goes. The honor guards are of no individual importance and are sort of crowded and heaped up over on the edge of things. They are overlapped by a shield bearing a monogram devised by Constantine the Great, the first Roman emperor to be converted to Christianity. This device is called the *Chi-Rho* (X-P) and represents the first two letters of the word *Christ* in Greek. But it means still more. An *X* is, literally, a cross and must be taken to refer to the Crucifixion. The *P*, especially when given an elongated form, is not unlike a shepherd's crook; it stands for the pastoral mission of the Church and harks back to the parable of the Good Shepherd.

Like many backgrounds in Christian art of the Middle Ages, this one is flat and gold. Golden things in a spiritual context recur constantly in Christian art, and it may seem odd that this should be so. After all, one might think, what could be more closely associated with worldly materialism than gold? Such a reaction is sponsored by innocence of the reasons for man's love of the yellow substance. Gold was and is valued not merely because of its rarity. It is unique among metals in that it does not corrode or oxidize. Even silver tarnishes. But gold remains unblemished. Therefore, ancient peoples considered it "immortal" and invested it with magical powers and supernatural meaning.

You may have noticed the circle ringing the head of the emperor. It is a halo. This symbol was originally Persian and signified the descent of the Persian religious figure Zoroaster from the sun, so indicating his godlike origin and his holiness. The Greek Christians applied it to their emperor, in effect deifying him. There was a tradition in the ancient Roman world of deifying pagan emperors—both Julius Caesar and Augustus were considered demigods—and it was not difficult for early Christians to accept the idea. That would have been particularly true in Byzantium. Byzantium was a "caesaropapacy," that is, a system of rule in which the emperor is not only the secular ruler but also the final ecclesiastical authority, the pope. The laws of the Church and those of the state are one with the law of God, and it is the emperor who administers them.

The application of the Persian halo to secular authorities did not persist, but the motif itself became a convention of all Christian imagery. Throughout the Middle Ages the halo appears over and over again, designating spiritual radiance. It is used to indicate the sacredness of certain individuals—Jesus, His family, the disciples and apostles, various sainted prophets, martyrs, and so forth. It is interesting to observe what became of this symbol as it was subjected to the aesthetic conventions of various periods. For, while the halo remains even today a meaningful convention, the character of the halo has undergone radical transformations.

Economics and Artistic Convention

Although art underwent many changes during the medieval era, the really profound modifications of treatment and convention occurred as the Renaissance began to emerge during the 1300s. In the work of the Italian artist Cimabue (c. 1240–1302?) one already sees marginal changes that are tokens of a new direction. In his *Madonna Enthroned* (fig. 49) the prophets in the lower region are

49
CIMABUE. *Madonna Enthroned.* c. 1280–90.
Tempera on panel, 12′6″ × 7′4″.
Uffizi Gallery, Florence

treated much more realistically than the
principals above. Still, the picture is very
much like those of centuries past, with many
of the medieval conventions. Mary and the
infant Jesus are very large relative to the
other figures, an indication of their importance; the work is quite flat in effect, and
there is little feeling for these people as anything but emblems of worship. The halos are
simply signs of holiness. They don't look like
anything in particular; we know that they

are not meant to have an objective referent
in the real world.

Cimabue's pupil Giotto (c. 1266 or 1267–
1337) carried the realism hinted at in the
lower part of the Cimabue far, far further in
his own *Madonna Enthroned* (fig. 50). The
advances are much more radical than the
casual observer is likely to recognize, and we
are going to deal with their importance later
on. For now, it is enough to say that here, too,
the halos are merely emblematic—flat golden
circles behind the heads.

It is in the work of the short-lived Masaccio
(1401–c.1428) that the seeds sown by Cimabue and Giotto come to flower in a style that
can safely be called Renaissance. In his *Tribute Money* (fig. 51) the halo is no longer a
mere emblem. Now it resembles an element
of the visible world, like nothing so much as a
golden plate hovering over the head of the
holy being. The appearance of the halos is
subsidiary to the effect of the whole painting,
which, compared with the other works, is
more substantial and real looking.

The sudden emergence of Masaccio's realism is connected with a more general modification of convention—the whole set of
changes that are known, collectively, as the
Renaissance. The emergence of this set of attitudes, social forms, and artistic conventions
has never been completely accounted for.
Certainly, it was the product of many things.
One of the most profound influences was undoubtedly the creation of a middle class.

In the United States we tend to associate
the term *middle class* with middle-income
groups. But this is a peculiar usage. Historically speaking, the middle class is the one
which stands between the lower classes and
the aristocracy; it is made up of those who
have either wealth or education but are untitled. For the most part its members are
merchants, and their principal goal in life is
the making of a profit.[3] During the Middle
Ages this group was too small and insignificant to constitute a social class. Indeed the

50
GIOTTO.
Madonna Enthroned.
C. 1310.
Tempera on panel,
10'8" × 6'8".
Uffizi Gallery, Florence

51
MASACCIO. *The Tribute Money.* c. 1427.
Fresco. Brancacci Chapel, Sta. Maria del Carmine, Florence

whole idea of profitmaking was in eclipse from the fall of Rome until the beginning of the fourteenth century.

The idea of gain as a positive social good is a relatively modern one. Throughout most of recorded history it has been conspicuous by its absence. Even our Pilgrim forefathers considered the notion of "buying cheap and selling dear" nothing short of satanic doctrine. Nonetheless, a genuine middle class appeared as a social force in the Mediterranean region during the course of the fourteenth century. Its development coincided with an increase of trade occasioned by two related discoveries. The first was the invention of the technique of tacking against the wind, a procedure that made sailing much less subject to the whims of nature than it had been before. The other was the compass. Marco Polo had brought one of these magical instruments back from Cathay in 1295 (although it does seem to have been known in Europe a century earlier), and general use of the device by mariners made

navigation a good deal more certain than it would otherwise have been. Soon new trade routes opened up all over the world. Surplus capital came into existence and, with it, new ambitions. By the beginning of the fifteenth century a number of merchants had become wealthier than any king. The fortune established by one of these, Giovanni de' Medici (1360–1429), created what we know as the Florentine Renaissance. The history of the city of Florence was for centuries the history of the banking house of the Medici. For the Medici became the discreet dictators of the city—ostensibly a republic—without ever holding public office. The Medici were bankers to all of Europe. Their home base, Florence, became a cultural center to rank with the Athens of ancient Greece.

Although the Medici held social views that you and I might, loosely, call "aristocratic" and although they eventually became a line of dukes by marriage and through papal action, their fundamental attitude toward life was very different from that of the medieval nobility. In many respects their world view was distinctly middle class. The middle class is dynamic and businesslike; it distrusts class privilege when that privilege is based on nothing more than a birthright, and it at least gives lip service to the idea of an aristocracy of proven ability. This is the class which supported the republican revolutions in England, France, and America. As a class it tends to be highly opportunistic, hard-headed, and pragmatic.

It is hardly surprising that whenever the middle class makes its tastes felt in art the resulting art is apt to be rather down-to-earth. But the effect is not unmixed. The art sponsored by the Medici was not *just* realistic. Not only did the weight of tradition influence everyone's taste in art; there was also the influence of the preferences of the genuine nobility, which maintained greater or lesser power into the nineteenth century. And there was the mitigating factor of abstract thought. Bankers and merchants, after all, do deal constantly with ephemeral abstractions such as market values, profit and loss, relative quality, interest rates, and so on. Even for their practical minds reality is not just what shows on the surface; beneath everything there is a sort of hidden substructure. Throughout its history the art of the Italian Renaissance exhibits a marriage of mimesis and formality; that is, realistic effects are packaged in unnatural form.

This excursus seems, perhaps, to have taken us far from anything to do with halos. Nothing could be further from the truth. Masaccio, whom we were discussing, is singular in the whole span of history. Within the short space of six years he moved from the late medieval style into a full-blown Renaissance manner. This genius, who died at twenty-seven, was the creative descendent of Giotto, and he revolutionized painting by incorporating into it a whole repertory of pictorial devices that constitute what, for most people, is "real

art." Not only do his halos look like solid objects, the figures themselves are profoundly three-dimensional in appearance. And his picture contains cast shadows, scientific perspective, plausible drapery, and a high degree of anatomical exactitude. *Tribute Money* looks a good deal more like a segment of real space than does Giotto's *Madonna Enthroned*. Even the halos, purely symbolic things, look substantial. They express a middle-class preference for the straightforward and true to life over and above aristocratic acceptance of the purely emblematic.

Sandro Botticelli's *Madonna of the Pomegranate* (fig. 52), painted by a man born twenty years after Masaccio's *Tribute Money* was completed, takes advantage of all that the earlier painters had accomplished and contains halos that are far more illusionistic. Now they seem to be made of glass. They are not so obtrusive as the golden plates, but they seem even more like things that might be seen on earth.

Still later, Raphael (1483–1520), in his *Madonna of the Beautiful Garden* (fig. 53), uses the kind of halo that is the commonest symbol of holiness even today; above the Christ Child's head hovers a slender golden ring. Hardly noticeable, the ring halo is more of a concession to the demands of the middle class for what is palpable and easily accommodated into its matter-of-fact image of what is true.

By the sixteenth century, when the middle classes are burgeoning, buying titles and otherwise moving toward suzerainty, Tintoretto (1518–1594) has substituted for a disk or ring a nimbus of flame that blazes in the dark behind his figures' heads (fig. 54). But it remains for Rembrandt van Rijn (1606–1669) in that most middle-class of all nations, the Dutch Republic, to reduce the halo to ambiguity. In his *Christ at Emmaus* (fig. 55) is the halo radiated by Jesus, or is it a coincidental flash of light from a firelight to his right? All that one can be certain of is that mundane

52
SANDRO BOTTICELLI.
*Madonna of the
Pomegranate.* c. 1487.
Tempera on panel, diameter
56¼". Uffizi Gallery, Florence

53
RAPHAEL. *Madonna of the
Beautiful Garden.* 1507.
Oil on panel, 48 × 31½".
The Louvre, Paris

54
TINTORETTO. *The Last Supper*. 1592–94.
Oil on canvas, 12′ × 18′8″. S. Giorgio Maggiore, Venice

55
REMBRANDT VAN RIJN. *Christ at Emmaus*. 1628–30.
Oil on paper, mounted on panel, 15⅜ × 16½″.
Musée Jacquemart-André, Paris

56
JOHN SYLVESTER. *Tupai Kupa.* c. 1800.
From *The Childhood of Man* by Leo
Frobenius. Lippincott, 1909.
Reprinted by permission of Lippincott,
New York, and Seeley, Service & Co.
Ltd., London

57
TUPAI KUPA. *Self-Portrait.* c. 1800.
From *The Childhood of Man* by Leo
Frobenius. Lippincott, 1909.
Reprinted by permission of Lippincott,
New York, and Seeley, Service & Co.
Ltd., London

reality has been invested with significance. And to do that is common to the middle classes. A belief in Christian doctrine prevails, the faith that gives believers hope remains; but the symbol of divinity is cast in a form that presents the miraculous as a direct experience. How different the Rembrandt is from the Cimabue, where everything unworldly is simply accepted and the solicitations of the material world play an incidental role. The halo is a traditional symbol, and both Cimabue and Rembrandt use it. But the artistic conventions of their respective periods are as different as the economic and social bases of their times, and the way the halos are rendered shows it.

Social Convention and Artistic Convention

Whether the paintings of Rembrandt would look as conventionalized to Cimabue as the Cimabues look to us is impossible to say. Probably they would not. Most likely Cimabue would consider the Rembrandt "profane." His concept of religious truth probably would not have room for the Dutchman's conventions of realistic rendering. All we can do is guess at such things. There is no way to verify our suppositions.

We do know that certain kinds of cultures are so removed from any notion of direct depiction that photographs mean nothing to them. There is a famous story of some anthropologists who showed a photograph of Queen Victoria to a group of African tribesmen on the Gold Coast. The nearest guess the tribesmen could make as to the identity was that the picture might be of a British man-of-war. Well, the old girl was pretty formidable-looking at that. But the tribesmen would have had similar reactions to a snapshot of a lovely maiden from their own circle. Those men were not stupid or uncultured. They had a

highly developed social structure, a complete metaphysics, even an epistemology. But they were unfamiliar with the conventions of realistic portrayals. All the photographic print showed them was blotches of variegated gray. Theirs was quite a common reaction for so-called primitives. Usually, however, they can be taught to comprehend the meaning of photographs very swiftly if they are permitted to trace outlines with their fingertips. The tactile sense of an outline indicates the nature of the three-dimensional thing the flat picture represents in a way that vision unaided cannot.

The disparate ways in which men see other men and nature in terms of artistic conventions is made clear in a comparison of figures 56 and 57. Figure 56 is a drawing of the Maori chieftain Tupai Kupa made by Englishman John Sylvester about 1800 Figure 57 is a self-portrait by Tupai Kupa. The self-portrait is a flat, bisymmetrical pattern. It is, however, the way the chief saw himself. He identified his entire appearance with the ornamental pattern of his facial tattoo. But it is a true likeness, an authentic self-portrait. Among the Maoris of New Zealand each tattoo is peculiar to its owner. No two are alike; the convention is such that by his scarified design every tribesman is set off from the others. In one sense the tattoos are more individual than bone structure, as distinctive as fingerprints.

A likeness of a person means something very different to a Maori than it does to a European. Conceiving of an accurate likeness in terms of relative values of light and shade, in terms of specific kinds of proportions, in terms of detached, mechanical optometrics, is a peculiarly Western convention. Our technology has given it a certain universality, but the conception itself is no more correct or civilized than its alternatives. Still, it is *your* way of looking at things. And it scarcely matters whether your ancestors were

58
Guardian figure, from the Bakota
area, Gabon. 19th–20th century.
Wood, covered with brass and copper,
height 30″. Ethnographical Museum
of the University of Zurich

59
PABLO PICASSO. *Les Demoiselles
d'Avignon.* 1907.
Oil on canvas, 96 × 92″. The Museum
of Modern Art, New York. Lillie P.
Bliss Bequest

Europeans, Africans, Asiatics, Americans,[4] or
Oceanics.

All of us have learned to look at pictures
through the eyes of the West. Yet the
world of art is not a provincial place to live.
White artists have been influenced by the
power of black insight (figs. 58 and 59) and,
in Nigeria, there is sculpture from the 1100s
(fig. 60) rivaling the harmonious realism of
the far later Renaissance. The human adventure is a single adventure upon which all
races and cultures have embarked together.
If this primer helps the reader to a greater
awareness of what art has to do with his own
role in that adventure, it will have served its
purpose well.

60
Male half figure (probably Oni),
from Ife, Nigeria. 12th century.
Bronze, height 14½″. The American
Museum of Natural History, New York

3
Line and Form

All I have done so far is emphasize that art has many faces and make an issue of the fact that the relationship between art and reality is relatively obscure. We have given incidental attention to ways in which artists of various ages and places have translated reality into pictures, but we have not paid much attention to the things common to all visual art, to what are called its "elements." The visual elements are fundamental, basic. Without them no imagery could exist. Usually, they are identified as *line, form, space, texture, light,* and *color*. But to label them in this way is merely a convenience; in fact, the attributes described by these words merge into one another so that it is impossible to draw hard and fast distinctions among them. They are quite a lot like the interrelated components of music:

melody, harmony, rhythm, meter, and timbre. Artists and composers don't very often think of such elements as separate entities. They use the words, however, to make it easier to talk about certain aspects of their works. To a layman they and their critics sometimes seem to be playing fast and loose with the English tongue, as when artists discuss the "line" in work like that of Mark Rothko (fig. 61). Here again, however, a common-sense approach can help us understand precisely what is meant.

There are ten different black marks in figure 62. They are all the same height; the widths vary. Which of them would you refer to as "lines" in casual conversation and which would you call "forms"? The most common reaction is to call "lines" those marks which are so thin that you don't really pay attention

61

MARK ROTHKO.
Orange and Yellow. 1956.
Oil on canvas, 91 × 71″.
Albright-Knox Art Gallery,
Buffalo, New York. Gift of
Seymour H. Knox

62
Lines and forms

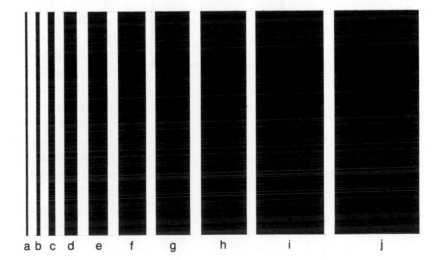

a b c d   e   f   g   h   i   j

63
Square

64
Geometric forms indicated
by isolated dots

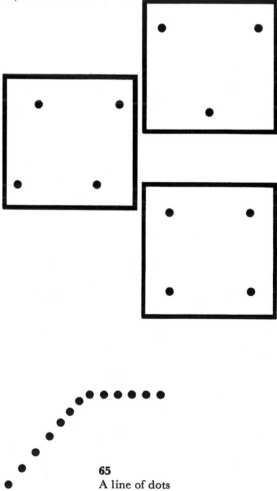

65
A line of dots

to their ends. They have a noticeable length —they terminate—but the look of the ends themselves is not an important feature of their appearance. With respect to the "forms," though, the character of the end is of sufficient thickness that we are apt to call it the "top" or "bottom" of the shape. Now in fact *all* the marks are forms; some are long and thin, some are not. We are aware that *C* is wider than *A*, but nonetheless it is true that what predominates in *C* is its length; our eye seems to run up and down *A*, *B*, and *C* whereas it seems to run around *H*, *I*, and *J*. We might go so far as to say—as some readers undoubtedly already have—that *H*, *I*, and *J* have lines *around* them, that their edges are the same as lines. And this is perfectly correct. A line can describe the edge of a form, or it can be a long thin mark enclosing an area (fig. 63). In both cases we could call them "boundaries" or out*lines*.

That is not the close of the matter. For we also have invisible lines. Thus, in figure 64 our tendency will be to link up the isolated dots into a square, a parallelogram, and a triangle. And with a few more units (fig. 65) we provide the viewer with a *line* of dots.

What is important to the concept of line is the impression of movement. When someone says, "Lines do not exist in nature," he simply means that your arm, say, is not bounded by long thin marks. But we commonly refer to such things as the *line* of the horizon, the tree*line*, and the receding hair*lines* of older men. And, in a sense rather close to that of the artist, we speak of the *lines* of a car. The line of an automobile design is not just the outline of the machine. It is also the general flow of the forms. Figure 66 is identical in silhouette to figure 67; but the "lines" are not the same, only the outlines are. Such language is very inexact, of course, but the meaning is quite clear.

When the artist or critic speaks of the lines in such a work as Raphael's *Madonna of the*

66
Automobile

67
Automobile

Beautiful Garden (fig. 68) or *Orange and Yellow* (fig. 61) by Mark Rothko (1903–1907) he is talking about movements. Most often such movements are along the edges of forms, that is, they are lines of boundary as in the Raphael. Sometimes, though, they are as diffuse and generalized as the movement around the hazy rectangles in the Rothko. My meaning is fairly obvious when I speak of lines existing in something like the Degas *Self-Portrait* (fig. 69). In this work there are actual drawn lines[1]—that is, thin forms—and there are also the outlines of the larger forms or shapes which result from the accumulation of the thin black marks.

In a very real sense all drawn lines can be thought of as forms that serve to emphasize movement. For example, the lines in figure 70 indicate the directions the edges would take if Tarzan were treated in terms of bold masses (fig. 71) instead of in terms of thin black forms. All lines are pathways that connect up shapes and forms in a work of art. If we put Tarzan back into the original compo-

sition (fig. 72) by Burne Hogarth, we can see that he is at the crest of a general sweep of lines and forms beginning at the bottom of the picture and curving up and back to the assassinated chieftain. This is a very important use of line in pictorial composition. It is the result of an alignment of forms, in this case a lining up of shapes so insistent that one's eye is drawn through the illustration almost as if by a powerful magnetic force. Even the streaked sky contributes to Hogarth's little drama.

The same kind of movement occurs in the Raphael, although in a far more subtle way. Notice how the forms of Christ's body establish a curved movement that is carried on through the arm of the Virgin. There are a number of such linear developments throughout the work. I have diagrammed some of them in figure 73. Of course, a diagram is not the work itself; there are other alignments and pathways that I have overlooked or deliberately ignored. Indeed, one is wise to be suspicious of critics who engage

68
RAPHAEL. *Madonna of the Beautiful Garden.* 1507.
Oil on panel, 48 × 31½″.
The Louvre, Paris

69
EDGAR DEGAS. *Self-Portrait.* 1855.
Etching, 9 × 5⅝″. National Gallery of Art,
Washington, D. C. Lessing Rosenwald Collection

70
After *Tarzan* by Burne Hogarth

71
After *Tarzan* by Burne Hogarth

72

BURNE HOGARTH *Tarzan.*
© 1949, Edgar Rice
Burroughs, Inc.

73
Diagram of movements in Raphael's
Madonna of the Beautiful Garden

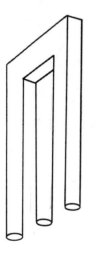

74
Three-legged arch

in very much of this kind of analysis; truth is apt to exist in inverse proportion to the number of schematic diagrams. But it is sometimes necessary to sacrifice a bit of truth to understanding. Which brings me to another caution.

I have had frequent recourse to such phrases as "the eye runs up and down," "the eye runs around," "our eye is drawn," and "pathways through the picture." While these phrases are commonly used among artists and critics, there is no real evidence that we comprehend pictures in this way. Certainly it is not true that the focus of our vision is actually along the lines in a picture. If it were so, the bizarre image in figure 74 would not disturb us in the least; we would accept it as a matter-of-fact array of long thin marks. But we see it in its totality, and the top half doesn't go with the bottom part. The notion of movement of line in art has more to do with a generalized sensation that it has to do with the actual mechanics of vision. Yet the *feeling* that one's eye moves along pathways is so pronounced in something like the Hogarth cartoon of Tarzan or the Raphael Madonna that it is both convenient and convincing to talk as if it were true that vision finds its way through pictures by using stepping stones and pathways.

A painter of the American West, Charles Russell (1864–1926), made very obvious use of such pathways in his oil painting *Loops and Swift Horses Are Surer than Lead* (fig. 75), which shows a couple of wranglers roping a bear. The lariats establish a bold, looping curve through the middle of the work. This same curve is repeated in the shapes of the valley beyond, carried through the slant of the horses' legs, and echoes in the posture and movement of the cowboys. Notice, too, that the sagebrush is not so random in disposition as one might at first suppose. The clumps are lined up in curves; some correspond to the line of the lariat, others lead up from the

75
CHARLES RUSSELL. *Loops and Swift Horses Are Surer than Lead.* 1916.
Oil on canvas, 29½ × 47½″. Amon Carter Museum of Western Art, Fort Worth, Texas

foreground into the center of the action. At first glance the painting looks perfectly natural. But a little analysis reveals the artist at work, arranging things in terms of movements.

It would be difficult to find a more contrasting painting than *Composition in White, Black and Red* (fig. 76) by Piet Mondrian (1872–1944). Here there is no action, not even a portrayal of any kind—nothing but black lines on a white panel with a thin rectangle of red at the base. What Mondrian was interested in, obviously, was outlining different size zones on his canvas. This looks simple, but it is a difficult sort of problem and Mondrian has handled it very sensitively.

Because his style was associated with a certain development in architectural design, reflected in such structures as Mies van der Rohe's buildings (fig. 77), it is common to teach people to "appreciate" it by suggesting that they think of the black stripes in the work as steel members, the white spaces as glass, and the red strip as brick. Yes, it resembles a storefront of the sort one might see on a fashionable street. This approach demonstrates, perhaps, the relevance of Mondrian's ideas to our daily lives, but it misses what is most intriguing about the painting itself, namely, the relationships of the forms.

May I suggest that you try looking at the work not as if it were produced by placing

76
PIET MONDRIAN. *Composition in White, Black and Red*. 1936.
Oil on canvas, 40¼ × 41″. The Museum of Modern Art, New York. Gift of the Advisory Committee

77
MIES VAN DER ROHE.
Crown Hall, Illinois Institute of Technology, Chicago. 1952–56

black stripes on a white background but, instead, as if Mondrian had placed large white units on a black background? The exquisite proportioning of the various elements may be more apparent when seen in this light than when looked at in the expected fashion. However, it might not; some people find this kind of thing dull no matter how expertly it's done. In any case, you may get some idea of Mondrian's seriousness of purpose. He was deeply in earnest about his art, feeling that it was a purified representation of the kind of harmony and equilibrium toward which all nature strives but never experiences in fact.

Charles Russell, like Burne Hogarth, was a popular illustrator who appealed directly to a mass audience. His audience was interested first and foremost in the anecdote, that is, in the story the picture told. They were somewhat less concerned with imagery, although the authenticity of details had a decisive bearing upon reception of the anecdote. As to the composition, the fans of Russell were indifferent. Russell organized his forms in order to present the anecdote effectively, not out of some noble, artistic motive. Mondrian was far more serious-minded and self-sufficient about his picture; he was devoted to an ideal and he wished to express it. He organized his composition for the sake of the composition itself. For him it had a value in and of itself. Russell was not indifferent to artistic form by any means, but he looked upon the forms as means to another end.

It would be misleading to say that the painters of the Italian Renaissance wanted

78
LEONARDO DA VINCI. *The Last Supper*. 1495–98.
Mural. Sta. Maria delle Grazie, Milan

79
Leonardo's *The Last Supper*

to achieve the same ends as Mondrian. They did not. Yet they were somewhat more like Mondrian than like Russell. They sought far above themselves for inspiration and turned their backs on the details of everyday existence. In its way the famous *Last Supper* (fig. 78) by Leonardo da Vinci (1452–1519) is as good an example of the Renaissance search for harmony as Mondrian's painting is of twentieth-century seriousness. Let us examine it in terms of line and form.

The work is remarkably symmetrical. Leonardo assembled the twelve apostles in four groups of three with two groups to the left of Christ and two groups to his right. Christ himself is posed and drawn so as to form a pyramid (fig. 79). He is the most stable shape in the entire work, and the most isolated and self-sufficient figure. The moment is immediately after He has spoken the words, "One of you shall betray me." The party is alive with speculation. Judas, whose head is fourth from the left, draws back in fear and hatred. His outline is as triangular as the Master's but is lopsided, scalene, and far less stable. Of the disciples only he has a face

caught by darkness. His left arm is parallel to the left arm of the disciple seated between him and Jesus, and the two disciples' arms are at an angle to the table which is precisely opposite to the angle struck by Jesus's right arm. This establishes between Christ and His neighbor a wide V that echoes His own silhouette inverted. At the point of the V He is in contact with the adjacent disciple. But the width of the V and the repetition of its left side in Judas's arm bars Him from the traitor. By means of this geometry Leonardo conveys both the historical closeness and the moral distance between the Messiah and Judas. Their shared triangularity accents the fact that they are the principal actors in this historic event. Of course, Christ is the focus of the tale. And He is, quite literally, the focus of the picture. Not only is He on center stage, He is the spot on which the lines of the ceiling converge. Similarly, the tops of the tapestries on either wall are in line with His forehead. So are the edges of the table. He is seated before a rectangular window accented by a curved molding that resembles a halo. Too, there are linear developments through the disciple groups, leading us to the central figure. It is a very austere, harmonious, and thoughtful work.

Leonardo's *Last Supper* is the most famous of them all, but the subject has been treated by many other painters. Nearly a century later, the Venetian painter Tintoretto undertook the same theme on a similar scale (fig. 80). But how different from Leonardo's is his conception of the event! The main point of convergence is no longer Christ's face but is over on the far right. The whole thrust of the room is opposed to that of the viewer's eye, which is yanked across the picture toward Jesus. This effect is achieved partly by means of Christ's bright halo; all the halos are like shouts in the night in this dark and smoky inn, but His is largest. It is also the most radiant, and it casts a light so powerful that sharp shadows fall from it across the figures in the forefront of the picture. A very distinct pathway is created by the coincidence of the shadow beneath the foot of the nearest person in the right foreground, the folds in the garments of the kneeling maid, the shadow of the maid's head, Christ's plate, and the edge of His robe. The cherubim and seraphim boiling down from the oil lamps in the ceiling

are coordinated with the figure of Christ. There are numerous other chains of this general type, such as the one leading from the basket up through the serving table and on to Christ.

The Tintoretto is far, far more dramatic than the Leonardo. It is theatrical. This has a good deal to do with the history of the Church. The Leonardo was painted before the beginnings of the Protestant Reformation. Leonardo was, personally, a skeptic in matters of the faith. But he was not self-conscious about depictions of gospel stories. He took them for granted. In fact, the stability of Rome, the permanence of the Church, and the patronage of the devout could all be taken very much for granted. After 1517, however, this was no longer true. Once Martin Luther had successfully challenged the authority of Rome, the Church was on the defensive. Tintoretto was a painter of the Counter Reformation, Rome's answer to the threat of Protestantism, an increasingly powerful influence in northern Europe. Tintoretto did not take the Last Supper for granted; he wished to thrill viewers with his portrayal, wished to move them to accept the continuity of the Roman Church from Christ through

80
TINTORETTO. *The Last Supper*. 1592–94.
Oil on canvas, 12′ × 18′8″.
S. Giorgio Maggiore, Venice

Peter all the way up to their own day. Notice that Leonardo keeps us down in the orchestra pit, as it were, while Tintoretto sets us upon the stage. Leonardo shows us a tableau; Tintoretto invites our participation. Tintoretto was a propagandist for the Catholic position, and his work is devoted to propagation of the true faith. He marshals every resource available to him to dramatize events from Christ's life, to invest mere paint with hints of the truly miraculous. Thus his use of line and form is charged with dynamic energy, full of grand sweeps, thrusts, and counterthrusts. He enlists the capacities of line and form to touch the viewer emotionally so as to simulate the effect of a mystical experience. Leonardo's pacific symmetry is an emblem of a time when the permanence and order of the Church were exempt from challenge. Tintoretto's style is a shout for attention.

The Shapes of Venus

Line and form are characteristics of all images, not just those produced by artists with pencils, pens, and brushes. The photograph of a nude woman (fig. 81) is subject to the same kind of analysis as a painting or a

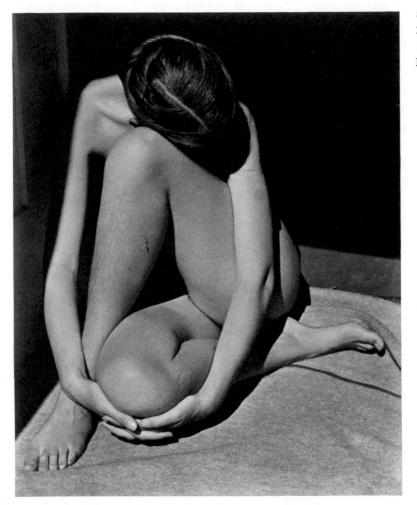

81
EDWARD WESTON. *Nude.*
1936.
Photograph

drawing. The photographer cannot control the line as decisively as a painter; but he can, by means of pose and lighting, articulate his images. The woman portrayed in figure 81 is composed. The photographer has studied her in terms of massings of anatomical forms and their outlines to produce a very cohesive work. And she is treated as a female human being, an animal having certain physical properties distinct from other beings. The commercial photographer who makes pictures for the enjoyment of readers of men's magazines such as *Playboy* approaches women with a quite different objective in mind. He does everything possible to make the figures resemble those depicted by pinup artists like Vargas. Such renderings have proved highly provocative to most males in Western culture. They don't look like real women, though, despite the tremendous stress on female secondary sexual characteristics. You've only got to study them dispassionately to see this. Vargas's young ladies are so drawn as to be quite impossible; their internal organs would be in disarray. One can't use that fact alone to put them down, however. Many of Michelangelo's nudes are equally unsound from a physiologist's point of view.

What is most striking about the treatment Vargas gives the female form is that he invests it with an overall tenseness. He and his colleagues treat womankind as if every bit of female flesh were made of erectile tissue and were utterly lacking in the softness more typical of the female body in repose.

A human breast is a gland surrounded by fatty tissue, a form on which gravity exercises some effect. In Vargas it looks like some sort of pneumatic pillow. This kind of rendering has the effect of making women look like male athletes with female appendages. The aggressive "femininity" of the pinups is barely skin-deep; a young man is hiding under there.

The popularity of such treatments insinuates something unsettling about our civilization. But the point I wish to make here is that the pinup photographer does everything he can to duplicate them. The *Playboy* model tends to be posed with her arms raised, her thorax inflated, her stomach held in, her legs tensed. The photographer cannot overcome the effect of gravity in fact; but he can choose a model with an unusually high bosom, tilt the set so that the forces of nature are cancelled out, and then tilt the camera so that the picture looks straight. And he can retouch the negatives and prints to erase certain blemishes, unwanted lumps, and other evidences of humanity—particularly female humanity.

In ages past, men were less nervous about the female form. This is particularly evidenced in the many statues and paintings of the goddess of love and beauty, Aphrodite (or, as the Romans called her, Venus). In the fourth century before Christ a great Greek sculptor named Praxiteles (active 375–330 B.C.) carved a statue of her (fig. 82) for the city of Kos. As it happened, that city was nervous about uncovering the beauties of Aphrodite and rejected Praxiteles' nude in favor of a draped figure. The people of another city, Knidos, were to profit by this piety, for they became the owners of the nude version of the goddess, possibly the most famous statue in all antiquity. The original work is lost, and only imperfect Roman copies remain. Still, it is easy enough to see the general approach chosen by the artist.

The Knidian Aphrodite is a bit heavy for modern tastes (as for the Flemish of the seventeenth century, she'd have been too slim), but she is nonetheless of an extraordinary perfection of form. She is relaxed, unselfconscious, and posed with her hip swung out in the way the French call *déhanchement*. The arc of her right hip, sweeping up to the sphere of the breast, is balanced by the long graceful undulation of the left side. No one of the time questioned that the statue was intended as an embodiment of physical desire; for a Greek that would be connected

82
PRAXITELES. *Aphrodite of Knidos.*
Roman copy after an original of c. 330 B.C. Marble, height 80″. Vatican Museums, Rome

83

PRAXITELES. *Hermes and
Dionysus.* C. 330–320 B.C.
Marble, height 7′1″.
Museum, Olympia

with religious veneration of the goddess of
love. Indeed, a Greek author of late antiquity tells how a companion was overcome
by erotic frenzy at the sight of the sculpture.
Granted, it is hard to believe in his story on
the basis of the Roman copy before us. Just
how imperfect an imitation it must be can be
estimated by a glance at the sole remaining
work that is pretty surely from the hand of
Praxiteles, the *Hermes and Dionysus* (fig. 83).
The translucent delicacy so astonishing in
this work is altogether absent from Roman
copies. The only surviving marble from the
ancient world that today imparts some hint
of the sensual thrill the Knidian Aphrodite
must have provoked is the far later *Aphrodite of Cyrene* (fig. 84), where stone seems
nearly turned to flesh.

Female nudes occur throughout art history. Even in medieval times there were
isolated examples, usually of Eve. But between the fall of Rome and the emergence of
the Renaissance, the representation of the
sensuous was proscribed. When Venus re-
appeared, she exhibited the same mixture of
sensual realism and abstract harmony ob-
servable in all other art of the fifteenth and
sixteenth centuries. The earliest of these
masterpieces is Botticelli's *Birth of Venus* (fig.
85), but the most influential of all Renaissance
nudes was the *Sleeping Venus* (fig. 86) by the
Venetian artist Giorgione (c. 1476/8–1510).

Giorgione's *Venus* established a pose so
satisfying to painters' eyes that she has served

84

Aphrodite of Cyrene. 1st century B.C.?
Marble, height 60″. Terme Museum, Rome

85
SANDRO BOTTICELLI.
The Birth of Venus. c. 1480.
Tempera on canvas,
5′8⅞″ × 9′1⅞″. Uffizi Gallery,
Florence

as a model for the greatest painters of female nudes—for Titian, Rubens, Manet, Renoir, and even Picasso. Sir Kenneth Clark has said of the painting:

Her pose seems so calm and inevitable that we do not at once recognize its originality. Giorgione's *Venus* is not antique. The reclining figure of a nude woman does not seem to have been the subject of any famous work of art in antiquity . . . She lacks the weighty sagging rhythm, as of a laden branch, in which the antique world paid equal tribute to growth and to gravity.[2]

The treatment of the figure is such that she is, as Clark remarks, like a bud enfolded. Giorgione has given to the female form a compression of shape that brings about perfectly smooth transition from shape to shape. The lines flow insensibly from one place to another. The forms of the beautiful cloth on which Venus lies express the same kind of coherence and are a sort of reflection of the graceful outline of her body. She sleeps a gentle sleep, removed from immediate reality, in a landscape that is suffused with mellow golden light.

Titian's *Venus of Urbino* (fig. 87) is very like

the Giorgione in pose, yet the mood is different. The *Venus of Urbino* is awake; she invites us to her side with her eyes. And Titian (c. 1487/90–1576) has turned the torso a bit more toward us. By intensifying certain darks he has produced stronger contrasts of form within an outline that is almost as cohesive as the silhouette of the Giorgione *Venus*.

The appeal of these Renaissance nudes is sensuous and direct, largely achieved through the manipulation of line and form. While it would be going too far to say that the artists have revealed the carnal nature of Venus, it is well within the bounds of truth to note that their treatment of female anatomy in terms of enclosed forms which have the solidity of spheres and cylinders points up woman's physical being. Only those who accept the human body in an open, straightforward manner have such a command of line and form.

By the middle of the nineteenth century the naturalness of Titian had been supplanted by a stuffy, high-minded attitude toward the female nude. The nineteenth century wor-

86
GIORGIONE. *Sleeping Venus* c. 1508–10.
Oil on canvas, 42¾″ × 69″.
State Picture Gallery, Dresden

87
TITIAN. *Venus of Urbino*. 1538.
Oil on canvas, 47 × 65″. Uffizi Gallery, Florence

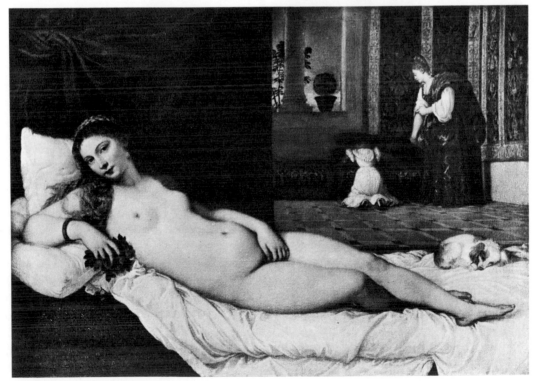

88
ADOLPHE WILLIAM
BOUGUEREAU.
Nymphs and Satyr. 1873.
Oil on canvas, 8′6⅜″ × 5′10⅞″.
Sterling and Francine Clark
Art Institute, Williamstown,
Massachusetts

shiped women in the sense that Victorian men put their ladies on pedestals and idealized them. But the nineteenth-century view depended upon a rejection of women as human beings. The successful painters of the day—whose names are now known mostly by professionals only—had one thing in common: when it came to depicting naked women, they glossed over the facts.[3] An artist like Adolphe William Bouguereau (1825–1905) imitated the mannerisms of the Renais-

sance but had no feeling or interest in the substance of the women he depicted. He substituted for the articulate volumes and coherent lines of Giorgione and Titian a slick, waxy-looking surface and placed his women in a mythological fantasy (fig. 88). Their geometry corresponds to a genuine ideal but it is explicitly sexual in a way intended to appeal to men by turning rather realistic young girls into identically unblemished objects of desire. In 1863 Edouard Manet (1832–1883) challenged this popular image with the exhibition of his *Olympia* (fig. 89).

The *Olympia* is based on Titian's *Venus of Urbino*. Manet was perfectly open as to that. But while the poses are similar, the women are quite different. This is not Titian's loving creature; this is a hard and cold professional —a high-class prostitute, a courtesan. Her stare is not inviting; it measures one. Moreover, the girl is very much an individual; her face and figure are rendered with an eye to their specific characteristics. We could probably recognize Manet's model on the street. And we encounter her here in probable surroundings. The picture is a fine example of the style art historians know as French Realism, a movement opposing the high-flown fancies of men like Bouguereau with the realities of the everyday world. Titian had been concerned with reality too, but it was a reality that went beyond the one that Manet represents. The Renaissance artists strove to reveal the substance that lay beneath superficial appearances. The Realists were obsessed with appearances only. That they were so concerned drew upon them the charge that their works were both shallow and ugly.

Still, Manet's *Olympia* is as significant for the painting to follow as its prototype, the *Venus of Urbino*, was for the art that succeeded it. Generally, the *Olympia* is considered the first example of truly "modern" art. This may

89
EDOUARD MANET. *Olympia*. 1863.
Oil on canvas. 51¼ × 74¾". The Louvre, Paris

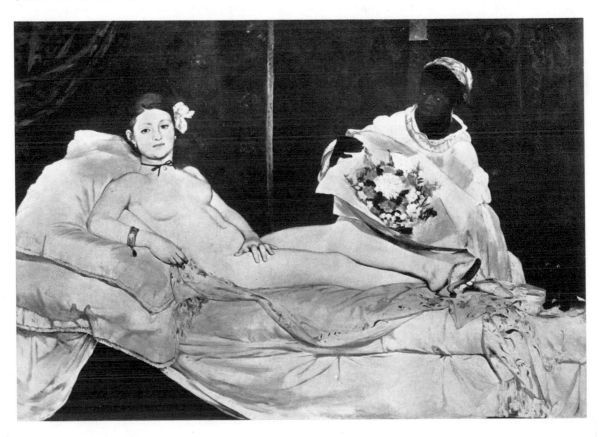

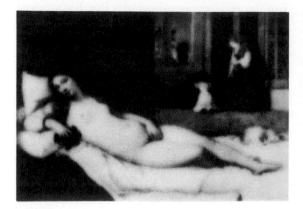

90
Titian's *Venus of Urbino* out of focus

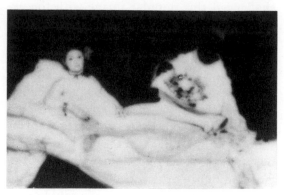

91
Manet's *Olympia* out of focus

sound odd. The term *modern art* connotes to most of us a kind of art that doesn't resemble anything—the sort of thing Picasso, Kandinsky, Mondrian, and Rothko do—and the *Olympia* is very true to life. What makes Manet modern is the way he employs the elements of art.

Certainly, the *Olympia* doesn't look much like the *Venus of Urbino*; she is flat, pale, and the lines are crisp and rather cold. Compare figures 90 and 91, out-of-focus photographs of the Titian and Manet, respectively. The two photographs are blurry to the same degree, but the lines and forms in the Titian remain relatively clear while those in Manet's nude are nearly lost. The one line in the Manet that does remain clearer than any in the Titian is the outline of the pale silhouette containing the girl, the bed, and the maid's clothing. This large light area has some of the impact of a gigantic poster. Within it there are no deep shadows to produce an impression of deeply rounded forms. The outline of the nude *Olympia* is a faintly shaded edge as narrow as a drawn line. Thus, the form of the *Olympia* produces an entirely different effect from that of the *Venus of Urbino*.

The image of woman in the work of Richard Lindner (1901–1978), an American art-

ist, evokes still other thoughts. His work (see fig. 92) constitutes a statement on the kind of society in which men get their "kicks" from looking at women presented in the way the pinup artists show them—as non-women. Lindner's figures are armored, corseted, and otherwise constrained. They are grotesque caricatures of the painted, pampered American Woman, a woman who (Lindner seems to say) is about as yielding as a chunk of sidewalk. The lines of his figures are of an inhuman regularity; their forms are geometric to the extent that nothing animal is left. They are robots in the form of sex machines. They represent the pinup view of woman carried to its logical conclusion.

Clearly, the image of Venus changes with the role of women in society, and artists convey their feelings about that role by the way they describe woman through the medium of art. It is also true that the moods peculiar to the individual pictures are produced in part by the varying character of the lines and forms.

Line, Form, and Feeling

There is a kind of folk-art knowledge em-

92
RICHARD LINDNER.
119th Division. 1965.
Oil on canvas, 80½ × 50½″.
Walker Art Center,
Minneapolis

bodied in the name of the weeping willow tree. Everyone knows that drooping lines are supposed to convey sorrow or fatigue. A calm sea is placid, and placidity is marked by horizontal lines. When you're "up" you are happy, and upcurving lines are often used to indicate joy. These associations of line direction with mood probably derive from somatic identifications; that is, with their occurrence in our own bodies. Figure 93 illustrates the presumed relationships. Actually, the inference that downturned lines are sad and up-

turned ones joyous is simple-minded. For instance, the face made up of only upturned lines is not as gleeful-looking as the top-left face in figure 32 because the latter corresponds more closely to actual configurations in a smiling face. But simplistic or not, it is obvious that there is *something* to the idea that line movement and mood are connected.

Leonardo's *Last Supper* (fig. 78) conveys a pacific feeling. It is a calm picture. The Tintoretto version (fig. 80) boils with energy; its line movements are highly charged. In

joy

calm

sorrow

93
The supposed physiognomy
of linear moods

viewing it one feels less at rest because it is not at rest. Its mood is intense and aims at provoking a feeling akin to ecstasy, religious fervor. In an analogous fashion, two famous works from the late nineteenth century, *The Starry Night* by Vincent van Gogh (1853–1890) and *A Sunday Afternoon on the Island of La Grande Jatte* by Georges Seurat (1859–1891) evoke different moods because of the different ways the artists have used line and form.

The brushstrokes in the Van Gogh (fig. 94) are exceptionally linear, and their movement is torrential. *Starry Night* is emotional to the point of being vehement. The nebulae raging across the heavens of the night are not things seen but something felt. In *A Sunday Afternoon on the Island of La Grande Jatte* (fig. 95) the painter has employed little dots of color. His lines are regulated, predictable, serene. Everything is thought out. Even the forms between the figures are calculated; they resemble jigsaw cutouts. And the repetitions of line are very clear. Compare the back of the lady in the bustle on the far right with the line movement from the seated girl ahead of her up through her companion's parasol to the hip of the oncoming mother. Such similarities can be discerned throughout the painting. The mood? It is one of calm, appropriate to a quiet Sunday afternoon in Paris.

Line and form are but two of the elements of art. They are, as you have seen, so closely related as to be almost interchangeable. The other elements are similarly dependent upon each other. Without contrast between dark and light we could not perceive form, and without form we would not have line. Darkness or lightness is an aspect of color. In fact, the aspect of color summed up by the terms *dark* and *light* is perhaps the most important aspect of all. One can be colorblind and still see very well indeed. But without the contrast between lights and darks one would be unable to see at all.

94

VINCENT VAN GOGH.
The Starry Night. 1889.
Oil on canvas, 28¾ × 36¼".
The Museum of Modern
Art, New York. Lillie P.
Bliss Bequest

95

GEORGES SEURAT.
*A Sunday Afternoon on
the Island of
La Grande Jatte.*
1884–86.
Oil on canvas,
6'9½" × 10'1¼".
The Art Institute
of Chicago.
Helen Birch Bartlett
Memorial Collection

4
Light and Shade

In discussions of light and shade it must be ever borne in mind that the painter works with pigment and not with real light. He cannot make us squint into his painted sunsets, cannot actually blind us with the radiance of his desert skies. We need not shield our eyes from the glare on Turner's water (fig. 96). The artist creates his illusions within a very limited range. But he always has our help, our willingness to go along with the tricks.

A good example of just how tolerant we are when it comes to accepting deviations from reality in pictures can be had by studying a slide of Jan van Eyck's (c. 1390–1441) *Giovanni Arnolfini and His Bride* (fig. 97) projected onto a screen in an appropriately darkened room. Pick out something in the picture that looks very dark, even black. It will not be as dark as any number of things in the room around it. The slide is, in other words, a very pale image of reality. Yet, until you make an effort to notice this effect, it is not apparent. Even when you are aware of it, the image on the screen continues to look "right." This is because the relationships among contrasts in

96

JOSEPH MALLORD
WILLIAM TURNER.
*The Dogana, San Giorgio
Maggiore, le Zitelle from
the Steps of the Europa.*
1842.
Oil on canvas, $24\frac{1}{2} \times 36\frac{1}{2}''$.
The Tate Gallery, London

97

JAN VAN EYCK.
*Giovanni Arnolfini and
His Bride.* 1434.
Oil on panel, $32\frac{1}{4} \times 23\frac{1}{2}''$.
The National Gallery,
London

98
Gray strip in
graduated background

99
Natural light

100
Artificial light

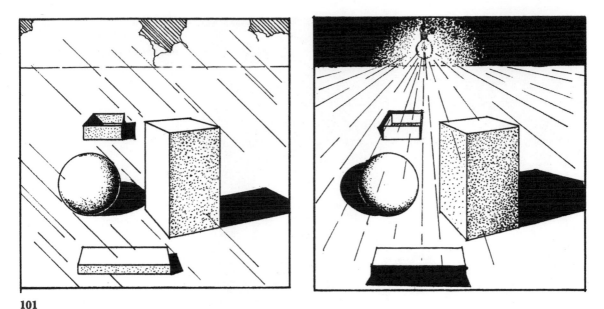

101
Diagram of light sources and effects. Slanting lines indicate parallel sunbeams
and radiating artificial light rays

the original painting and its slide reproduction remain pretty constant. It's like playing an instrument at higher or lower pitch; the difference is obvious, but the relationship between tones doesn't change much.

One can see the importance of such relationships by glancing at figure 98. The background is graduated from black to faint gray, the central strip remains a constant gray; the strip only *seems* to change because its relationship to the background is inconstant.

Convincingly realistic pictures, such as photographs, preserve the principal relationships that obtain for vision. Thus, in figure 99 sunlight, falling in parallel rays, lights the sides of things in a consistent fashion. Everything to our left is light, and what is to the right is in shadow. Of course, the shadows are not utterly black, because air itself is reflective and holds light even in the shade. Artificial light, emanated by candles, lanterns, electric bulbs, and the like, radiates so that

the things in figure 100 are lighted on the side toward the torch. The effect is obvious to everyone. Figure 101 diagrams it. What is toward a light is lighted; what is away from it is darker. *Giovanni Arnolfini and His Bride* is based on the assumption that light is entering the bedchamber from our left, and Giovanni Arnolfini's face is light on the left and dark on the right. Similarly, all the things in the room —the oranges on the sill, the folds in the bride's gown, even the individual hairs on the little dog—are light on the left and cast shade to the right.

Georges de La Tour (1593–1652) was fascinated by the effects of artificial light, and in his painting *Joseph the Carpenter* (fig. 102) he has used a flame to illuminate the figures. They are consistently light on the side of the light source and lost in deep, deep shadow elsewhere. It is not magic that makes it look so like a firelit scene; it is the artist's consistency.

102
GEORGES DE LA TOUR.
Joseph the Carpenter.
c. 1645.
Oil on canvas, 53⅞ × 40⅛″.
The Louvre, Paris

Chiaroscuro and Modeling

The Italians have a word for the effect of light and shade in art. They call it *chiaroscuro*. This is the term artists apply to the general effect; the specific applications of it to noses, lips, eyes, drapery folds, and so forth are called *modeling*. Chiaroscuro always refers to light and dark, but there are some specialized uses of the term that you should know about. It is often applied to a kind of drawing (fig. 103) emphasizing light-and-shade effects. In such drawings the artists work on tinted paper, usually gray, indicating shadows with a dark crayon or ink and noting the lightest places with a white crayon or paint. There is a woodcut technique called chiaroscuro (fig. 104) in which light in the print is indicated by white paper, semishade by some medium tone, and dark shade by black or extremely dark gray. But these usages are just special applications of the term. Chiaroscuro is literally *chiaro*, meaning light, plus *scuro*, meaning dark.

103

PIERRE PAUL PRUD'HON. *Study for La Source.* c. 1801.
Black and white chalk, 21¼ × 15¼". Sterling and Francine Clark Art Institute, Williamstown, Massachusetts

104

UGO DA CARPI. *Raphael and His Mistress.* 16th century.
Woodcut, 7 × 5½". The Metropolitan Museum of Art, New York. Rogers Fund, 1922

105
Shadow lettering

106
Metallic strips forming letters

107
High contrast drawing

108
Stipple drawing

We can best understand how artists use light and shade to create an illusion of solidity if we ignore the subtleties of modeling. A very good example for our purposes is the kind of lettering in which the letter forms are indicated by what would be the shaded side if they were made of metal strips (fig. 105). Viewers perceive the letters as if they were as I have rendered them in figure 106. But of course there is no thin band along their thickness in figure 105: the viewer merely "fills in" with such a band; he pretends it is there.

You do the same thing when you look at an ink drawing such as the picture of Lincoln (fig. 107); you imagine the intermediate grays that are actually defined by tiny dots in figure 108. In both figure 105 and figure 107 you are projecting your expectations onto emptiness. The empty surface is as much a part of the image as the black forms are. A number of art styles are based on precisely this effect. Milton Caniff's cartoon style (fig. 109) derives its documentary appearance from it; and Jim Steranko (fig. 110), Jeff Jones (fig. 111), and others make constant use of it for dramatic impact and design. The Chinese created an entire aesthetic tradition based on the power of expressing things through the absence of ink. The whiteness of the silk in figure 112 is not just a void; it is as palpable a part of the depicted scene as are the brushstrokes that evoke hillocks, trees, and mounds of earth. It is also true that a number of media, such as wood engraving (fig. 113), rely on the willingness of viewers to fill in absent information.

That the contrast between the large masses of shade and the blankness of light is fundamental to the painter's illusions is borne out by the practice of the great masters of representational art. When Caravaggio (1573–1610) painted *Christ at Emmaus* (fig. 114), he detailed every surface, and we luxuriate in the satiny perfection of his tones. In his preparatory studies, however, Caravaggio, like his followers (fig. 115), was brusque,

109

MILTON CANIFF. *Steve Canyon.*

110

JIM STERANKO. *At the Stroke of Midnight.*

111

JEFF JONES. *Alien.*

112
MA YUAN. *Landscape with Bridge
and Willows.* Sung Dynasty,
early 13th century.
Ink and colors on silk, 9⅜×9⅝″. Museum
of Fine Arts, Boston

113
ROCKWELL KENT. *Northern Light.* c. 1928.
Wood engraving, 5½ × 8⅛″. Philadelphia
Museum of Art

114
CARAVAGGIO. *Christ at Emmaus.* c. 1598.
Oil on canvas, 55 × 77½″. The National Gallery, London

115
FOLLOWER OF
CARAVAGGIO. *A Feast.*
17th century.
Pen, brown ink and wash,
6½ × 7¾″. The Fine
Arts Museums of San
Francisco. Achenbach
Foundation for Graphic Arts

116
HENRI ROUSSEAU.
The Dream. 1910.
Oil on canvas, 6'8½" × 9'9½".
The Museum of Modern
Art, New York. Gift of
Nelson A. Rockefeller

117
JAN VERMEER. *Head of a
Young Girl.* c. 1665.
Oil on canvas, 18¼ × 15¾".
Mauritshuis, The Hague

searching not after subtleties of light and
shade but studying their larger disposition.
Since it is known that Caravaggio worked
directly on his paintings, without recourse to
careful preparatory drawings, it is likely that
the initial sketching onto the canvas was
similarly bold, perhaps something quite like
figure 115.

In learning to draw, it is important for art
students to come to the understanding that
the big relationships are primary. If the
general effect is plain, precise detail is relatively easy to attain, but no amount of fussy
detail will convey an impression of reality.
Such itemizing may be charming (fig. 116),
may even possess its own distinctive kind of
genius; but it does not provide a convincing
illusion. Many amateur works of art look
naive because the painter has approached his
subject "backwards."

The reduction of the complex world of light
and shadow into simpler contrasts also has
the effect of packaging the volumes more
coherently than they come to us in ordinary
life. For example, look at Vermeer's *Head of a
Young Girl* (fig. 117). Jan Vermeer van Delft
(1632–1675) may be the very greatest master
of light and shade. He modeled his forms with
such certainty that this girl seems extant in
space as no real person could ever be. The
volumes are so explicit that one knows almost
exactly how this head would look if the girl
were in profile or if she were looking up or
looking down.

Whenever in painting a light meets a dark,
an accent is obtained, just as a contrast in
tone creates an accent in a musical sequence.
When this accent is formed by the junction of
two areas, one uniformly light relative to
another that is uniformly dark, an apparent
change of plane occurs. In other words, if
nothing else opposes the illusion, such a contrast is read as though it were a corner carved
from space. Thus, in figure 118 we have a Y
in a hexagon, but with one segment darkened
we have a cube (figure 119). Whether such a

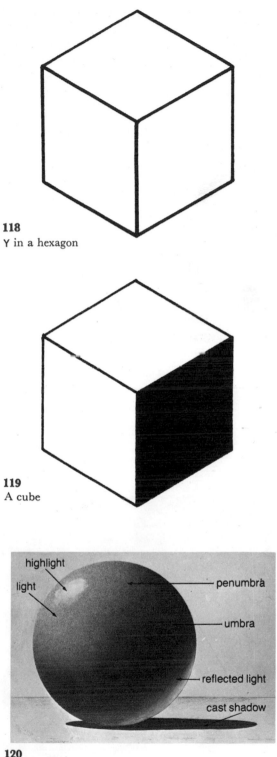

118
Y in a hexagon

119
A cube

120
The nomenclature of
chiaroscuro

corner seems carved into space or seems to project outward depends on its relation to the other contrasts. Thus, had Vermeer darkened the top of the young lady's nose instead of its side, the nose would appear to be a hideously deep scar. As this suggests, darkening the nose on its side—the side corresponding to the dark side of the face—made it stand away from the head. Likewise, placing a continuous series of accents over the turban, down the forehead, by the eye, down the neck, and across the shoulder creates the impression that the planes to either side are moving back into a dark void. The girl's head and body constitute one large volume containing smaller volumes (like noses and ears) and are not merely aggregations of little details.

Of course, it is not really possible to describe the Vermeer in terms of light versus dark. There are all sorts of in-between tones; some parts of the shadow are darker than others, some lighted surfaces are much lighter than others, and everywhere there are transitions. The technical term in physics for a space of partial illumination between perfect shadow and full light is *penumbra*. This is the

term applied to the "twilight" area of the moon, to the hazy edge of an eclipse, and also to graduations from dark to light in pictures.

Figure 120 illustrates the traditional way of describing form as it is revealed by light and shade. The *highlight* represents a reflection of the light source; it is nearly pure white. On a dull surface the highlight will not be reflected in so clear a fashion; it is then merely part of the *light* area. The *penumbra* provides the transition to what is known as the *umbra* (or core of shadow). The *cast shadow* is, of course, the shade of the object on another surface and is usually the darkest of all these components. The final element is *reflected light*.

Reflected light is perhaps less well understood by laymen than are the other components of chiaroscuro. So far as that is concerned, the paintings by Jan van Eyck and Vermeer at which we've been looking contain hardly any reflected lights. The Caravaggio (fig. 114) has some, but they are not treated in a very obvious fashion. The most familiar demonstration of reflected light is the child's game where a dandelion is held beneath the

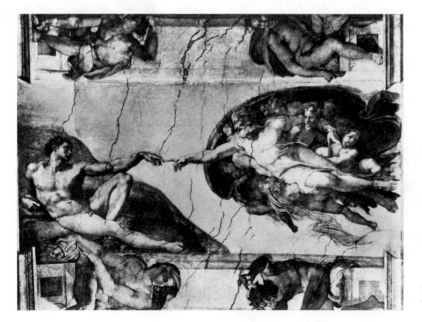

121
MICHELANGELO.
The Creation of Adam.
1508–12.
Fresco. Sistine Chapel,
Vatican, Rome

122

IVAN LE LORRAINE
ALBRIGHT. *Into the World
Came a Soul Called Ida.*
1929–30.
Oil on canvas, $56\frac{1}{4} \times 47''$.
The Art Institute of Chicago

123

SALVADOR DALI.
*Apparition of a Face and
Fruit Dish on a Beach.*
1938.
Oil on canvas, $43\frac{1}{2} \times 57''$.
Wadsworth Atheneum,
Hartford, Connecticut. The
Ella Gallup Sumner and
Mary Catlin Sumner
Collection

GIRL RIDING
ON
VIKING

124
VIRGIL FINLAY. *Untitled.*
Courtesy Mrs. Virgil Finlay

chin to see whether the subject "likes butter." Invariably, a yellow glow appears. It is sunlight reflected from the blossom. In sunlit atmosphere such reflections are all around. Most people aren't aware of their presence, but without them things on earth would look a good deal more stark than they do. In fact, the absence of an atmosphere on the moon decreases the chance for reflection with predictable consequences—the shade is black. The photographer, in his studio, often uses both a primary and a secondary light source in order to enhance his illusions, with the secondary source doing duty for reflected light. But the value to artists of representing reflected light goes beyond the duplication of sunlit reality.

Michelangelo's *Creation of Adam* (fig. 121) makes good use of reflected light on the upper arm of God the Father. Without the glossy light touching the curve of His triceps, the thrust of the entire arm would be less powerful. And a similar treatment of God's right leg brings the leg out from the mass of nudes supporting Him. In the same way, the glisten of a light under God's left wrist helps distinguish His arm from the background. These reflected lights also help continue certain linear patterns which compose the picture into a unified whole.

Ivan le Lorraine Albright of Chicago (born 1897) paints "uglies" (fig. 122). Even his paint surfaces look corrupt. And his shadows have the phosphorescent glow of utter putrefaction, a unique use of reflected light.

The Spaniard whose name is synonymous with the bizarre in art, Salvador Dali (born 1904), has turned chiaroscuro into a game in his *Apparition of a Face and Fruit Dish on a Beach* (fig. 123). What seems one thing is quickly transmuted into another. Take the bridge over the river at the upper right. It is also a dog's collar! A little attention will reveal the entire animal. The hole through the hillside is the dog's eye. His hindquarters seem to be of a holocaust at sea. Dali accomplishes these shifts of meaning through a clever use of the principles of chiaroscuro, turning one set of lights into relative darks (in the sea scene, for instance), making the reflected light serve double duty, and so on. It is very ingenious, if rather tricky and superficial.

The mechanical procedures for producing chiaroscuro modeling are more easily observed in drawings than in paintings, simply because the procedures are more direct. Anyone can see how fantasy-science-fiction illustrator Virgil Finlay (1914–1971) did his ink drawing (fig. 124): very *care*fully.

Finlay's technique involves both cross-hatching, in which lines are drawn over one another, and stippling, in which dots are made with the pen. His work is particularly useful in discussions of light and shade because he is a painstaking craftsman in love with simple artifice. With a kind of puritanical insistence his lines follow every curve of flesh; they are incredibly controlled as pen lines go,

almost as precise as the engraved lines he imitates. The stippled dots are used to intensify a few darks and to moderate the lighter areas of the sea god's face. Notice that the illustration contains every facet of chiaroscuro. By bringing the umbra—the darkest part of a shadow—right up against the light on the girl's back, Finlay even obtains a highlight. This produces the illusion of increased whiteness nearest the dark. It is a well-known effect —Finlay is not at all imaginative in terms of artistic approaches—which can be observed in El Greco's *Resurrection* (fig. 19). It derives from the illusion we noted in figure 98.

The means of operation in the Finlay is the

125
Pen scratches

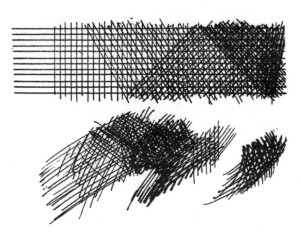

126
Cross-hatching

127
EDGAR DEGAS.
Self-Portrait. 1855.
Etching, $9 \times 5\frac{5}{8}''$. National
Gallery of Art, Washington,
D.C. Lessing Rosenwald
Collection

128
GEORGES SEURAT.
Seated Boy with Straw Hat.
1882.
Conté crayon, $9\frac{1}{2} \times 12\frac{1}{4}''$.
Yale University Art Gallery,
New Haven. Everett V.
Meeks, B. A. 1901, Fund

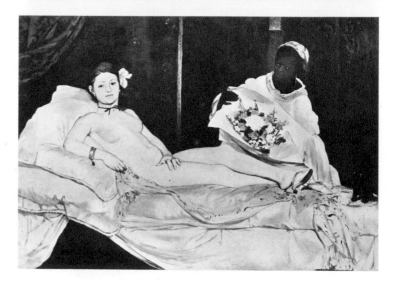

129
EDOUARD MANET.
Olympia. 1863.
Oil on canvas, $51\frac{1}{4} \times 74\frac{3}{4}''$.
The Louvre, Paris

a   b

130
Shading techniques

same as that in any pen-and-ink drawing, line etching, engraving, or similar image. The darkness or lightness of an area is the result of the relative density of units. Where there are more lines or dots per square inch, there is the deepest shade. Obvious? Of course. But it has some consequences. It is, for example, a good deal easier to control the relative concentration of lines or dots if a rather systematic procedure, like Finlay's, is used. In the work of professional artists you rarely see scratchy effects like those in figure 125. Normally, the artist will crosshatch by going from light to dark, building up the darks by adding new lines at different angles from the ones he puts down first (fig. 126).

In his *Self-Portrait* (fig. 127) Edgar Degas presents himself lighted from behind, his face and body in shadow faint enough to reveal his features and details of his clothing. The shading entails several levels of cross-hatching, each one growing progressively darker.

First, there is the general half-light of the silhouette. It is rendered as a haze of very, very thin marks. Over this, Degas applied a layer of slightly heavier lines, following the contours of his flesh and his clothing. Finally, another set designates the darkest shadows, the eyes, mustache, beard, and so on.

A slightly later painter, Georges Seurat, did many drawings with black crayon on a very distinctively textured paper (fig. 128). One can see that he was very conscious of the crayon as a granular substance. Again, the relative density of units (in this case particles of crayon) determines relative darkness, and light and shade in Seurat's drawings take on a curiously crepuscular quality.

You may have noticed that most of the artists discussed in this chapter contrive to work with a light source that is above and to the left or right (usually to the left) of the subject. There are various advantages to proceeding in this fashion, but it is not essen-

131
CIMABUE. *Madonna Enthroned.*
c. 1280–90.
Tempera on panel, 12'6" × 7'4".
Uffizi Gallery, Florence

132
FERNAND LÉGER.
The Card Players. 1917.
Oil on canvas, 50⅝ × 76".
Kröller-Müller Museum,
Otterlo, The Netherlands

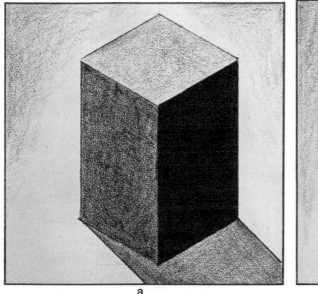 

a   b

133
Treatments of a cube

tial to do so. Manet's *Olympia* (fig. 129) seems to be lighted from directly in front, as if by a flashgun; and the faint shadows curve around the edges of the model's torso, head, arms, and legs. This relationship of lights and darks can be turned to advantage by artists who wish to give an impression of the third dimension without making use of the full range of light and shade effects. Figure 130 contains some geometric solids treated in terms of a light source in panel *A* and, in *B,* on the assumption that light areas stand for advancing or protruding forms and dark ones for receding edges. *B* is not consistent with any real light source, not even one out front, but it is an effective way of representing the objects. Cimabue (fig. 131) and other late medieval painters attempted to convey solidity in this way, generally, but a certain timidity stood in the way of the kind of exaggeration I have employed in my drawing. That is not true of the modern painter Fernand Léger (1881–1955). In his *Card Players* (fig. 132) and in other works he turns everything into a series

of mechanical forms by means of the same technique.

Léger also uses a related device whose basis is demonstrated in figure 133, where *A* is treated as if sunlit and *B* as the result of a simple alternation of dark-light contrasts.

What is important in every one of these images is that they depend upon contrast between light and dark. The impression can be of greater or lesser verisimilitude, depending on the degree to which the drawings or paintings approximate actual light effects; but the presence of dark-light contrast is essential. In figure 134 I have taken an exquisitely subtle still life (fig. 135) by the eighteenth-century Frenchman Jean-Baptiste-Siméon Chardin (1699–1779) and ruthlessly reduced it to gross relationships which derive from a theoretical light source and mechanical alternation of darks and lights. Despite some passages that would be inexplicable in nature—such as the darks on the wall behind the objects—the result is an image of solid objects occupying space.

134
After Chardin's *Still Life:
The Kitchen Table*

135
JEAN-BAPTISTE-SIMÉON
CHARDIN. *Still Life:
The Kitchen Table.* 1733.
Oil on canvas, $15\frac{1}{2} \times 18\frac{5}{8}$".
Museum of Fine Arts, Boston.
Gift of Peter Chardin Brooks

136

REMBRANDT VAN RIJN. *The Descent from the Cross: By Torchlight.* 1654.
Etching, 8 × 6¼″. Rijksmuseum, Amsterdam

The Meaning of Light and Dark

Darkness means more to us than just the absence of light. It conjures up within our minds notions associated with the night—concealment, mystery, danger, evil. In nearly every culture blackness has some identification with evil. It is not true that white racism is the sponsor of such associations;[1] they grow out of the long ages of mankind when night was filled with terrors, before artificial lighting had mitigated the hazards of darkness in the forest, on the prairie, and in the jungles. Even today the lightest streets are the safest ones.

Rembrandt's etching *The Descent from the Cross: By Torchlight* (fig. 136) uses light to dramatize the scene and also to heighten the symbolic meaning of the event. Whiteness is associated with Christ, the Light of the World, and darkness with the great sin of humanity. The hand raised to receive Christ's head is as eloquent as the ancient symbol of the drowning man; it reaches out of the gloom as if in hope of salvation.

The Spanish painter Francisco Goya (1746–1828) makes use of dramatic lighting in a rather similar fashion. In *The Third of May, 1808* (fig. 137), representing French troops crushing a rebellion by the people of Madrid, the principal victim is in the center of a veritable explosion of light. The effect is all the more striking because his flesh is dark. He throws his arms out in a gesture of defiance and signifies that he, like Christ, is being "crucified." In the distance a tiny cross on a church building drives home the point. The firing squad is shadowy and featureless: the soldiers have no individual personalities; they are merely instruments of French imperialism, the tools of the oppressor.

Works of art that are highly dramatic, such as the Goya, the Rembrandt etching, Tintoretto's *Last Supper* (fig. 80), or El Greco's

137
FRANCISCO GOYA. *The Third of May, 1808.* 1814–15.
Oil on canvas, 8'8¾" × 11'3⅞".
The Prado, Madrid

138
RICHARD CORBEN. *Den.*
© 1973, Richard Corben

139
THÉODORE GÉRICAULT.
The Raft of the "Medusa."
1818–19.
Oil on canvas, 16′1″ × 23′6″.
The Louvre, Paris

140
HONORÉ DAUMIER. *The Laundress.*
c. 1861.
Oil on panel, 19¼ × 13″. The Louvre, Paris

141
JOSEPH MALLORD WILLIAM TURNER.
The Dogana, San Giorgio Maggiore,
le Zitelle, from the Steps of the Europa. 1842.
Oil on canvas, 24½ × 36½″. The Tate
Gallery, London

142
AD REINHARDT. *Abstract*
Painting, Blue. 1952.
Oil on canvas, 75 × 28″. Museum of
Art, Carnegie Institute, Pittsburgh

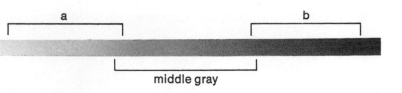

143
Value scale

a

b

middle gray

Resurrection (fig. 19), frequently contain areas of extremely high contrast. Usually the drama is produced by bright light in dark surroundings. But once in a while the artist will do the opposite and show us a dark shape against the light, as Richard Corben does in his underground comic strip *Den* (fig. 138), as Théodore Gericault (1791–1824) did in his famous *Raft of the "Medusa"* (fig. 139), and as Honoré Daumier (1808–1879) did in *The*

Laundress (fig. 140). In any case, the extreme contrast between dark and light areas makes for a highly charged impact.

Not all painters wish to be so dramatic as Goya or Tintoretto, and not every subject lends itself to collisions between dark and light. The later works of the Englishman J.M.W. Turner (1775–1851) are so light as to approximate luminous phantoms on the canvas (see figure 141). The typical Rem-

144
WILLIAM HARNETT. *After the Hunt.*
1885.
Oil on canvas, 11 × 48″.
The Fine Arts Museums of San
Francisco. Gift of H.K.S. Williams
to the Mildred Anna Williams
Collection

145
JAN VAN EYCK.
Giovanni Arnolfini and His Bride. 1434.
Oil on panel, 32¼ × 23½".
The National Gallery,
London

brandt tends towards gloominess. An American painter, the late Ad Reinhardt (1913–1967), did abstractions so dark that when you walk into a gallery full of them your first impression is that the place has been hung with dark brown and black rectangles (see fig. 142). His pictures contain very, very somber rectangles, and there is a kind of magic in their emergence out of sunless depths.

Paintings and photographs in which the majority of tones are, like Turner's, lighter than a middle gray (fig. 143A) are called high key. Those in which most of the tones fall below middle gray (fig. 143B) are referred to as low-key pictures. (These terms have nothing to do with tension and relaxation; they refer only to the comparative lightness or darkness of things.)

The key of a painting has an important bearing on its general character. It is not altogether true that dark paintings are sad and light ones joyous, although there is a kind of affinity between the mood and the key. It is true, though, that the representation of miniscule detail can be achieved only in the lower register. Notice that the two most detailed works we've so far examined, the Harnett (fig. 144) and the Van Eyck (fig. 145), are dark.

The impression of complete and absolute fidelity to nature achieved in a work like *After the Hunt* derives from the artist's handling of the sparkle of reflections on the various surfaces. For it is in the treatment of the reflection of the light source that the variety of textures is revealed. The same thing is true of *Giovanni Arnolfini and His Bride*. But, since the highest possible highlight is nothing but white pigment, it is necessary that lightness not be approached too rapidly. The reason for this has to do with something we barely touched on earlier. I mentioned above that there would not be distinct highlights on a dull surface, that the highlight there would be merely a part of the lighted area. The art historian E. H. Gombrich once made use of an old-fashioned textbook example similar to

146
Light and luster

figure 146 to make a point about the difference between light and luster. The way light falls on an object reveals its form. The way the object's surface reflects the light reveals its texture. The matt-surfaced top hat exemplifies light's operation; the shiny silk top hat is filled with highlights that are reflections of the light source distorted by the curvature of the tissue of fabric.

It is a commonplace of art criticism that

147
MASACCIO. *The Tribute Money.* c. 1427.
Fresco. Brancacci Chapel, Sta. Maria del Carmine, Florence

148
CARAVAGGIO. *Christ at Emmaus.*
c. 1598.
Oil on canvas, 55 × 77½″.
The National Gallery, London

149
Pale and dark underpainting

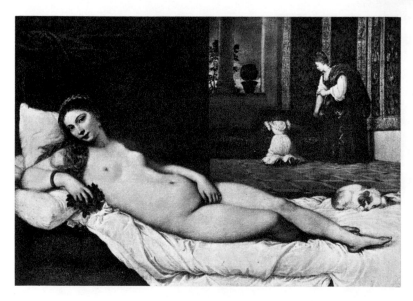

150
TITIAN. *Venus of Urbino.*
1538.
Oil on canvas, 47 × 65″.
Uffizi Gallery, Florence

151
EDOUARD MANET.
Olympia. 1863.
Oil on canvas, $51\frac{1}{4} \times 74\frac{3}{4}''$.
The Louvre, Paris

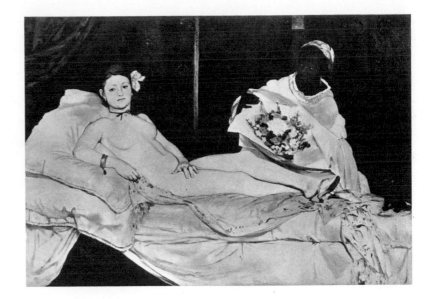

works like the Harnett and the Van Eyck are less secure in rendering forms in space than are works in which surfaces have not been treated with such miraculous precision. Thus, a Masaccio (fig. 147) is far more solid-looking than a Van Eyck, although not nearly so detailed. When Caravaggio, in his *Christ at Emmaus* (fig. 148), placed his objects on a table, moving back into space, he sacrificed some of the illusion Harnett retained. The Harnett is convincing partly because it is shallow, because the need to use dark and light to handle spatial relationships has been suppressed.

You will notice that in figure 146 the highlight of the matt-surfaced hat is no less white than the highlight on the shiny one. Consider then my treatment of a jewel (fig. 149). In both *A* and *B* I have begun by painting the jewel so as to reveal its form, without indicating anything of the texture. Below, in each case, I have tried to render the texture of the jewel on the basis established above. But the highlights in *A* don't sparkle as they should, and the gold setting has none of the sheen of real metal. The finished rendering

in *B* is much more convincing simply because I began with a lower-key representation of the form and could, therefore, vary the lightness of the highlights, achieve different contrasts, and simulate the flashing variability of vision. This condition prevails for all renderings of meticulous detail. You can't have high-key pictures that are impressively detailed in the way that the Harnett and Van Eyck are.

The condition of relatively far-ranging contrast between the highest light and the darkest dark holds for all powerful illusions of three-dimensionality too. This is the reason that the Masaccio looks more solid than the Van Eyck. Masaccio didn't expend his highest lights on detailing; he used them to model bold forms in space. It is also the reason that Titian's *Venus of Urbino* (fig. 150) gives an impression of roundness and fullness that the more photographic *Olympia* (fig. 151) does not.

Manet, however, was onto something else. But it is something that cannot be understood without an understanding of color theory, the subject of the next chapter.

5
Color

In our discussion of light and shade we were already dealing with color theory, for lightness and darkness are aspects of color. Everyone must be aware of that. Navy blue is dark and sky blue is light, and all that the two colors share is their common blueness. In every other respect they are different. Scarlet is different from crimson, but both are reds. If we want to be precise in our description of a color, we must refer to three specific attributes: (1) the *value*, (2) the *hue*, and (3) the *intensity*. I would describe a "passion pink" as having a high value (it is light) and being in the hue of red at full intensity.[1] Since we are going to be talking about some

features of painting that depend upon hue and intensity as well as dark-light relationships, it will be necessary for you to understand exactly what the terms mean.

Before getting into a more elaborate discussion of the meaning of value, hue, and intensity, however, I wish to remind you once more that the painter is not working with light; he is using pigments. Of course, he sees only in terms of light rays, like everyone else, but he cannot imitate light effects in a direct way. What is true of the brightness of sunlight as compared with the brightness of white pigment is true of everything else in painting. For instance, in light theory the

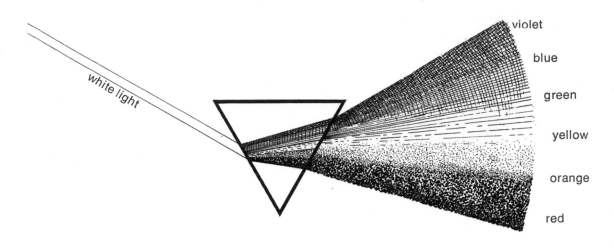

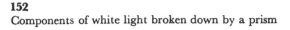

violet
blue
green
yellow
orange
red

152
Components of white light broken down by a prism

presence of all colors equals white light, but if I were to mix all the colors on my palette together, I'd end up with a dark brown muddle. White light, when broken down into its components by a glass prism (fig. 152), produces a full range of spectrum colors: violet, blue, green, yellow, orange, red, and all the intermediate gradations. White light striking white pigment reflects back almost entirely, while nearly all of it is absorbed by dull black paint. Red paint absorbs some of the white light but no red; the red is reflected back to our eyes and therefore we see the paint as a red area. Of course, this doesn't apply just to paint. It applies to everything. Lemons absorb some of everything but yellow, the green felt on a billiard table reflects back nothing but green.[2] (To ask what these substances "really" look like makes no sense. That is like wondering what a guitar sounds like apart from the sensations it produces in the ear, or asking what sugar tastes like apart from what it does to the taste buds in the mouth.)

We have already discussed *value* at some length because it is the basis of chiaroscuro. There will be more to say about it, but color is most easily approached by beginning with the notion of *hue*.

Hue

Hue is what most people think of when they think of color. When you are arguing with a friend about whether a sports car you saw was blue or blue-green, you are arguing about the hue. A simple way of describing hue would be to say that it represents a segment of the spectrum. In discussing color, artists often make use of a color wheel (colorplate 1). This is nothing more than the hues of the spectrum bent into a wheel. (There is, however, one color in the wheel that does not appear in the rainbow of hues the prism gives us. Red-violet is used to tie the ends of the spectrum together into a circle.) It would be possible to make the circle of hues continuously graduated into one another, but it is customary to divide color wheels into twelve units.

You will notice that three of the hues are labeled with the numeral *1*, three with a *2*, and six with a *3*. The colors labeled with a *1* are called *primary hues*. You cannot mix these from any other hues; you must begin with them. Given these three primary colors, red, yellow, and blue, you can mix any of the other hues.

If you mix two primaries together in equal amounts, you will get one of the hues labeled *2*, hence the name *secondary hues*. Red+yellow=orange. Yellow+blue=green. Blue+red=violet. And, of course, the hues labeled *3* are the tertiary hues, the mixtures standing between the primaries and secondaries. Red+orange=red-orange. Orange+yellow=yellow-orange, and so forth. By adding a little more red to the orange one gets a redder red-orange, a scarlet. By adding quite a lot of red to a red-violet you can produce a red red-violet, a crimson. All such intervening colors are referred to as *tertiary hues* even though the number of variations is infinite. All of them are the result of combining any two of the three primaries.

Hues that are very similar—adjacent to each other on the color wheel—are called *analogous hues*. Analogous relationships always involve a tertiary color, since these fall between primaries and secondaries. Analogous hues tend to be harmonious and restful when used together in a design. *Orange and Yellow* (colorplate 2) by Mark Rothko (1903–1970) has an analogous color scheme involving oranges, red-oranges, yellows, and yellow-oranges. Those luminous rectangles float effortlessly, tensionlessly, in a cottony atmosphere.

The Last Supper (colorplate 3) by Emil Nolde (1867–1956) is different from the Rothko in many ways, but one of the most striking differences is in the color organization. Nolde's painting is the opposite of an analogous design; the hues are highly contrasting. Greens and reds, yellows and violets, contest for our attention in much the way that dark and light do in Tintoretto's *Last Supper*. Nolde's color scheme is a *complementary* one involving hues that are com-

plements, that is, directly opposite each other on the wheel. The effect is one of excitement and intensity.

Rarely do artists work exclusively with analogous hues or complementary ones. More often they use complex arrangements in which analogous areas contrast with each other or in which zones of highly contrasting hues are played off against harmonious ones. In Picasso's *Girl Before a Mirror* (colorplate 4) much of the upper portion is made up of analogous hues, and the background and the girl herself are constituted of complementary and primary contrasts. *Girl Before a Mirror* is a particularly bold and well-orchestrated example of such balance, but you will find some hint of this kind of equilibrium of hues in most paintings.

Another feature of color is the relative *warmth* or *coolness* of hues. The identification of reds, yellows, and oranges as warm colors, and blues, blue-greens, and violets as cool colors, derives no doubt from our experience of nature. Extremely hot things are usually red or orange, and the ocean, the sky, distant mountains, and ice cubes are bluish. Artists have come to term hues lying toward the red-orange side of the color wheel "warm" and those lying toward the blue-violet end "cool." Within the various hues, too, there are different temperatures; a red-violet is a cooler red than a red-orange and a yellow-green is warmer than a green. But the connection between hues and actual temperature is extremely vague—as observe "white heat" and "blue flames." For the moment it is best to consider "warmth" and "coolness" as descriptive of the placement of hues on a spectrum or color wheel and ignore the other implications.

Value

Value refers to the lightness or darkness of a color. The hue of a color depends on the

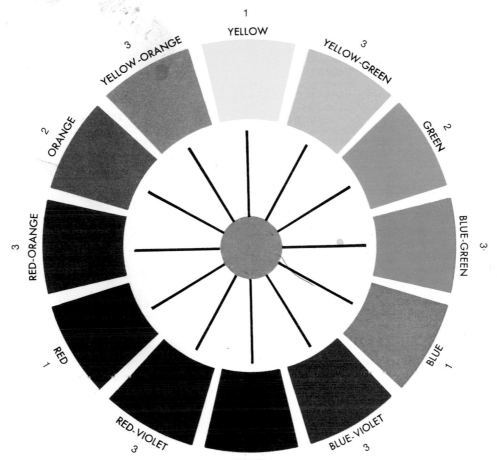

VALUE SCALE

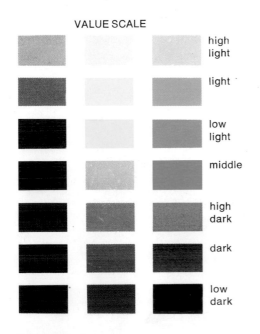

high
light

light

low
light

middle

high
dark

dark

low
dark

INTENSITY SCALE

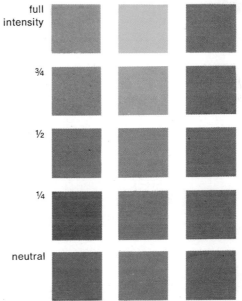

full
intensity

¾

½

¼

neutral

Colorplate 1
Color wheel

Colorplate 2
MARK ROTHKO. *Orange and Yellow.* 1956.
Oil on canvas, 91 × 71″.
Albright-Knox Art Gallery,
Buffalo, New York. Gift of
Seymour H. Knox

kinds of white light rays the color absorbs and which one or ones it reflects back. The value of a color depends on how *much* of the light is absorbed. Pure violet absorbs far more light than pure yellow. If we wish, however, we can lighten the violet to the point where it is as light as pure yellow by introducing white into it. When this is done, the resultant color, orchid, is a *tint* of violet. A tint of a hue is a lightened version of the hue. There are various ways of darkening the yellow. We could add black to it, for instance. A yellow so darkened would be called, technically, a

shade of yellow. (Yes, I know, paint salesmen and interior decorators, among others, use the terms *tint* and *shade* interchangeably. Color theorists don't.) Generally speaking, artists do not add black to hues to darken them, because it deadens them. All the same, the term for a color darkened by the addition of black is *shade*.

There is very little to be said about dark and light values in art that we have not already covered. In colorplate 1 a value scale gives an indication of possible comparisons and contrasts among hues. Needless to say, the lightest of all colors is white and the darkest is black. (These *are* considered colors even though they have no hues.)

Intensity

Of all the attributes of color the most difficult to explain is intensity. *Intensity* is the term used to describe the brightness or dullness of a color, and there is a tendency for people to confuse intensity with value. But if you look at the intensity scale that is shown in colorplate 1, you will realize that intensity has to do with how much of the hue is present in a given color sample. Anything you do to a color that neither tints it nor changes its hue will vary its intensity. That is, if you mix white into a pure red, you tint it: it becomes a bright pink.[3] If you mix yellow into red, you modify the hue: the red turns into red-orange or orange. If, however, you add black to the red, you change its shade and also its intensity (it becomes less bright), but you do not change its hue. And, as odd as it may seem, the introduction of green into the red also will make the red duller without changing the hue.

Look at colorplate 1 again. Notice that

Colorplate 3

EMIL NOLDE. *The Last Supper.* 1909. Oil on canvas, 33⅞ × 42⅛". Royal Museum of Fine Arts, Copenhagen

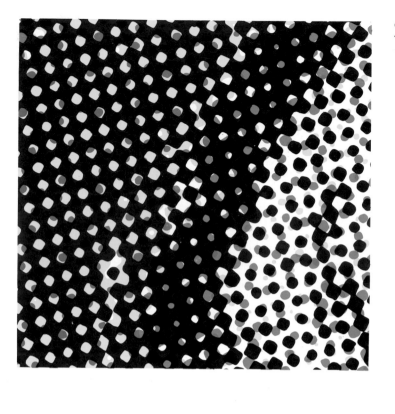

Colorplate 10
Vastly enlarged color
halftone dots

Colorplate 11
RICHARD ANUSZKIEWICZ. *All
Things Do Live in the Three.* 1963.
Acrylic on canvas, $21\frac{7}{8} \times 35\frac{7}{8}''$.
Collection Mrs. Robert M. Benjamin,
New York

that reaches one's eyes is the optical color. Another example would be a burning cigarette in a room lit by a red bulb. The coal of the cigarette appears bright white in such circumstances, although we know that in white light it would be red orange. If the smoker is wearing a green shirt, the shirt will look black in the red light. Again, red orange is the local color of the cigarette tip, and white the optical color. Green is the local color of the shirt, black the optical color.

The example of the distant mountain shows that painters and laymen accept without qualm the substitution of optical color for local color when the effect is sufficiently obvious and universal. The example of the red-lighted smoking room should demonstrate just how arbitrary the idea of a local color is. That is, in these special circumstances the cigarette tip *is* glowing white. And the green shirt *is* black. All that local color means is that an object seen under white light will have that particular hue.

But Monet wanted to show in his paintings that vision is not constant even in sunlight—to depict such phenomena as the simultaneous contrasts on the green vase. The major difference between Monet and a traditional painter is that he was willing to substitute optical color for local color at all times and without exception. So far as Monet was concerned, what he saw was what was. He painted the colors of the haystack just the way they looked to him, the exact color and shape, until he had, in his own words, a "naive impression of the scene." And by "naive" he meant to indicate a more honest and truthful rendition. Now Monet couldn't really portray the thing precisely as it appeared; that is impossible. What he did do was rely on visual sensation to the exclusion of intellectual knowledge about local color. And he eliminated chiaroscuro to retain the purity of the hues he saw.

Monet was the outstanding representative of *French Impressionism,* a movement about which I shall have more to say later. Its influence was not restricted to the acceptance of optical color in place of local color, but this was the most striking thing about it. When the public was first exposed to Impressionist painting, it reacted with incredible hostility. The reaction was due partly to the kind of brushwork the Impressionists used and to some extent to the kinds of subject matter typical of the style, but it was due more than anything else to the use of optical color. After all, the average person perceives optical color as differing from local color only under very unusual circumstances, as in a room lit by a red light. To him the Monet would look fantastic. A fellow Impressionist, examining the Monet, would see it as a refreshingly accurate recording of visual reality. The Impressionists had trained themselves to see such things. The cliché about the beholder's eye was never more true than it is in this case.

Georges Seurat invented a later style typified by *A Sunday Afternoon on the Island of La Grande Jatte* (fig. 158). He retained in this work the Impressionist interest in purity of hue and intensity of color, but he did something very radical: he looked at the whole matter from a reverse point of view. Monet had copied optical color sensations with little dabs of oil paint. Seurat attempted to *create* optical color sensations with little dots of oil paint.

Paint also has its local color. There is no difference, so far as optical receptivity is concerned, between light reflected from a green leaf on a living tree and light reflected from dead pigment of the same hue if both are viewed under similar conditions. This is obvious, of course, but we don't often look at pictures from just this angle. Seurat did. He conceived of his paints not so much as colors that could imitate the hues of nature, but as colors that were themselves sensation-producing. He was thereby led to apply himself to the science of optics and devise a set of princi-

157
Haystacks lighted from the side and from behind

ples to guide his intuition. These principles were largely derived from the writings of the physicists Ogden Rood and Michel Chevreul and were later jotted down by another painter, Lucien Pissarro, for his own use. Among them is the following:

Two complementaries mixed in unequal portions destroy each other partially and produce a broken color which is a variety of grey, a tertiary color. The law of complementaries permits a color to be toned down or intensified without becoming dirty; while not touching the color itself one can fortify or neutralize it by changing the adjacent colors.[5]

This is a description of simultaneous contrast. Monet copied the effect. Seurat used it. Not content with Impressionism's copies of the world of visual phenomena, Seurat aimed at constructing a phenomenal image at first hand, an image that would possess all the brilliance and variability of the world of light itself because it was constructed according to the laws governing the mechanics of vision.

In order to accomplish his ends, he had to control the color relationships very precisely. This is one of the reasons for his use of thousands of separate dots of color instead of the usual brushstrokes. The technique of application is known as *pointillism,* the style itself either as *Neoimpressionism* or, by Seurat's own preference, *Divisionism.* Most critics and authors of art appreciation books assert that the way to view a Seurat is to stand far enough away so that the dots fuse and only the effect is plain, as if Seurat's style were a kind of handmade halftone reproduction like the one in colorplate 10—so blue dots and green dots together give you blue-green. Nonsense! The optical mixtures and contrast effects will not occur at such a distance. To appreciate the picture you must be standing just close enough to comprehend the dots as separate areas of color.

There is a somewhat related set of experiments with color in art which has come in recent years to be called *Op Art.* Among the outstanding practitioners of the mode is the American Richard Anuszkiewicz (born 1930). His *All Things Do Live in the Three* (colorplate 11) is an example of Op Art and also a good illustration of what a small but distinct area of color can do to adjacent hues. The red background is continuous but appears to change according to the influence of the colored dots upon it. Notice, too, that the effect of the blue-green dots on the red is different from that of the blue dots going to the outer edges. If you have someone hold the book up far enough away for the dots to become invisible, the outer edge is indistinguishable in color from the internal form. This supports my point about not standing so far from the Seurat as to cause the dots to merge.

Emotional Effects of Color

This chapter has been almost exclusively concerned with the visual attributes of color. But color also has another side, as noted in such common terms as "black mood," "the blues," "green with envy," "seeing red,"

158
GEORGES SEURAT.
A Sunday Afternoon on the Island of La Grande Jatte. 1884–86.
Oil on canvas, 6′9½″ × 10′1¼″.
The Art Institute of Chicago. Helen Birch Bartlett Memorial Collection

"a yellow coward," "purple prose," and "brown funk."

For reasons not understood at all well, specific hues are associated with certain moods. Folk knowledge of this fact led the famous football coach Knute Rockne to have the team dressing rooms at Notre Dame painted red for the home team and blue for the visitors. The assumption was that red would maintain the emotional "heat" of his players during the half-time break while blue would cause the visitors to relax. Rockne won a lot of football games and was noted for his half-time pep talks that sometimes snatched victory from defeat. Whether the wall colors had the effect he hoped for is impossible to say, but he did recognize that cool colors are more restful than warm ones. Motivational psychologists have made considerable use of such recognitions in packaging products, marketing automobiles, and selling political ideologies.

Painting a locker room red would have at least one disadvantage, because warm colors tend to advance and cool ones to recede. A claustrophobic quarterback would concentrate much better in a blue room. When interior decorators wish to make a room look larger, they use cool colors and minimal contrast. If, conversely, they want to make a large room seem more intimate and cozy, psychologically smaller, they will tend to use warm hues and plenty of contrast. Hotel rooms are apt to be cool in hue and to use analogous color schemes. The lobby of a large ski lodge is likely to be full of browns, yellows, and reds, with a few highly contrasting hues and values to make the setting seem less institutional. These colors will also make the lobby seem literally warmer than it otherwise would.

The terms *warm* and *cool* are well chosen to describe the effect of color on the inhabitants of a room. It has been discovered that personnel working in offices painted with warm tones, such as red-orange, are physically comfortable at lower temperatures than those working in offices painted blue, green, or violet.

Painters make use of the emotive content of color. In chapter four I discussed at some length the feelings evoked by darks and lights and their relationships. Van Gogh, speaking of *The Night Café* (fig. 153), said that his colors were not entirely true to life but were meant to "express the terrible passions of humanity by means of red and green." The café, he said, is a place where one might run mad, commit a crime. The violent contrasts of the complementaries are no longer so garish as they must have been when these words were written, but Van Gogh's understanding of the emotional function of color is made quite clear in a beautiful passage from a letter written to his brother Theo in September, 1888. "I am always between two currents of thought," he said, "first, the material difficulties . . . and second, the study of colour. I am always in hope of making a discovery there, to express the love of two lovers by a marriage of two complementary colours, their mingling and their opposition, the mysterious vibrations of kindred tones. To express the thought of a brow by the radiance of a light tone against a somber background. To express hope by some star, the eagerness of a soul by a sunset radiance."

I have one last statement to make about the psychology of color. For years I have heard psychologists, art theorists, and others make reference to studies which have shown women to be slightly superior to men in color discrimination. Usually, the relevant experiment was supposed to have involved equal numbers of males and females sorting strands of differently hued yarn into piles; the women tended to discern more kinds of blue, of green, and so on, and consequently ended up with more piles of yarn than the men. I say that the experiment is "supposed" to have been like this because no such experiment seems to be on record. It's a myth. There are, however, experiments *refuting* such claims. Women may be more expert in using color names because of tradition and social influences (just as men are more apt to know about machinery) but there is no evidence that they are fundamentally better at judging color likenesses or differences.[6] The only difference between men and women so far as color is concerned would appear to be the well-known fact that color blindness is vastly more common in the male, the proportion being 8 percent for men and 0.5 percent for women.

6

Space

You cannot help but notice that we have been talking about two different kinds of forms in the previous chapters. There are the kind that make up the Mondrian (fig. 159)—flat, two-dimensional areas—and the kind that seem three-dimensional (fig. 160). In actuality the Titian is no more three-dimensional than the Mondrian, of course; it's just that chiaroscuro provides an illusion of roundness and relief. Physically, the works are much the same. Psychologically there is a world of difference.

And the difference is mostly spatial.

There are two primary alternatives a painter has when he creates a picture. He can treat the canvas as if it were a window or *picture plane* through which the world is seen, or he can treat the canvas as a window on which forms are placed. Psychologically, it is the same with paintings as with real windows. If you focus on the world beyond the window, you are not aware of the window (fig. 161); and if you focus on the window itself (fig. 162), the world beyond has little

159

PIET MONDRIAN.
*Composition in White,
Black and Red.* 1936.
Oil on canvas, 40¼ × 41".
The Museum of Modern
Art, New York. Gift of the
Advisory Committee

160

TITIAN. *Venus of Urbino.* 1538.
Oil on canvas, 47 × 65". Uffizi Gallery, Florence

161
Focused beyond the window

162
Focused on the window

prominence. Thus, *The Marriage of Isaac and Rebekah* (fig. 163) by the French painter Claude Lorrain (1600–1682) really does somehow seem "in" the page, while Picasso's *Girl Before a Mirror* (fig. 164) is more easily accepted as being printed on the page.

Since pictures are flat, not deep, laymen are usually more intrigued by the illusion of depth than they are by an arrangement of zones on a surface. And well they might be. The creation of spatial illusions is a major achievement of Renaissance art. In some respects, the deep space of the Claude Lorrain depends even more upon conventions than do chiaroscuro or line drawing. But these particular conventions have proved their effectiveness over and over again through the medium of photography, which incorporates them. Indeed, the impression these conventions make is so powerful that, once you've learned them, the illusion is apt to remain even when you are doing your damnedest to destroy it. The humorous engraving (fig. 165) by William Hogarth (1697–1764) is an at-

tempt to defy the conventions. Yet the space of the picture is not flat or nonexistent; it's just that some of the things contained in the space look bizarre.

The primary clue to spatial order is overlapping. What blocks out something else is ahead of it. Basic to all spatial *illusions* is the fact that things distant from the viewer appear smaller than things close to him. If an artist wants something to look far away in a picture, he draws it small relative to something he wants to look near. While it is necessary to use this device to convey depth, it is not, as the Hogarth engraving proves, in itself sufficient. What is absolutely essential to the spatial illusion—apart from overlapping and relative size—is the one other thing Hogarth preserved (whether by design or inadvertence): a clear notion of the viewer's station relative to the scene. The artist and the viewer must both understand the vantage point from which a scene is viewed. That is, if the picture were reality, where would you have to be standing in order to see the objects as they ap-

163

CLAUDE LORRAIN.
*The Marriage of Isaac
and Rebekah (The Mill).*
1640.
Oil on canvas, 58¾ × 77½".
The National Gallery,
London

164

PABLO PICASSO.
Girl Before a Mirror.
1932.
Oil on canvas, 63¾ × 51¼".
The Museum of Modern
Art, New York. Gift of
Mrs. Simon R. Guggenheim

165
WILLIAM HOGARTH. Frontispiece to *"Kirby's Perspective"*
(Joshua Kirby's edition of Dr. Brook Taylor's *Method of Perspective*). 1753.
Engraving, $8\frac{1}{4} \times 6\frac{3}{4}''$. The British Museum, London

166
NEAL ADAMS. *Green Lantern.* © 1970,
DC Comics Inc.

167
CIMABUE. *Madonna
Enthroned.* c. 1280–90.
Tempera on panel,
12′6″ × 7′4″.
Uffizi Gallery, Florence

pear in the picture? Hogarth's objects look implausible, but you do know, intuitively, that you are standing on the ground looking out between the two sides of the image, about on center. In the first panel of Neal Adams's *Green Lantern* (fig. 166) you, the viewer, are standing approximately on line with the older man. In panel two you are very, very close to him but lower and looking up. The third panel puts you above the superhero and his questioner. Adams adapted this kind of presentation from Milton Caniff (born 1907), the first cartoonist to make effective use of shifting points of view. Caniff got it from the movies. So far as this book is concerned, there is no difference between a pictorial vantage point and a camera angle except that, historically, the former was necessary to the latter. What photographers and commercial artists take for granted was hard won by geniuses of the past.

Cimabue's *Madonna Enthroned* (fig. 167) reveals the artist fumbling after an illusionistic space in the lower part of the painting. The concave steps below Mary's feet are an indication of his attempt. He tried to carry the effect on down into the arch above the anonymous prophets' heads, but the marriage of arches and concavity gave birth to ambiguity. Is the arch an arch like the ones that flank it, or is it an indentation that happens to look like the flanking arches? No one can say.

About thirty years after Cimabue painted his *Madonna Enthroned*, Giotto, who was probably a student of Cimabue's, did a rather similar one (fig. 168). Both of them are displayed in the same room in the Uffizi Gallery in Florence, Italy, and thereby invite comparison. The Giotto is vastly more advanced in the direction of Renaissance realism, despite the retention of many medieval characteristics such as larger scale for the more important figures. Giotto didn't know scientific perspective—it wasn't invented until after his death—but he did establish a vantage

168

GIOTTO. *Madonna Enthroned.* C. 1310.
Tempera on panel, 10'8" × 6'8".
Uffizi Gallery, Florence

point. The viewer is conceived of as standing slightly to the left of center and being approximately as tall as the two angels standing on either side of Mary's throne. Your position to center left is very certain; you can see slightly more of the left end of the step than the right end, and you see a little more of the inside of the throne on the side that is to your right. This explicitness is important. Cimabue gives you no good clues as to your position. You might say that you are meant to see the Cimabue as if from dead center but you'd be

169
Photographic perspective

170
MASACCIO. *The Tribute Money.* c. 1427.
Fresco. Brancacci Chapel,
Sta. Maria del Carmine,
Florence

wrong. Yes, you *would*. Because you can see the inside of both sides of all three arches, and this would be impossible if you were viewing them from on center.

As for the relative height of the viewer, I must confess that this is somewhat uncertain in the Giotto. We can see the tops of the throne arms, which means that our eyes must be above them. And we can see the underside of the throne's canopy, which means our eyes must be below that. So we feel that we are somewhere on the level of the standing angels. But the viewer cannot be sure which rank of angels is at his level. Even so, the Giotto is a considerable advance over the Cimabue.

In the Cimabue there is no sense whatever for the vertical position of the observer. When looking at a reproduction in a book, our first impulse is to identify with Mary's eye level, as if we were looking straight across at her. (Confronted with the actual work, which is over twelve feet tall, one is less likely to suppose this.) But there is nothing to prevent us from supposing that we are on the level of *any* of these painted figures. The only consistent pattern is of looking down onto elements of the throne. And we always see the throne from the same angle no matter how high or low its elements, unlike Giotto's throne, parts of which are obviously above our gaze, parts of which are obviously beneath our gaze.

Giotto does numerous things to make his picture like a segment of real space. Cimabue drew Mary's halo in line with the collar of her blouse, a procedure that makes for flatness. Giotto gave the collar a different contour. He also drew the Virgin's cowl in such a way that you can see the outside of it on one side of her head and the inside on the other. This gives one a greater sense of looking at a three-dimensional object. The light in Cimabue seems to come from up front, if anywhere. It is somewhat realistic. But Giotto shifted the light source to the right so that it is obviously a light *source*. His angels are shaded on the left side and lighted on the right.

Finally, there is a sense of gravity in Giotto's work. This is due partly to the greater roundness of his figures; they look solid and heavy compared to Cimabue's. But what really enhances the effect is the distribution of the figures. In Cimabue they are all over the place, from top to bottom. Giotto masses his figures toward the bottom of his picture, and this makes them seem like things tied to earth. It helps convey to us the notion that we are related to them as fellow creatures sharing a common gravity. The total effect is a feeling of being presented with an extension of our own space. The illusion is incomplete and unconvincing to us because we are surrounded by images like that in figure 169. But without Giotto or someone like him, photography might not have come to be.

Masaccio's *Tribute Money* (fig. 170) is by the next artist of Giotto's stature. It is in his work that we first encounter scientific perspective. Perspective was not invented by Masaccio; it seems to have been the invention of the architect Filippo Brunelleschi (1377–1446).[1] But it is in Masaccio's work that it becomes part of the vocabulary of art.

Geometric Projections

I am going to tell you enough about perspec-tive to give you a pretty good notion of how it works. You should understand at the outset, however, that perspective drawings are not really realistic. Rather, they are mathematical approximations of the way you see with one eye closed and your head in a fixed position. Too, perspective is just one way of projecting objects in space.

Consider figure 171. It is not a projection; it is a plan with elevations. People speak of the different elevations as "views," but they are not. If the front elevation were a view of this object, the cabinet section would appear to be on a different plane from the bookcase section. Moreover, you would be able to see the undersides or the tops of at least some of the shelves in the bookcase. All an elevation does is give you a drawing of measurements: if something on the side is to be one inch wide, it is drawn to the same scale as anything else that is to be one inch wide whether it is on the nearest face, six inches back, or two hundred feet back. A plan drawing is made to be worked from rather than looked at. But even carpenters, machinists, and masons find it helpful to have pictures of the things they are constructing. For their purposes a method of drawing pictures that offers a high degree of accuracy and clarity is required. There are two techniques of mechanical drawing which provide this kind of clarity. Neither requires the slightest talent for freehand drawing.

Cabinet projection (fig. 172) simply combines the plan with the front and side elevations from the original diagram. It gives a fairly good approximation of how the object will appear when finished and also provides measurements in scale. It is not, however, a particularly popular method because it requires that the measurements of top and side undergo at least one translation—into halves—even when the projection is exactly the size of the object itself. Usually it requires two translations. After all, if you want to make a drawing that is not too cumbersome for normal use, you usually want something

plan

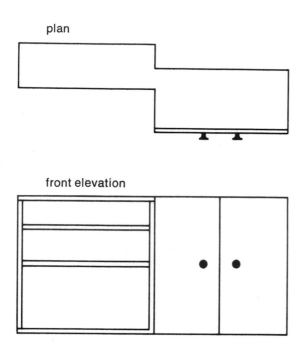

front elevation

side elevations

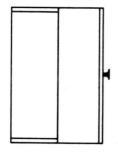

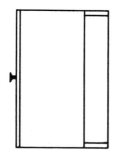

171
Plan drawing with elevations

smaller than the object you are going to build. In cabinet projections the ratios become annoying to deal with because what is a quarter of an inch on the front elevation has to be an eighth of an inch on the side. And what happens when something turns out to be seven thirty-seconds of an inch? A more popular method of projection avoids this sort of tiresome chore.

Isometric projections (fig. 173) are commonly used wherever exact conceptions of shape and scale are required. Tool- and diemakers use them, the aircraft industry relies on them, and industrial designers frequently present their ideas in this form. The word *isometric* means "of equal measure." All measurements in an isometric projection are to the same scale; but the front, side, and top of the object are at a thirty-degree angle to the vertical axis. The general impression is of looking down onto the object. And some of you will feel that it looks distorted, that the distant end of our piece of furniture is taller than the nearer end. If you measure them, you'll find that the ends are exactly the same height. The reason they don't seem to be is that in isometric drawings everything that will actually be parallel is drawn parallel. The edges of the top and bottom of the bookcase are parallel in the plan, and they are therefore parallel in the isometric projection. It looks peculiar to see the bookcase in an isometric projection because we expect the edges to appear to converge as they will when we look at the real object. In a photograph they would. In perspective drawings they do.

Scientific Perspective

Perspective drawing is another form of projection. The technical name for scientific perspective is *central projection*. The center of this projective technique is the center of one eye—or any point of focus. The German artist

Albrecht Dürer (1471–1528) once did a woodcut of an experiment to show, in one quick
step, how the system works. His *Demonstration
of Perspective* (fig. 174) depicts two men doing
a drawing of a lute as it would look to us if we
were standing so that our eye was at the spot
on the wall marked by the hook, the center
for a central projection. One man attaches
the string (which represents a light ray) to the
point on the lute to be noted. The other man
drops a plumb down to where the string
passes through the frame (representing a picture surface), then loosens the string and
swings the drawing board around to mark
the dot. Such a procedure will give you an
accurate perspective drawing of the lute.
Perspective theory accomplishes the same
thing and doesn't require awkward appara-
tus. Photography does the same thing with a
convenient mechanical device. I could describe the relationships between the Dürer
illustration, the human eye, the camera, and
scientific perspective. I'm not going to, because I don't believe these things have much
relevance to the appreciation of artists' work.
What I am going to do is give you a quickie
course in perspective drawing . . . the sort of
thing I give beginning drawing students as
an introductory lecture.

Perspective theory depends upon the idea
of a functional infinity. Ordinary perspective
drawing depends upon two basic notions: (1)
the horizon line or *eye level* and (2) *vanishing
points* toward which the edges of things converge.

Figure 175 contains three pictures of a
telephone pole. In *A* we are above the pole, as
if in a helicopter. In *B* we are standing looking
at the pole. In *C* the pole is higher than we are
—it's floating. The drawing of the pole is the
same in all three pictures; the only change is
the position of the line of the horizon relative
to the pole. When you arc above the pole,
the line is above it. When you are on the
ground, the horizon line passes through the

172
Cabinet projection

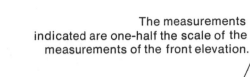

The measurements
indicated are one-half the scale of the
measurements of the front elevation.

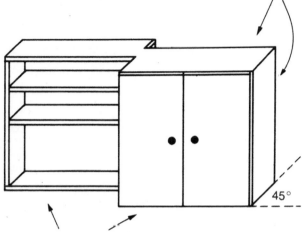

45°

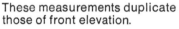

These measurements duplicate
those of front elevation.

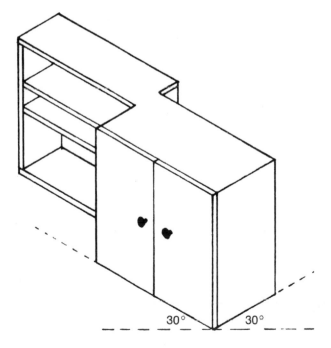

30°   30°

173
Isometric projection

174
ALBRECHT DÜRER. *Demonstration of Perspective, Draftsman Drawing a Lute.*
From the artist's treatise on geometry. 1525. Woodcut, 5¼ × 7⅛".
Kupferstichkabinett, West Berlin

pole. When you are below the pole, the line is below the pole. The horizon line is *always* at the same level as your eyes. *Always!* (Okay, so if you're in outer space it isn't. But within the gravitational field of the earth it is.) Even if you are flying in an airplane, the horizon is level with your eyes. You can check me out by looking through a sash-hung window, a casement window, or any window with open venetian blinds. Stand looking at the horizon so that some other horizontal (sash, crossbar, blind slat) matches the line of the Earth against the sky. Squat. The horizon will de-

scend with you. Stand on a chair. The horizon will ascend with you. If you happen to live in a mountainous region, in an urban apartment, or in densely wooded suburbia, this may not work, because "horizon line" as I am using it refers to the edge of the globe, and things like mountains, buildings, and trees get in the way if they are close enough. Figure 176 shows you what I mean by the horizon line or eye level. In perspective theory the two terms are identical.

Imagine that you are standing in the desert in the middle of a railroad track (fig. 177).

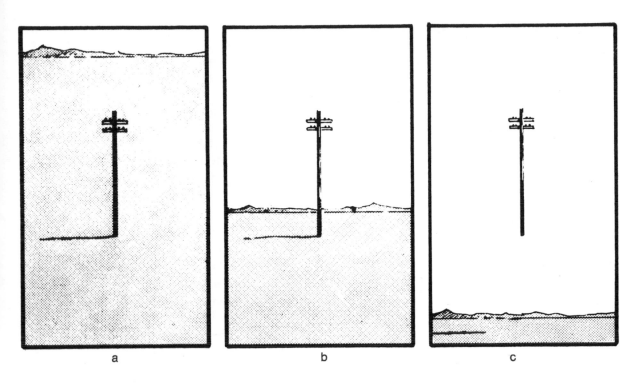

a   b   c

175
Horizon line and viewer's eye level

176
Horizon line

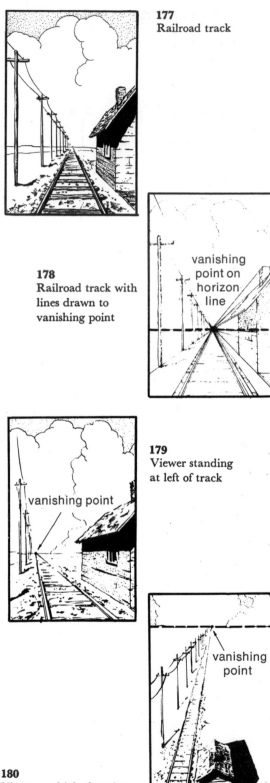

177
Railroad track

178
Railroad track with
lines drawn to
vanishing point

179
Viewer standing
at left of track

180
Viewer on high elevation

Of course, the rails converge at a single point. What you may not realize is that every edge or alignment parallel to the rails is directed to the same spot (fig. 178). This is a perspective drawing. The horizon line establishes the viewer's presumed eye level relative to the scene. The point at which all the diagonals converge is called a *vanishing point*. The vanishing point establishes the viewer's position. In figure 179 the viewer has moved just left of the tracks. In figure 180 he has climbed up onto a watertower. (By the way, so far as the artist is concerned, *he* is the viewer.) This kind of image involves one vanishing point.

What if the viewer is supposed to be standing way, way around to the side of the tracks —so they go off to the edge of the picture as in figure 181? Where do the ties go? How do you know how to draw the crossbars on the poles? In such a case the artist sets down a second vanishing point and directs anything that is at a right angle to the rails to the new point, as in figure 182. (Don't worry about how I knew where to put the second one. It's too complicated to explain in a nontechnical book. The main thing is not to get them too close together.) Actually, as you can see, I have established a third vanishing point for the nearby crate and two more for the box that is over by the tracks. So we have, altogether, five vanishing points on our horizon line. The system, however, is called two-point perspective because it never involves more than two vanishing points for any single object. In somewhat the same fashion an image like either figure 178 or 179 is called one-point perspective because most of the principal elements are directed to one point. There is also a three-point perspective system, used for drawing things like skyscrapers (fig. 183), but it is very uncommon in the fine arts. In drawing certain sorts of things—such as houses with pitch roofs—there are elevated vanishing points (fig. 184), but the system itself is included in two-point perspective.

Regardless of the number of points, any

181
Viewer standing at far right
of track

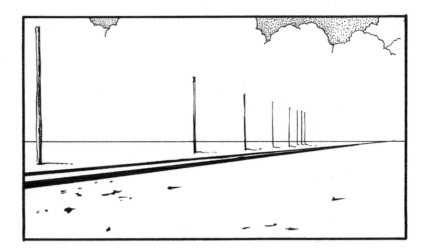

circle drawn in correct perspective will appear as an ellipse (fig. 185)—unless, of course, it is parallel to the picture plane (as in the upper left) or exactly on eye level (as in the center of the cylinder). There are many, many special rules and exact procedures for doing scientifically correct perspective renderings; they have to do with the optimum angle of vision, the procedure for establishing relative distances among objects as they recede into the distance, techniques for doing things like roller coasters, spiral staircases, and so on. None of these need concern us here. But I do want to confirm the utterly mathematical and theoretical nature of central projections. And one way to do this is to show you how an

architectural draftsman would go about making a perspective drawing of our bookcase.

People who do technical illustration and architectural studies are not often required to have ability in freehand drawing. I have done both, and I know. When an architect shows you a perspective drawing of a building to be put up, he is not showing you an artist's sketch. He is showing you a drawing that was produced mechanically, by application of the techniques of projective geometry. The mechanical procedure for drawing the bookcase is described in figure 186: (1) The plan is put down at an angle to a line representing the picture plane, with one corner just touching it. (2) A point is fixed directly below that

182
Two-vanishing-point
perspective

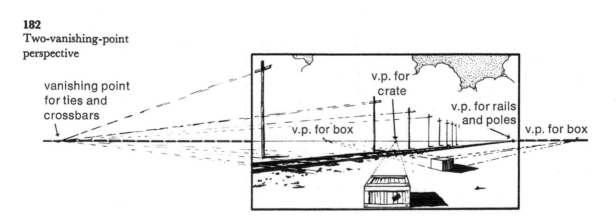

vanishing point
for ties and
crossbars

v.p. for
crate

v.p. for rails
and poles

v.p. for box

v.p. for box

corner. This point represents the viewer's eye and will be nearer to or farther from the plan depending on how far from or near to the object the viewer is supposed to be. (3) From this point lines are run out parallel to the edges of the plan. (4) A second horizontal line is placed at some arbitrary, convenient distance below the picture-plane line. This line is going to be the eye level. (5) Below this line the draftsman will draw a third horizontal line known as the *base line*. (6) Two dots are drawn on the eye-level line directly beneath the spots where the diagonal lines intersect the picture-plane line. (7) Lines are drawn from important points on the plan to the

viewpoint and marked off where they intersect the picture-plane line. Vertical lines are dropped from those points of intersection through the eye level. (8) An elevation is placed on the base line. (9) Measurements on the elevation are carried across to the line connecting the nearest corner of the plan and the viewpoint. Using these coordinates, the draftsman can make a perspective drawing (10) of any object from the blueprints alone. And he can vary the angle of the plan to produce whatever point of view is desired.

That photography's images closely correspond to drawings produced by the application of strict perspective (fig. 187) is not sur-

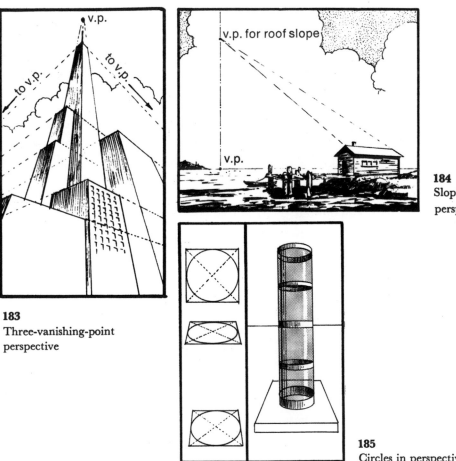

183
Three-vanishing-point
perspective

184
Sloping roof in
perspective

185
Circles in perspective

186

Perspective drawings of a
bookcase derived
mechanically from
plan and elevations

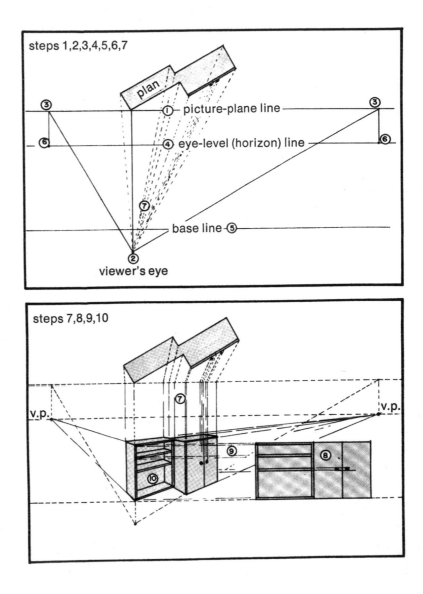

steps 1,2,3,4,5,6,7

③ ① picture-plane line ③

⑤ ④ eye-level (horizon) line ⑥

⑦

base line ⑤

②

viewer's eye

steps 7,8,9,10

v.p. v.p.

⑦

⑨ ⑧

⑩

prising, since most camera lenses are ground in accordance with the geometry of central projection. Both perspective and photography do, of course, have something in common with the way a single human eye functions. (An obvious difference is the matter of focus. If you hold your eye completely still, very little of what it sees will be in sharp focus. But a fixed camera lens or perspective rendering puts *everything* into clear focus.)

Renaissance painters, from the time of Masaccio on, made constant use of scientific perspective. It affected them powerfully because it seemed the ultimate example of an abstract, theoretical system that revealed a visual truth. Out of mathematical order illusion is produced. And the orderliness of perspective, with its completely unified space, appealed to them almost more than its realistic effects. In chapter three I remarked apropos of Leonardo's *Last Supper* (fig. 188) that the convergent lines of the ceiling, the

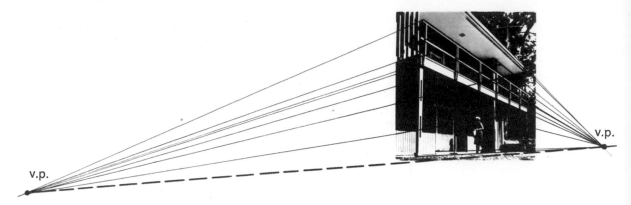

187
Photograph with lines superimposed to show perspective.
Dotted line represents eye level of slightly tilted camera

188
LEONARDO DA VINCI. *The Last Supper*. 1495–98.
Mural. Sta. Maria delle Grazie, Milan

tops of the tapestries, and the table edges all pointed to the face of Christ. It will now be obvious that this is a consequence of one-point perspective. In Masaccio's *Tribute Money* the vanishing point for the architecture is on Christ's face. Tintoretto, in his *Last Supper* (fig. 189), has used a distorted one-point perspective to accomplish his ends. The viewer is conceived of as standing way over on the right, more or less in line with the nearby male figure. If the table were drawn in two-point perspective (which, technically, this span of the room demands), the viewer might well imagine himself over to the left. Since the ends of the table are parallel to the eye level while its sides converge on the same vanishing point as other major elements of the room, we know the viewer is remote

from the center of the room, in line with the vanishing point. For in one-point perspective the viewer is always directly ahead of the point of convergence. Tintoretto's aims are not scientific but emotional, and it is to his advantage to break the rules. His "error" is partially hidden by the glamorous chiaroscuro.

One of the most famous examples of deliberate deviation from the rules is a painting by an artist who was a contemporary of Leonardo, Andrea Mantegna (1431–1506). Mantegna's *The Dead Christ* (fig. 190) is a perspective study which is "wrong" from a technical point of view. Again, though, the artist knew what he was doing when he made his mistakes. If he had projected the body of Christ mechanically from this angle, the feet would have dwarfed the rest of the figure.

189
TINTORETTO. *The Last Supper*. 1592–94.
Oil on canvas, 12′ × 18′8″. S. Giorgio Maggiore, Venice

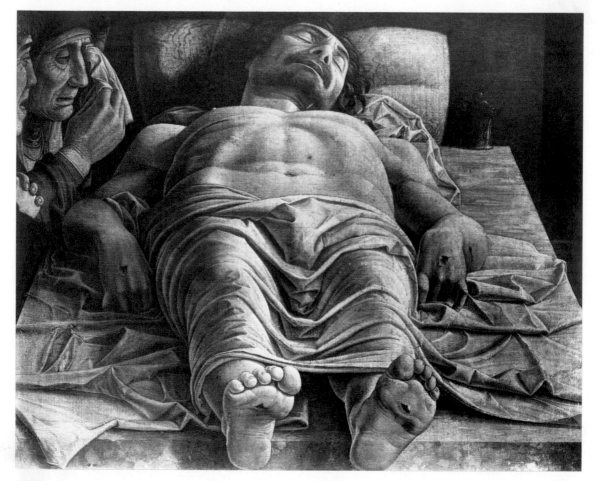

190
ANDREA MANTEGNA. *The Dead Christ.* c. 1501.
Tempera on canvas, 26 × 30″. Brera Gallery, Milan

Given the nature of the subject matter, the result would not be humorous, but it would demean the sacred spirit of the work. So Mantegna has adjusted his projection in order to preserve the dignity and solemnity of Jesus. When you realize this, it becomes very obvious that the legs and feet are smaller than one would expect them to be. Until just now, however, you probably didn't notice it.

Usually, in the fine arts, the absence of scientifically correct perspective is neither deliberate nor the result of ineptitude. It is the consequence of an antipathy for mechan-ical exactitude. Edgar Degas was actively interested in perspective drawing, but his mature work (fig. 191) is full of inconsistencies. He's always doing things that would drive a mechanical-drawing teacher up the walls. He takes in too much of the floor; he paints things from slightly different points of view. His receding parallels don't have a common vanishing point. *Foyer of the Dance* proves him guilty on every count. Yet the painting doesn't look unreal; on the contrary, it gives an impression of considerable accuracy. Degas's perspective is not inaccurate so much as empirical. He knew the rules and they assisted his intuition. But it was an impression of the room he wished to project onto his canvas and not a geometric diagram. His perspective is sensed rather than constructed. Most artists' drawings are done freehand in the way Degas drew in his picture.

Even an artist like Canaletto (1697–1768), famed for his perspective vistas, did not do paintings with the precision theory would require. Still, it is obvious that when he painted *Santa Maria della Salute, Venice,* showing the Molo as seen from the Piazzetta (fig. 192) he began with a pretty systematic central projection. The figures are distributed in such a way as to measure off distance in the picture, and he used the lines in the pavement as well as the architectural components of the buildings to mark off the square with exceptional clarity.

Francesco Guardi (1712–1793) was another painter of eighteenth-century Venice, and he has given us a very similar view (fig. 193). But in his picture the perspective is empirical, felt, much as it is in the Degas. Guardi sacrificed a lot to atmospheric effect. His perspective is not exact. All the same, the space of the picture is deep and dramatic. And in his work we are conscious of the essentials of the perspective scheme. The eye level is firmly established, and the ideal of the vanishing point remains even though the actual points

191
EDGAR DEGAS. *Foyer of the Dance.* 1872.
Oil on canvas, 12½ × 18″. The Louvre, Paris

192
ANTONIO CANALETTO.
*Santa Maria della Salute,
Venice.* 18th century.
Oil on canvas, 23¼ × 36⅝".
The Wallace Collection,
London

193
FRANCESCO GUARDI.
*Santa Maria della Salute,
Venice.* 18th century.
Oil on canvas, 17¾ × 28".
Galleria Giorgio Franchetti,
Ca' d'Oro, Venice

at which edges of things converge stray far from the ideal. Fortunately for painters like Degas and Guardi, those of us who see their pictures are very tolerant of such positionings and are not disturbed by shifts away from geometric perfection. As a matter of fact, since buildings settle and human constructions are rarely so regular as drawn diagrams, the "sloppiness" of Degas and Guardi may actually make their scenes appear more true to life.

Atmospheric Perspective

One reason for the effectiveness of both the Canaletto and the Guardi is that neither relies entirely on central projection. Guardi, especially, achieves depth through so-called *atmospheric perspective.*

Everyone must be aware of the influence atmosphere has on the appearance of things that are far away. The layer of air between us and distant mountains is one of the causes of their appearing blue. They are also less clear; even relatively nearby things are somewhat blurred by atmospheric haze. Artists copy this effect to represent the near and far in their works. But in paintings it is not blurriness that is the deciding factor in creating the impression of depth. The lucid, transparent light in which Canaletto's scene is bathed is one of the most appealing things about it. We feel that this is a clear day indeed, because distant buildings are almost as sharp as things nearby. Despite the universal clarity, those domes do look far away. And the illusion is due to more than scientific perspective.

The Return of the Hunters (fig. 194) by Pieter Bruegel the Elder (1525/30–1569) does not depend for its spatial illusion on scientific perspective, because the landscape contains few elements that are geometrically regular. The same can be said of the Claude Lorrain (fig. 195). Both pictures rely for their impression of depth upon atmospheric perspective, a perspective whose character is only incidentally related to air. What this system really has to do with is value contrast. *Things high in contrast appear closer than things low in contrast.* That is, the difference between lights and darks is greater close up than far off. Thus, in the Bruegel, the trunks and branches of the nearby trees are far darker than distant ones, and those in the middle distance are darker than the ones that are far, far away. At the

same time, the foreground snow is whiter than that of the valley, and the snow in the valley is not so dark as that on the mountainside. Everything gets grayer toward the horizon.

In Claude Lorrain, too, one is led back through passages of diminishing contrast. As you go back, the darks get lighter and the lights grow somewhat darker. What is important to the illusion, however, is the decrease of contrast *between* lights and darks. One could simply make all the lights grow darker, leaving an impression of the distance shrouded in gloom. Conversely, a painter might lighten darks and preserve the same lightness throughout. Because Claude Lorrain lightened his darks a bit more than he darkened lights, his picture suggests far-off things lost in a luminous haze. The isolated panels of my comic strip *Maxor of Cirod* (fig. 196) make use of the principle of atmospheric perspective by eliminating large black spots from the distance, by reducing the amount of unbroken white space in the end of the arena and the mountains, and by treating the out-

194

PIETER BRUEGEL THE ELDER. *The Return of the Hunters.* 1565. Oil on panel, 46 × 63¾″. Kunsthistorisches Museum, Vienna

line of the clouds with a faint, broken line.

From the close of the Renaissance to the middle of the nineteenth century, painting underwent many stylistic changes without forsaking the spatial conception that gave birth to both scientific and atmospheric perspective. John Constable (1776–1837) was one of the great masters of English landscape painting. His *Hay Wain* (fig. 197) was really quite radical in its treatment of nature. It was painted straight onto the canvas from studies done at the scene, and Constable employed spontaneous, sketchy brushwork designed to capture the transitory aspects of nature—the flicker of light on water, the leaves fluttering in the breeze, the clouds crawling lazily across the sky. This painting made so profound an impression on the French painter Eugène Delacroix that he revised the background of his *Massacre at Scio* in imitation of Constable. The *Hay Wain* is not a timid work. It is anything but conservative. But the space of the picture is no different from the space in the Pieter Bruegel or Claude Lorrain.

A contemporary of Constable, J. M. W. Turner, became so fascinated with the corre-

195
CLAUDE LORRAIN.
The Marriage of Isaac and Rebekah (The Mill). 1640.
Oil on canvas, $58\frac{3}{4} \times 77\frac{1}{2}''$. The National Gallery, London

196
JOHN ADKINS RICHARDSON.
Maxor of Cirod.
© 1971, John Adkins Richardson

197
JOHN CONSTABLE.
The Hay Wain. 1821.
Oil on canvas, 51¼ × 73″.
The National Gallery,
London

198
JOSEPH MALLORD WILLIAM TURNER.
*The Dogana, San Giorgio Maggiore,
le Zitelle, from the Steps of the
Europa.* 1842.
Oil on canvas, $24\frac{1}{2} \times 36\frac{1}{2}''$.
The Tate Gallery, London

199
JEAN-BAPTISTE-CAMILLE COROT.
*Bridge and Castle of St. Angelo
with the Cupola of St. Peter's.*
1826–27.
Oil on paper, mounted on canvas,
$8\frac{5}{8} \times 15''$.
The Fine Arts Museums of San
Francisco. Collis Potter Huntington
Memorial Collection

lation between light and color that his work foreshadows Impressionism. In essence, however, his paintings (see fig. 198) share the spatial effects of Claude Lorrain. Corot's (fig. 199) solidity exists within the same general scheme as that of his predecessors. It is with the French Impressionists that the concept began to change.

Space in French Impressionism

Actually, the modification of traditional space was just a by-product of the Impressionists' concern with sensation. Monet's procedure of painting scenes in terms of color notations without regard for much except his "naive impression of the scene" (fig. 200) would have itself denied the deep space typical of his predecessors. The scientist Hermann von Helmholtz pointed out that if you look at the world from an unusual position it looks flat.

In the usual mode of observation all we try to do is judge correctly the objects as such. We know that at a certain distance green surfaces appear a little different in hue. We get in the habit of overlooking this difference, and learn to identify the altered green of distant meadows with the corresponding color of nearer objects. . . . But the instant we take an unusual position and look at the landscape with the head under one arm, let us say, or between the legs, it all appears like a flat picture. . . . This whole difference seems to me to be due to the fact that the colours have ceased to be distinctive signs of objects for us, and are considered merely as being different sensations.[2]

Monet's haystack picture makes no distinction between the spots of color used to indicate farm buildings in the distance and those which indicate light on stubble just behind the stack. Because of this the houses are hard to identify. (They are strung out in line with the division between the hump and sides of the haystack.) Does the horizontal line between the houses and the top of the picture represent the edge of a hillside or the crest of a cloud bank? You'd have to know the locality to make a good guess, and even then

200
CLAUDE MONET. *Haystack at Sunset Near Giverny.* 1891.
Oil on canvas, 29½ × 37″. Museum of Fine Arts, Boston. Juliana Cheney
Edwards Collection

you'd not be sure. Colors have ceased to be distinctive signs of objects and are treated merely as different sensations. It is just as Helmholtz said.

The kind of spatial ambiguity exhibited by the Monet is called *frontality*.[3] The nude and bedclothing in Manet's *Olympia* have the same property. Most Impressionist paintings have it to some extent. It is not the result of a doctrinaire denial of the perspectives of the past; it is merely one consequence of the outlook of painters who wished to be true to their sensations. Our discussion of scientific perspective should have proved its abstract, impersonal character if nothing else. Monet would have considered the rules of central projection an imposition upon his sensations which was inconsistent with his purposes. And he would have been correct. The rules dictate certain proportions that are not in accord with sensational responses. They substitute measurement and magnitude for intuition. Atmospheric perspective is similar insofar as it presupposes an ideal range of value relationships.

Degas did not consider himself an Impressionist, although he exhibited with them. He did not concern himself with color sensation in and of itself until quite late in life. To cite him as an example of Impressionist divergence from abstract principle is to select the poorest example—for he was interested in perspective more than any other Impressionist. Yet, even in his work, the perspective is never scientifically correct; it is Impressionistic.

Two French Impressionists who were not particularly fascinated by perspective drawing were all the same disturbed by what seemed to them the superficial nature of the Impressionist method. Both Auguste Renoir (1841–1919) and Paul Cézanne (1839–1906) became disenchanted with the relative looseness of Impressionism. Renoir attempted to combine Renaissance form with Impression-

ist color. Cézanne is often said to have done the same, but his accomplishment goes far beyond Renoir's rather obvious synthesis of Titian's drawing with Monet's hues. He invented what the English critic Roger Fry called a *perspective of color*.

Cézanne's Perspective of Color

Cézanne's art is very complicated. It is rather like the music of Bach; solemn contemplation of each part and its relationship to the whole is necessary if one is to come to an appreciation of it. Perhaps the following remarks will not convey what I want them to. Roger Fry thought that the method Cézanne employed was inexplicable. Fry was a lyrical critic of art, and he didn't attempt to analyze the specific functions of line, form, and color. What a poet would not try, I perhaps should not attempt. But I am going to, anyhow. Maybe I can give you some notion of the majesty of Cézanne's accomplishment.

Let us examine the panoramic landscape entitled *Mont Sainte-Victoire* (colorplate 12). At the base of the lone central tree there is a dark clump of brush. It is juxtaposed with the yellow-brown wall of a little house. The house is nearly hidden by foliage. It has a lavender roof. Notice, now, that the ridgepole along the middle of the roof and the eaves on its right-hand side form a single line, interrupted only by the tiny chimney. The house is virtually a continuous plane because of this line. Almost as if unbroken, it leads the eye back into the picture from the accent of the brush. But it is not unbroken. It is divided by hue into two parts, the yellow-brown of the wall and the pale violet of the roof. From this simple division emerge the many relationships that, together, identify a Cézanne.

When you place a cool color (blue-green) against a warm color (yellow-brown) and the two hues are of different value, they tend to separate. Thus, the brown wall pulls away from the green shrub. And space, thereby, comes to exist *within* a receding plane. But the effect has another side. Put together, colors dissimilar in hue temperature but of approximately the same value suggest a "folding" of space; that is, they create the illusion of an angle. For this reason, the single segmented plane of the house can also be viewed as composed of a wall parallel to the viewer and a rooftop slanting away from him. Having such a duality of recession, the form is doubly cogent. Moreover, the plane of the little house is but a section of a still larger plane which penetrates the house, the trees on the left, and drifts into the ground plane of the valley. Such planes, of which the entire work is composed, are like great slabs of light superimposed over the volumes of the landscape. And what is most intriguing about it all is that Cézanne managed to make the picture deep and frontal at the same time.

Frontality in *Mont Sainte-Victoire* stems from the fact that elements of the foreground participate in the illusion of deep space. For example, the bit of foliage to the left of the lone pine tree belongs to the tree and also acts as an accent for a set of shifting planes that tip up and backward to become Mont Sainte-Victoire. We'd think the green was a clump of trees, except that they would have to be the largest trees in the world if they towered as they seem to over the ancient Roman aqueduct. A branch on the right of the pine projects a corresponding spot of green out over the landscape. This spot is the accent for a plane that passes along the branch to the aqueduct. Numerous elements of this kind predominate. The projecting branch aligns the two green spots and also lies parallel to the roof of the little house and to the general direction of the distant river. The meanderings of that river are almost exactly repeated in the line of the mountain range against the sky.

The entire shape between the river and the mountaintops can be relished as an independent chunk of the picture. When you look at that segment of the picture, you can see just *how* frontal it can seem. The picture is an exquisite marriage of Classical structure and harmony with Impressionist sensitivity and frontality. It contains both and resembles neither.

The Uncanny Space of Cubism

Five years after Cézanne's death in 1906, two young artists invented a style that was to revolutionize painting in modern times. The artists were Pablo Picasso and Georges Braque (1882–1963), and the style came to be called *Cubism*, although it had nothing to do with cubes. It is the first truly nonrepresentational or "abstract" movement in modern art, and we shall have more to say about it later on. For now, I am interested in its curious spatial quality.

The space of Cubism is so unusual that it has led to all kinds of speculations: that it is derived from multiple viewpoints of objects, that it is dependent on a mystical fourth dimension, and that it has something to do with Einstein's Theory of Relativity, which was enunciated about the same time. These speculations are almost always based on a misunderstanding of both the style itself and the scientific ideas.[4] What we are presently concerned with is the space of painting.

Picasso's *Ma Jolie* (fig. 201) looks, at first glance, like a jumble of forms which doesn't make much sense at all. Select one of those forms and try to figure out whether it is ahead of or behind another one. Things *do* look as if they are ahead or behind; the picture doesn't look flat. Virtually any form you select can also be construed differently, however. If the one selected seemed to be on top of an adjacent one, imagine it beneath. You can shift assumptions this way with great

201
PABLO PICASSO. *Ma Jolie*. 1911–12.
Oil on canvas, 39⅜ × 25¾″. The Museum of Modern Art, New York. Lillie P.
Bliss Bequest

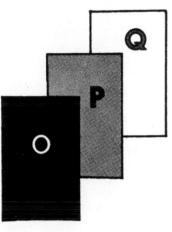

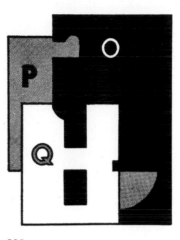

202
Overlapping planes

203
Cubistic treatment of space

ease. Picasso has taken to its ultimate conclusion Cézanne's method of rendering things so that they retain their volume as well as their frontality. The space doesn't depend on the color variations of Cézanne; it does derive from the ambiguities he used. It should be easy for anyone to see that in figure 202 plane *P* lies between *O* and *Q*. The illustration is typical of traditional overlappings. But what about the situation in figure 203? This schematic drawing takes a Cubist image as a point of departure. Where is *P*? Possibly it lies both ahead of and behind the other forms and lines. This ambiguity is not due to a transparency of the forms. It is due to the arrangement of masses and edges. The same is true of *Ma Jolie*.

The bizarre space of Cubism is of great interest because the whole character of a painting like *Ma Jolie* changes as you change assumptions about where in space the elements are. Take that one tiny form you took before. Look at the whole picture in terms of it. Then assume that the form is not where you at first supposed it was but is in the opposite relationship. The assumption makes the rest of the picture look different. Too, if you select another form and make alternative assumptions, similar changes will occur. This is the simplest version of what is most interesting about the painting: that it never "wears out." I have seen it many, many times, and it always shows me a somewhat different face. It is not a very decorative picture in terms of color (it is all browns and grays), but it is a work of art that one could live with forever.

Let me hasten to say that this is also true of Rembrandts, Caravaggios, and others. What is particularly intriguing about the Picasso is that its interest depends completely upon the way it was painted and not at all on what it represents.

7
Formal Composition

I have been using the word *form* interchangeably with *shape*. There is, however, another usage current in the fine arts. In writing about art, the terms *form* and *content* are frequently opposed. Like many terms in art, these have their counterparts in common speech. Suppose you are at a public forum dealing with the application of I.Q. tests to urban schools, a subject fraught with hazards. A speaker says: "White urban Jews do consistently better than white Protestants from rural Appalachia in I.Q. tests." You ask: "Are you saying that urban Jews are smarter than Appalachian whites?" He responds: "No, not at all. They just get higher scores on intelligence tests. Let me put it in a different *form*. The whole social structure and life-style of the typical Jewish child gives him the skills a normal. I.Q. test measures. This is not true of the mountain people." Now, the speaker has said essentially the same thing in both cases. The amplification didn't really add anything that was not implicit in his previous remark. The form made all the difference. What he said was the content of his remarks. The way he made them was their form.

In discussing artworks critics often distin-

204
JAN VAN EYCK. *Giovanni Arnolfini and His Bride.* 1434.
Oil on panel, 32¼×23½″. The National Gallery, London

guish between *form* and *content*. The content of a picture is what it's about, its subject matter. The form, of course, is what it looks like—what kinds of colors, lines, and shapes the artist used. This distinction is not as easy to make as you might think. In fact, sometimes it is hard to see exactly what the content is.

Content

Jan van Eyck's *Giovanni Arnolfini and His Bride* (fig. 204) seems to have a pretty obvious subject—a young man and woman standing behind a dog in a bedroom. That, along with all the subsidiary items in the room, might seem to be the content. As it happens, the content has further content. That is, the subject matter has a meaning, a theme, and the meaning is part of the total content of the work. There is a whole branch of art history concerned with content in this sense. It is called *iconography*. A closer, iconographic inspection of *Giovanni Arnolfini and His Bride* will quickly reveal what lies beyond the ostensible subject of the work.

Your first impression of Mrs. Arnolfini may be that hers was a "shotgun wedding," that the bride was pregnant. No, she was not. She is holding the folds of her gown against her midsection. True, she does have a slightly protrudent abdomen, but that was the stylish figure of her day. Her husband's posture is of greater importance. Notice how he holds up his right hand. He is taking an oath, the oath of marriage. At the time of the painting the Church did not require the presence of clergy for a valid marriage contract to be made between man and woman. The sacrament of holy matrimony was one that could be dispensed by the recipients. All that was required was a *fides manualis* (oath by joining of the hands) and a *fides levata* (oath by raising the forearm) on the part of the man. But this kind of private ceremony raised problems, since its proper performance could later be denied by a partner tired of his or her spouse. The

husband might, for instance, say that he had had his fingers crossed or something. The unhappy consequences of such unions caused the Council of Trent, in the sixteenth century, to issue a decree requiring (whenever possible) the presence of a priest as God's witness to the event. The Medici banker Giovanni Arnolfini took his bride long before that. And this painting was commissioned as a proof of the event. It is, if you will, a kind of document. Indeed, there is an inscription on the wall which reads "Jan van Eyck was here." And the mirror just above reflects the room, showing the backs of the couple and, tinily pictured, the painter and a companion. Van Eyck was witness to the exchange of marital vows, and his painting notarized it.

Despite the almost magical realism of the picture, it is more than a painstaking wedding "snapshot." It was painted in 1434, when the thoughts of men were still dominated by the thoughts of the Roman Church. For centuries in northern Europe there had been no reason to do an elaborate painting except for some purpose associated with God or the Church. Hence, for hundreds of years commonplace objects depicted in art had had a special "transfigured" meaning as things that functioned in some sacred moment. Van Eyck felt that the marriage of the Arnolfinis was inferior as a subject to a picture of Christ or an apostle. Probably his patrons agreed. So the artist invested everything with religious significance. He turned a relatively insignificant moment into a sacred symbol. It became not just a picture of two middle-class patrons but also a glorification of the Christian institution of marriage. The Arnolfini portrait is replete with symbols relating to this theme. The bed in the background is reminiscent of those in Northern medieval Annunciations—when the Angel Gabriel informs Mary that she is to bear the Christ Child. The little dog is doubtless a symbol of fidelity. In the chandelier a lone candle burns; a candle burning in a lighted room signifies the presence of God.

205
AGNOLO BRONZINO. *Exposure of Luxury*. c. 1546.
Oil on panel, 57½ × 45¾″. The National Gallery, London

Sunlight itself alludes to the purity of the bride, particularly since it bathes the fruit resting on the windowsill. The fruit harkens back to the story of Adam and Eve. Finally, the mirror is convex and takes in more than a flat glass would. It has been compared to the eye of God beholding the witnesses as well as the bride and groom.

A little over a century later the Italian artist Agnolo Bronzino (1502–1572) did a painting also having to do with sexual love, his *Exposure of Luxury*, formerly known as *Venus, Cupid, Folly, and Time* (fig. 205). It is characterized by a sort of cold lasciviousness. Venus was Cupid's mother, and here her adolescent son fondles her in a way that suggests anything but filial tenderness. She holds in her right hand an arrow taken from his quiver and in her left an apple. We take the word *sinister* from the Italian *sinistra* (left). Cupid can see the apple, but not the arrow. He is offered something that is delicious but dangerous. On the right a little figure (of a type called a *putto* in art) strews roses. He combines the ideas of pleasure and jest, something already hinted at in the apple and arrow. Venus's behavior also suggests deceit, and the picture is full of things relating to fraud. Beneath the putto there are masks, and behind him a curious creature sometimes referred to by critics of the painting as a Harpy. This being has the face of a precociously sensual little girl; the lower extremities are scaly, reptilian. In her right hand she is holding a honeycomb and in her left a poisonous lizard. But her right hand is formed like a left hand, and her left is like a right. Again, a sinister image, explicitly, the symbol of Deceit. Consider, too, the peculiar relationship of Cupid's head to his body; we have some question as to whether the head and body belong together. He kneels on a pillow, the standard symbol of idleness and luxury, just behind two billing doves signifying amorous caresses. Beneath his wing we observe an old woman tearing at her hair, a figure that has been identified as Jealousy. This highly suggestive group of weirdos is revealed to Truth by Father Time, who is shown drawing back a curtain. The subject is treacherous pleasure. It is a warning against luxury to the supersophisticated who would dismiss manifest evils as diverting pastimes.

Not all paintings are complicated in this way. *Giovanni Arnolfini and His Bride* was the result of a deliberate attempt to invest a dual portrait with religious significance. The Bronzino is an allegorical work; in fact, the title is sometimes given as *Allegory*. An allegory is a work (whether in the fine arts or in literature) in which symbolic figures and actions represent ideas about human conduct.

The majority of paintings and sculptures—the *vast* majority—are about just what they seem to be. The portrait of the German merchant Georg Gisze (fig. 206) by Hans Holbein the Younger (c. 1497–1543) is exactly that, a picture of a man surrounded by the materials of his trade. One might, of course, be interested in knowing who Gisze was, precisely how he earned a living, and what purpose each of the objects depicted served, but one can gain a pretty fair idea of all this just from the objective representation Holbein has given us.

What these pictures are of and about is their content; the way the artists painted them is their form. What is of more than passing interest is the way in which form can modify the meaning of the subject matter, that is, the way form influences content.

The Interdependence of Form and Content

Many of you are familiar with at least the general outline of the story of Othello, the Moor of Venice. It is famous because of William Shakespeare's play. Othello, a black

206

HANS HOLBEIN THE
YOUNGER. *Georg Gisze.*
1532.
Oil and tempera on panel,
38 × 33″. Staatliche Museen,
Berlin-Dahlem

man who is a gallant general in the service of
Venice, is married to Desdemona, daughter
of a white Venetian senator. He has offended
a cunning fellow named Iago by promoting
a younger soldier, Cassio, over his head. Iago
arranges it to seem that Desdemona and
Cassio are having an affair, and stirs Othello
to such a frenzy of jealousy that he murders
his wife in her bed. When it turns out that
Desdemona had been faithful and his fury
unjustified, Othello kills himself in remorse.

Even if you've not read or seen the play,
you can probably imagine how it was handled by Shakespeare. Fine. Imagine how it
might appear in the work of Sir Walter Scott.
Mark Twain? Ernest Hemingway? James

Baldwin? Mickey Spillane? LeRoi Jones?
Obviously, the same plot would have entirely
different implications in the hands of each of
these authors. Indeed, the meaning of the
events would take on different aspects because of the varying forms the writers would
give to them. Quite the same is true of painting and sculpture.

The Annunciation is a very common subject in Christian art. The essentials are the
Angel Gabriel and Mary. In terms of both
form and content one of the most elaborate
Annunciations ever painted is the Mérode
altarpiece (fig. 207), done by a painter whose
identity was for years uncertain. You will,
for this reason, sometimes see it credited to

the Master of Flémalle. Most scholars now identify the Master of Flémalle as Robert Campin (c. 1378–1444), who was the leading painter of Tournai.

The altarpiece is a *triptych* (three-paneled painting). The left panel depicts the couple who donated the picture to the church. They look toward the central panel through a garden door. The spring flowers denote the season of the Annunciation. Moreover, forget-me-nots stand for Mary's eyes, and the violets and daisies symbolize her humility. The rosebush is thorny (a reference to Christ's martyrdom) and full of beautiful blossoms (standing for Mary's love). The brick wall alludes to the Song of Songs in the Bible, where a virgin is described as "a garden en-closed." The man in the background is the broker who arranged the donors' marriage. The door is a symbol of hope. The lock symbolizes charity, and the key stands for the desire of God.

The central panel depicts the Annunciation itself, taking place in a fifteenth-century Flemish room. The room contains all sorts of references to purity: a basin, a lily, a white towel, white cloths, and white walls. The Infant Jesus, carrying a tiny cross, speeds through the window on a sunbeam. And the candle on the table has just gone out; its smoke trails up in a wisp. This signifies that God has assumed human form in Mary's womb.

The right-hand panel shows Joseph in his shop. The workbench is laden with sharp

207

MASTER OF FLÉMALLE (ROBERT CAMPIN?). Mérode Altarpiece of the *Annunciation.* c. 1425–28.
Oil on panel, center panel 25″ square, each wing 25 × 10″. The Cloisters, The Metropolitan Museum of Art, New York

208
FRA ANGELICO.
Annunciation. 1438–45.
Fresco. S. Marco, Florence

gouges and other tools, all of which summon up thoughts of torture and the Crucifixion. Joseph is boring holes in a board. There is uncertainty among scholars as to what he's supposed to be making. Erwin Panofsky, greatest of all iconographers, suggested a footwarmer. Another authority has said that it looks like a spike block. And Meyer Schapiro, another great scholar, thinks it may be a fish trap. The latter suggestion is rather persuasive, because fish symbolize Christ[1] and because there is another kind of trap in Joseph's shop, a mousetrap. It is by his elbow on the table. St. Augustine had written that the crucifixion of Christ was the bait in a trap that caught the Devil just as a mousetrap catches a mouse. Marilyn Aronberg Lavin, however, would seem to have come up with the best explanation. It is, she believes, from a winepress. Given the role of wine in the Eucharist and in Christian symbolism, it would be altogether fitting for Joseph to be drilling holes for a winemaker's sieve.

The Mérode altarpiece is heavy with content. But when one has seen what Campin's younger contemporary Van Eyck made of a simple marriage portrait, one can appreciate the care with which Campin inventoried all symbols connected with an event of universal significance. It is consistent with the style of fifteenth-century Flemish painting.

In the South during the same period, a little Dominican monk named Fra Angelico (1400–1455) decorated the monastery of San Marco in Florence with fresco paintings. One of these is an Annunciation (fig. 208). Again, the flower-carpeted garden symbolic of virginity is used. But nearly everything else is different. The event takes on a tender charm quite unlike the hard objectivity of the Flemish painting. Fra Angelico has used perspective and other Renaissance inventions for drawing the architecture, anatomy, and drapery, but has used them primarily with an eye to decorative effect. Even the secondary content is kept to a minimum so that attention is not distracted from the shy Virgin and God's messenger. (The dark halos, incidentally, have no significance. Originally, the halos were painted in gold leaf. The gold has long since vanished, leaving in its place the adherent of dark gum.)

Tintoretto, whose *Last Supper* has received quite a lot of attention in these pages, also did an Annunciation (fig. 209). It is as flamboyant as Fra Angelico's is restrained. Gabriel swoops down through the door, startling Mary half out of her wits.

The essential subject matter of all these Annunciations is the same. But the form in which the scene was cast makes the content rather different from one to another. It is also the thing that gives the works their quality. It would be easy to imagine me telling *you*, for example, everything to put into a picture of the Annunciation, even giving you the precise positions of the figures. It might not be quite so easy for some of you to imagine undertaking a picture according to my description, but let's pretend that I'm going to pay several hundred dollars if you do— regardless of how poorly finished the picture

is. Obviously, you are not going to be able to produce anything of the quality of the Campin, the Fra Angelico, or the Tintoretto, even when the content is exactly the same.

Since, in the final analysis, it is the form of the work that determines whether the work is good, bad, or indifferent, it is the form with which we shall concern ourselves in the rest of this chapter.

Formal "Rightness" and Families of Forms and Colors

All of us have had the experience of being asked whether something—an arrangement of furniture in a room, or a combination of clothing—looks "right." Sometimes we say, "No, there's something a little bit wrong. I'm not sure what. . . . Hmmmm. . . . Maybe if you changed—" and so on. You sort of play around with possibilities until everyone is happy with the situation or until it becomes obvious that it "just won't do." Of course, one person may be satisfied with what an-

209
TINTORETTO.
Annunciation. 1583–87.
Oil on canvas,
13′10″ × 17′10½″.
Scuola di S. Rocco, Venice

other cannot abide. There's no way of proving yourself right or wrong in such circumstances because there are no rules. It all depends on how the thing "feels." This is true even when you agree to decide taste by majority vote of a group; one set of feelings is being weighed against another. But let's face it, some people have feelings you can rely on and some don't; some of us have good sense about these things and some of us are stupefying clods. . . . whose opinion would you take on selecting draperies—the collective judgment of your father's bowling team or the suggestion of an interior designer?

Since ancient times men have tried to devise prescriptions for attaining beauty in art. None of the formulas have been confirmed by history. What seemed unquestionable in one age was overturned in the next. Even an abstract, objective system like scientific perspective, which *does* have hard and fast rules, cannot be employed strictly, without exception. When it's technically wrong, as in Mantegna's *Dead Christ,* it's artistically right for the picture—because content affects form just as form affects content.

There exists a geometric proportion called the *Golden Section.* Since its discovery by Euclid, some time during the third century before Christ, it has been considered the key to formal beauty by any number of theorists in art. It is a ratio between the two dimensions of a plane figure or the two divisions of a line such that the smaller element is to the larger as the larger is to the whole (fig. 210). There is something peculiarly natural and appealing about the proportion. It occurs all through nature, even in seashells and microscopic cell structures. I have tested its appeal in art appreciation classes by giving students identical strips of paper and asking each to cut out one "perfect" rectangle. When I collect all the rectangles from a class of one hundred, there are always a few silly ones— uncut long strips, tiny little bits, and so on— but the majority are so much alike that you

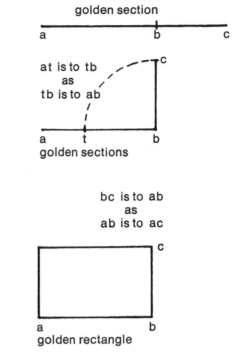

golden section

at is to tb
as
tb is to ab

golden sections

bc is to ab
as
ab is to ac

golden rectangle

210
Golden Section

can shuffle them like a deck of cards. And the rectangle in the deck is a Golden Rectangle; the short end is to the long edge as the long edge is to the end plus itself. Incredible! But true. A typical picture shape is a Golden Rectangle: most architectural forms subscribe to the proportion, painters employ it, and trees and eggs sometimes come in that proportion (fig. 211). Here, the temple, the Mondrian, and the Bakota sculpture contain many Golden Rectangles interlocked with one another.

As you might expect, many artists have attempted to paint perfectly composed pictures by applying the Golden Section to their designs. Unfortunately, the fact that this ratio is a persistent feature of great works does not mean that its presence will assure greatness. It does not even imply that a work con-

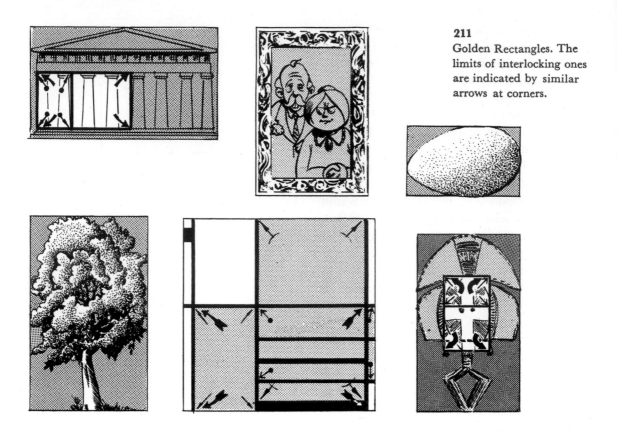

211
Golden Rectangles. The
limits of interlocking ones
are indicated by similar
arrows at corners.

taining it will be good. And, of course, it
certainly doesn't mean that works from which
the ratio is absent will be poor. True, there
are some zealots who insist that the Golden
Section and similar ratios can *inevitably* be
found in all great works of art. Their demon-
strations of this contention are frequently
ingenious and even fascinating. Sometimes,
too, they are a rarified form of mental torture.
I am convinced that whenever the ratios are
so well hidden as to require logarithmic functions to evoke them, they are not essential—
that in effect they do not exist. In any case,
it is possible to use the same techniques to
concoct similar justifications for paintings
that are hideous. All too often the measurements "come out" if you begin halfway over
on a fingernail but won't work if you measure

from either of the two sides of the nail. That's
altogether too "iffy" for this writer. Good
composition in art is less the result of ideal
proportions than it is a matter of consistency
of line, form, and color.

Consistency alone won't make for quality;
in fact, complete consistency would be monotonous. The trick, or so it seems to me, is to
attain unity without monotony. To pull off
the trick won't guarantee that a work of art
will be great, but it seems a basic attribute of
most fine painting and sculpture that it
treads a line between chaos on one side and
tedium on the other.

Confronted with a blank canvas, the artist
can, in principle, do anything at all. Compare
his situation with this: I hand you a piece of
white cardboard and a thousand scraps of

paper in a variety of colors. You are to create a design using no more than one hundred of those pieces. So you begin gluing them onto the cardboard. At first just any shape or color will be okay. But before long you will discover that certain things don't seem to fit in with the others. For instance, if you've used rounded forms in primary hues, a pentagon of chartreuse may look completely out of place. By the time you've put in ninety-nine shapes, the character of the one-hundredth one is going to be pretty well determined.

The American artist Stuart Davis (1894–1964) did paintings that might have been created by a method like the one just described. His *Colonial Cubism* (colorplate 13) contains choppy forms resembling paper cutouts. The white spots on the right might not look as if they went with the star in the lower left if it were not for the intervening shapes. The star is very like some of those shapes, the spots resemble parts of others, and when you have them altogether they "fit." A perfect square of pale blue-green wouldn't belong. (Incidentally, this picture is quite Cubistic in its space. If these were cut paper shapes, what would be on top and what beneath?)

What Davis did in *Colonial Cubism* was create a *family of forms*. That's also what you would have done with your cardboard and scraps. We can presume that Davis, as a practiced professional painter, did a better job of it than you would have, but the principle involved in the attainment of unity would have been the same.

Families of forms exist outside art just as Golden Sections do. Trees constitute such a family of forms. So do leaves. So do people. And designers in professions entirely removed from art take formal consistencies into account. Among the man-made objects most people would not consider "artistic" are handguns. Still, the family of forms making up my 9 mm Luger is entirely different from the family that constitutes the Colt .44 (fig.

212
Luger and Colt

213
Fantasy handgun

212). The harsh, knobby look of the Luger has made its silhouette immediately identifiable to generations of small boys. Those prominences are functional. The one on top is a hinge for the mechanism that ejects spent cartridge cases, the one on the bottom of the handle is a grip to remove the cartridge clip, and the one by the trigger is a button which releases the clip. The smooth contours of the Colt had some obvious advantages for a working cowboy in the 1880s. The weapon is easy to wipe clean, it comes out of a holster smoothly, and it isn't apt to get hung up on anything.

In figure 213 I have drawn a hybrid pistol made up of incompatible families of forms.

You might like it because of its exotic, bizarre look. Science-fiction illustrators sometimes mix up things in this way to make an object look alien by making it look implausible. But only in special circumstances will one actually encounter such an odd amalgam of forms. It is not absolutely necessary that the Luger's grip be of that particular contour; nothing requires the butt to have a knob pull. It would work just as well if it were formed the way other semiautomatic pistols are. The knob is consistent with the general character of the weapon, that's all.

The comic strip *Peanuts* (fig. 214) exhibits the same kind of formal consistency. The figures and backgrounds are sort of geometric in an irregular, carefree way that matches the mood of the strip. The "peanuts" are always striving for absolute order and facing frustration. The balloons in which the speeches appear have, generally, the same characteristics as the rest of the strip. In Hogarth's *Tarzan* (fig. 215) the musculature of every figure defines itself with unreal clarity. The same kinds of curves, even the same rhythms of darks and lights, are repeated in the masks, shields, spear tips, plumes, and knife hilts. The sweep of the figures itself echoes the same abrupt curvature of the individual bodies.

Doonesbury (fig. 216) is rendered with a wispy, rather negligent-looking line that fits the mood of the characters; at the same time, the variations in drawing of the same objects from panel to panel convey some sense of the uncertainties of everyday existence. The absence of speech balloons associates the drawing forms with the letter shapes and achieves a special kind of harmony in this very verbal comic strip.

Krazy Kat (fig. 217) by George Herriman (1881–1944) is perhaps the most poetic comic strip of them all. The dramatis personae are a black cat whose sex is never made clear, a white mouse named Ignatz, a white dog called Offissa Pup, and a brick. Black cat loves white mouse. Mouse has one goal in life: to hit the cat in the head with the brick. Cat considers these plasterings an ensign of Ignatz's affection. The Kop, Offissa Pup, strives to protect "that dear Kat" from Ignatz's sadism and Krazy's masochism. Herriman's scratchy drawing is well suited to the happenings and to the fantasy land in which Krazy and his/her companions live. It is a place where a distant house will turn into a more distant mesa and then into a tree—a metamorphosis that is taken for granted by the characters and never mentioned by any of them.

Prince Valiant (fig. 218), as drawn by its inventor, Harold Foster, was the cream of the adventure comics. Thoroughly researched (though full of anachronisms) and beautifully drawn, it established a standard that has never been surpassed. Foster's drawings are much more pretentious than those of the other cartoonists. The individual panels are really fairly elaborate illustrations of the text, and the family of forms they contain is discernible but too complicated for a quick definition. In figure 219 I've drawn Prince Valiant partly as Foster would have and partly with Hogarth's forms. It's easy to see that the things don't match. My conglomeration of Schulz, Gary Trudeau (born 1948), and Herriman in figure 220 is similarly uneasy.

Harold Foster picked up much of his style from the so-called Dean of American Illustration, Howard Pyle (1853–1911), particularly from Pyle's illustrations for his own books, published in the early 1900s (fig. 221). In this drawing Pyle used a specific kind of drawn line over and over and over, varying it only a little whether it described chain mail, tree bark, horsehair, or the masonry of the background turret. Contemporary illustrator Bernard Fuchs (born 1932), in his magazine portrait of John F. Kennedy (fig. 222), used

214
CHARLES SCHULZ. *Peanuts.*
© 1968, United Feature Syndicate, Inc.

215
BURNE HOGARTH. *Tarzan.*
© 1949, Edgar Rice Burroughs, Inc.

216
GARY TRUDEAU. *Doonesbury.*
© G. B. Trudeau/Distributed
by Universal Press Syndicate

blocky forms throughout, repeating a characteristic pose of the young president in the angles of the White House exterior. When the pseudonymous Moebius (born Jean Giraud, 1938), most versatile of the French comic-strip artists, did *Harzak* (fig. 223) he followed the same principle as Pyle, matching the rendering to the larger forms. The marks that make up the figures are matched by the configurations of the architecture and figure silhouettes. And the faint asymmetry of the central panel here is echoed in the deviant symmetry of the emblems above and below.

Let us now consider a serious work of art that is not much more complicated in its formal structure than the commercial illustrations. *American Gothic* (fig. 224) by Grant Wood (1892–1942) is unusually clear in the kinds of forms the painter has used as a basis for the composition. One of the most obvious forms is the pitchfork. Actually, it is somewhat

217
GEORGE HERRIMAN. *Krazy Kat.*
© 1938, King Features Syndicate, Inc.

218
HAROLD FOSTER.
Prince Valiant.
© 1943, King Features
Syndicate, Inc.

219
Figure combining forms from Burne
Hogarth and Harold Foster

unusual for a fork to have three tines; four or
five are far more common. But three-tined
ones are standard for handling bundles from
self-tying reapers in Grant Wood's Iowa.
Moreover, the trident shape is particularly
well suited to Wood's artistic purposes. It is repeated in the stitching of the man's bib over-
alls, in the stripes on his shirt, in the symmetry
of his face, in the first-floor windows behind
him, and in the pseudo-Gothic window of
the upper story. The curve of the fork recurs
in the rickrack border on the woman's apron
and in the trees behind the house.

Cézanne's *The Basket of Apples* (fig. 225) is
far more complex in its structure, although it
may seem at first to be ineptly drawn. It is
full of rather queer distortions. The bottle is
asymmetrical and tilted. The plate is not el-
liptical as it would be seen from this angle.
And that table is really strange; the near edge
loses its identity as it passes beneath the cloth.
We might suppose that there were two tables
placed together underneath the tablecloth if
it weren't for two things. In the first place,
Cézanne does this all the time. Secondly, the
table edge doesn't match up on the backside
either; a line drawn along the right side
through the plate won't meet the side on the
left of the plate. And there are other strange
things. Why is the basket of apples propped
up so that fruit spills out on the table? And
how about those cookies? Now, I ask you,
who would stack cookies that way?

...THEN THIS SMALL,
WHITE MOUSE...

220
Drawing combining elements from
Gary Trudeau, Charles Schulz,
and George Herriman

221
HOWARD PYLE.
Illustration from *The Story of the Champions of the Round Table.*
© 1905, Charles Scribner's Sons

222
BERNARD FUCHS.
Illustration for part one, "Kennedy," by Theodore C. Sorenson, *Look,* 1965.
Copyright 1965 by Cowles Communications, Inc.

223
MOEBIUS. *Harzak.* © 1976, *Heavy Metal Magazine*

224
GRANT WOOD.
American Gothic. 1930.
Oil on beaverboard,
29⅜ × 24⅞". The Art
Institute of Chicago. Friends
of American Art Collection

You can probably guess that I wouldn't point out these things if I didn't want to say something about them. And, after the analysis of Cézanne's *Mont Sainte-Victoire*, you most likely realize that the artist knew what he was up to.

The queer-looking bottle is a good place to begin. Notice how similar it is to the shape between itself and the basket; that space looks a little like the bottle inverted, flipped over, and painted a lighter color. The highlight on the bottle makes its left side resemble the dark shadow at the very bottom of the picture. And it is possible to draw a continuous line from the left edge of the bottle down under the basket through the cloth all the way to that dark spot. Also, notice how the lower half of the basket has its curve mirrored in the line from the apple on the far right along the edge of the folded cloth through the next apple and up to the apple adjacent to the basket. Not easily seen in a black-and-white reproduction is an echo of that movement in a depression beneath the lowest apple of the three directly below the basket. There are many such familial relationships. These are but a few.

A comparison of the two schematics in figure 226 should serve to illustrate the magnitude and meaning of Cézanne's departure from traditional drawing. One thing is apparent at a glance; of the two the "Cézanne" *(A)* is by far the most stable. It is more like the space it fills; its lines and forms are remi-

niscent of the outline of the rectangle containing them. *B*, a shabby composition, drawn in accordance with the rules of geometric perspective, has no comparable suitability to its particular space. It does, however, have a highly dramatic and effective space. By contrast *A* is "standoffish," like a wall. Its space is not dramatic at all. But the relationships within the space are dramatic. One must be aware that the table in Cézanne's drawing

225
PAUL CÉZANNE. *The Basket of Apples.* 1890–94.
Oil on canvas, 25¾ × 32″. The Art Institute of Chicago. Helen Birch Bartlett
Memorial Collection

a   b

226
Scheme of Cézanne still life contrasted with scheme of traditional still life

had no prior existence. This isn't true of the table in *B* because it is a projection, and projections have an existence in the rules according to which you draw them. Cézanne's table is unique. Yet it is not drawn in this odd way just to be perverse. It belongs, like everything else in his picture, to a whole series of relationships. Meyer Schapiro has said of this still life that "deviations make the final equilibrium of the picture seem more evidently an achievement of the artist rather than an imitation of an already existing stability in nature."[2]

Turn back for a moment to colorplate 4, Picasso's *Girl Before a Mirror*. Obviously, the forms are of a related family. Study for a while the way one shape fits into another and the way these join together to make still larger shapes. Look, for example, at all the shapes under the extended arm. Pick out the ones that contain black or touch a black zone of color. Do you see how they connect up into their own independent group and grow over into other areas of the painting? Try the same

thing with the white shapes, with cool ones, with those that curve, and so on. You will discover that new aspects of the work constantly emerge and that they awake new attitudes toward the painting.

Some Comparisons and Contrasts

In these pages such a point has been made of the fact that painters must depart from reality in order to portray it that you may suppose the same isn't true of sculptors. They are, after all, dealing with three-dimensional forms, and it is possible to model figures of wax that are so like living beings that they can be mistaken for humans at rest. Still, we do not consider Madame Tussaud's amazing craft an art of much importance. So close a copy of a human being or a piece of fruit is fascinating precisely because considerations of formal composition do not enter in. The moment you become aware of the artifice involved in creating them, the manikins in a

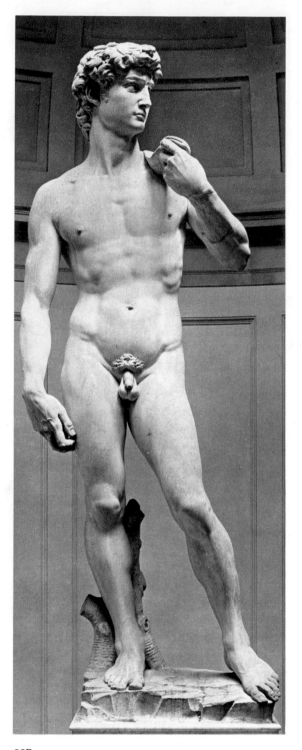

227

MICHELANGELO. *David.* 1501–4.

Marble, height of figure, 13′5″. Academy, Florence

wax museum look horribly stiff and dead.

Michelangelo's *David* (fig. 227) is clearly not a person—it is thirteen feet tall and made of solid rock—but it bursts with a vitality more potent than that of living creatures. The *David* is not shaped the way real men are, not even the way highly developed men are. Look at one of those magazines devoted to male "body-building." It does not take much study of figure 227 to disclose the modifications of the male torso Michelangelo made in creating his statue. The forms of the chest, thorax, abdomen, and pubic region are much more harmonious in their relationships than the similarly defined muscles of any weight-lifter. They constitute a more coherent family.

Within recent years there has been a movement towards waxworks-like realism among certain American sculptors. The works of Duane Hanson (born 1927) are made by taking plaster casts of people, making plastic molds from the casts, and finally adding real clothing and other paraphernalia (see fig. 228). The content is rather amusing as a comment on the vacuity of certain social values. The form is startling in its verisimilitude. But it hasn't the power of continuous interest of something like the *David*. Quite probably we in art would pay no attention to Fiberglas copies of people if it weren't for the fact that serious art has been dominated by nonrepresentationalism for the last three decades. It's kind of refreshing to see guys like Hanson flying in the face of all that art critics and professors have been saying is good for thirty years. But we must not forget that even during the days when abstract art was "it" no one doubted that Michelangelo's *David* was a masterpiece. Even Hanson is defended by his dealer, Ivan Karp, on the grounds that his work is interesting "because the volumes are right."

It may be of interest, at this point, to reexamine some of the masterpieces we've touched on before.

228
DUANE HANSON. *Tourists.* 1970.
Fiberglas and polychromed polyester, 64×65×47″. Collection Saul Steinberg, Hewlitt Bay Park, New York

229
CIMABUE. *Madonna Enthroned*. c. 1280–90.
Tempera on panel,12′6″×7′4″. Uffizi Gallery,Florence

230
GIOTTO. *Madonna
Enthroned*. c. 1310.
Tempera on panel, 10′8″ × 6′8″.
Uffizi Gallery, Florence

That Cimabue was aware of the necessity to maintain a pattern of similar forms is made clear in his *Madonna Enthroned* (fig. 229). There is so much repetition that the work verges on the monotonous. Giotto's version (fig. 230) is as advanced in its composition as it is in its spatial effects. Note that the upper third of the picture is light in value. The central section containing the standing angels and the body of the Virgin has a lot of darks. The lowest part, including the two kneeling angels and what's between them, contains large light areas. There is an overall pattern of large-scale value masses. Within that pattern many others operate. The dark area of Mary's robe contrasts with the lightness of

her face, blouse, and child. The impact of this large accent draws one's attention to the dominating personalities. The same kind of device was used by Holbein two and a half centuries later in the portrait of Georg Gisze (fig. 231). It would be easy to lose our way in the mass of detail surrounding Gisze were it not for the fact that the sitter's face and blouse constitute the largest and lightest area surrounded by the largest, darkest areas. In the Giotto the content also helps direct attention to the center of interest. In the Cimabue all the angels look out at us, Mary looks out, Christ looks out. Only the two prophets in the lower left and right direct their gaze toward anything within the work itself. In

231
HANS HOLBEIN THE YOUNGER.
Georg Gisze. 1532.
Oil and tempera on panel, 38 × 33".
Staatliche Museen, Berlin-Dahlem

232
RAPHAEL. *Madonna of the Beautiful
Garden.* 1507.
Oil on panel, 48 × 31½". The Louvre,
Paris

Giotto there is a psychological focus. The angels all look at Mary and her son. Mary looks at us. Christ is the most self-sufficient of all; He seems already to ponder the meaning of His life on earth.

Raphael's *Madonna of the Beautiful Garden* (fig. 232) is a later painting and is much more sophisticated. The artist has turned his figure group into an articulated whole by means of smooth, graceful curves. The line of Christ's

hip continues up through his mother's arm and proceeds in an *S* turn back over her shoulders. Her shoulders are themselves abnormally smooth and circular. The top of her dress matches them. The hills, the clouds in the sky, and even the arc of the frame relate to the gentle swelling curves prevailing in the figures.

Monet's *Haystack at Sunset Near Giverny* (fig. 233) and Van Gogh's *The Starry Night* (fig.

233
CLAUDE MONET. *Haystack at Sunset Near Giverny*. 1891.
Oil on canvas, 29½ × 37″. Museum of Fine Arts, Boston. Juliana Cheney Edwards Collection

234
VINCENT VAN GOGH. *The Starry Night*. 1889.
Oil on canvas, 28¾ × 36¼″. The Museum of Modern Art, New York. Lillie P. Bliss Bequest

234) were painted only two years apart (1891 and 1889) by modern artists of unquestioned genius. In some ways they are very much alike. Both are landscapes, both are frontal, both are concerned with private visions. The private vision of Monet was based on his attempt to render with complete objectivity the color sensations he perceived in a given time and place. That of Van Gogh was a blend of the objective condition of reality with his subjective feelings about it. Monet broke everything down into little spots of color, weaving a fabric of interlaced hues. His technique reduced the world down into brushstrokes, and they produced a cohesive pattern because of their similarity in scale and weight. The relative massings of strokes of various hues coalesced into shapes from which the larger composition grew. The brushstrokes in *The Starry Night* are more like drawn lines

235
VINCENT VAN GOGH.
Cypresses and Stars,
study for *The Starry
Night.* 1889.
Reed pen, pen, and ink,
18½ × 24⅝″. Formerly
Kunsthalle, Bremen
(destroyed in World War II)

than spots. They are filled with energy and drive that reveal the painter's feelings about the world. Nebulae rage across the heavens of the night, and cypresses spring up like dark flames against the sky.

It is easy to see why Vincent van Gogh has come to represent in the popular mind the example of a genius who created in the throes of maddened frenzy. He *was* mentally ill: he had delusions, once during a seizure he cut off the lobe of his own ear, and he finally committed suicide. But he was a great artist in spite of, not because of, his affliction. His study for *The Starry Night* (fig. 235) is excessive in its fervor; everything is sinuous, intertwined, overwrought. In the final painting such violence has been curtailed. The painting has been ordered, resolved, and made richer by pitting stable lines against wavy ones. The sketch is typical of sophomoric "Expressionistic" paintings, the oil an example of excellence.

One of the most famous paintings in the entire history of art is Leonardo's *Mona Lisa*

(fig. 236). Her strange smile is so haunting that it has become a part of the folklore of our civilization. The subject was Lisa,[3] wife of Francesco del Giocondo, but she never got the portrait; Leonardo liked it so much that he kept it for himself. A great deal has been written about why she looks at us in this way, about the circumstances under which the picture was painted, and so on. Most of it is nonsense. When you hear someone explain the smile, you must take into account something that most speakers don't—this is an oil painting done in a technique that is time-consuming. Such an expression occurs in this kind of oil portrait because the painter chooses to put it there.

In his *Mona Lisa* Leonardo is playing games with us. The ambiguity of the famous "gioconda smile" is the result of two things. One is the artist's skill in handling chiaroscuro so as to blur our perception of the second thing. The second thing is the radical asymmetry of the face. Cover up the left half and you will see that she is smirking rather superciliously.

Cover up the right half and you will observe that she is cool and reserved. All faces are asymmetrical, and all good portrait painters make use of this fact. But Leonardo has made La Gioconda's face do what a real face couldn't—maintain two expressions simultaneously without a hint of strain or unnaturalness. Also, the face has been harmonized by bringing the arc of the brows, the cheeks, the lips, and the chin into parallel. The same curve is repeated in the top of her dress, the slope of her shoulders, the shape of the top of her head, and in details of clothing. It is a masterful and ingenious work, in which form and content are so completely tied together as to be inseparable.

Leonardo did not much care for women, at least not as men usually do. Willem De

236

LEONARDO DA VINCI.
Mona Lisa. 1503–5.
Oil on panel, 30¼ × 21″.
The Louvre, Paris

237
WILLEM DE KOONING.
Woman and Bicycle.
1952–53.
Oil on canvas, 76½ × 49″.
Whitney Museum of American
Art, New York

Kooning (born 1904) does. But about 1950 De Kooning started painting gigantic pictures of women in a way that would make you think he hates the sex. His *Woman and Bicycle* (fig. 237) evokes the female as a crazed, maniacal, vampirish sex symbol. The forms are born of violent, smeary brushwork played off against flat zones of color. Yet all kinds of artistry are working here, revolting though their consequences may seem. To take a simple example, the feet of the figure merge with the immediate background so as to produce a whole area of sienna. An adjacent yellow area above (a skirt?) has a similar configuration. Seek out such comparisons and you will be able to see why critics speak of De Koon-

238
Anonymous comic-strip panel

239
ROY LICHTENSTEIN.
Brattata. 1962.
Oil on canvas, 42 × 42".
Courtesy of Greenberg
Gallery of Contemporary Art,
St. Louis

240
LARRY RIVERS. *Dutch Masters and Cigars III.* 1963.
Oil and collage on canvas, 96 × 67⅜″. Harry N. Abrams Family Collection, New York

ing's talents as a painter. I myself cannot abide the man's work; in my opinion it is vastly overrated. I can see, however, that it is not empty of value. Some of you may be as enthusiastic as most critics. You don't have to agree with my judgment, obviously. Neither do you have to go along with fashionable opinion. Who knows? I may change my mind about De Kooning. I have modified my opinion of Roy Lichtenstein.

Lichtenstein is what has come to be called a *Pop artist*. His early work was very delicate and sensitive. In the 1960s he developed a new manner. It involved turning comic-strip panels into huge paintings. Figure 238 is from a comic strip; figure 239 is a Lichtenstein painting. At first they look quite a lot alike, although perhaps the looseness of the cartoonist's rendering is more appealing than the tight, almost mechanical drawing in the oil painting. Art historian Albert Boime did a formal comparison of the panel with the painting, and it is worth quoting here:

In the *Brattata* the balloon is modified from the original to correspond more closely to the shape of the pilot's visor. . . . the balloon stem is carefully brought into compositional play with regularly recurring features in the picture. Departing from the straight stem of the original panel Lichtenstein repeats his own crescent shape in the speed lines of the falling plane, in the highlights of the visor and around the knob on the control panel. Its arc parallels the curve of the helmet and recurs in the contours of the pilot's profile. An even more significant change is Lichtenstein's formal emphasis of the cartoonist's visual "sound effect" of machine-gun fire (*Brattata*) not only in size and color but in the increased tilt which counterbalances the mass of the falling plane. A comparison with the original also reveals how Lichtenstein uses the balloon in his correction from two to four as the number of downed planes required "to make Ace."[4]

The paintings of Larry Rivers (born 1923), like those of De Kooning, marry Expression-

istic brushstroking to representational drawing. And, like Lichtenstein, Rivers sometimes paints pictures of pictures. His *Dutch Masters and Cigars III* (fig. 240) proves just how complicated this can get. First off, the Dutch Masters trademark is an old master, Rembrandt's *The Syndics,* and so while Rivers is using popular art as a point of departure, he is also closely tied to fine art. Using *The Syndics* for a trademark is a case of honoring greatness with levity, especially when the painting is animated for TV. Rivers reversed this by memorializing the trivial and making a cigar box into a cultural monument. The coupling of his drawing style with Rembrandt's figure composition produced an extraordinary effect of renewed vitality. And there is a kind of fascinating interchange of forms occurring between the top and bottom versions in Rivers's painting. The rhythmic play of the angular blotches that move through the pictures, seeming to erase them at one point, helping to articulate them at another, is almost like counterpoint in music. The cigars are handled with similar delicacy. The two at the base suggest the traffic lanes and divider strips of the Long Island Expressway, where the billboard that inspired this painting stood.

It would be misleading to say that formal composition comes down to nothing more than developing unmonotonous similarities of shape, line and color. Obviously, there is a good deal more to it than that. Proportions, painting and drawing techniques, spatial illusions, the nature of the content—all have a role in giving any work its unique form. In one way or another we've been dealing with formal composition all along, in discussing the elements of space, line, chiaroscuro, and form. What this chapter has tried to do is summarize the relationships critics refer to as "form." The next chapter will amplify the understanding.

8
Styles of Vision

The word *style* has so many different meanings as to be unwieldy. "She's not my style." "I don't care for the new styles in clothing." "His style evolved from folk music to hard rock." "When this Brother talks, he comes on with style." "The life style of young people during the 1950s was very different from that of young people today." At the root of all of these applications of the word *style* is the recognition that objects and individuals and groups of objects and individuals have certain things peculiarly characteristic of them, things which distinguish them from other objects, individuals, or groups. A man with hair to his shoulders, who customarily wears tie-dyed shirts and flared trousers of blue denim, has a different *style* from someone with a crew cut, a Botany 500 suit, and a "color-coordinated" shirt and tie. The grooming style of the first person identifies him with a completely different group from the one the second belongs to.

241

CHARLES SCHULZ.
Panel from *Peanuts*.
© 1968, United Feature
Syndicate, Inc.

242

GARY TRUDEAU. Panel
from *Doonesbury*.
© G. B. Trudeau/
Distributed by Universal
Press Syndicate

243

MILTON CANIFF. Panel from *Steve Canyon*.
© 1976, King Features Syndicate, Inc.

244

ALEX RAYMOND. Panel from *Flash Gordon*.
© 1939, King Features Syndicate, Inc.

But someone who shaves all his hair except for a short, four-inch triangle on top, who never wears anything but jump suits and slippers with pointed toes, and who affects a platinum ring through his lower lip could be said to have a unique style. Unless it should catch on, in which case he'd be the founder of a style.

The kinds of forms and lines in *Peanuts* (fig. 241) distinguish it from *Doonesbury* (fig. 242) at a glance. And one would not be likely to mistake a comic strip by Milton Caniff (fig. 243) for one by Alex Raymond (fig. 244), simply because the forms Caniff uses are consistently different from those employed by Raymond.

In art, *style* refers to the customary series of forms, colors, and techniques used by an artist. Sometimes these can be identified as characteristics of whole groups of artists; thus, we can speak of a fifteenth-century Flemish style in painting, of the French Impressionist style,

245

MASTER OF FLÉMALLE (ROBERT CAMPIN?). Mérode Altarpiece of the *Annunciation*.
c. 1425–28.
Oil on panel, center panel 25″ square, each wing 25 × 10″. The Cloisters, The Metropolitan Museum of Art, New York

246

JAN VAN EYCK. *Giovanni Arnolfini and His Bride.* 1434.
Oil on panel, 32¼ × 23½″. The National Gallery, London

247

CLAUDE MONET. *Haystack at Sunset Near Giverny.* 1891.
Oil on canvas, 29½ × 37″. Museum of Fine Arts, Boston. Juliana Cheney Edwards Collection

248
EDGAR DEGAS. *The Tub.* 1886.
Pastel, 23½ × 32⅜″. The Louvre, Paris

249
PABLO PICASSO. *Ma Jolie.* 1911–12.
Oil on canvas, 39⅜ × 25¾″. The Museum
of Modern Art, New York. Lillie P.
Bliss Bequest

250
GEORGES BRAQUE.
Man with a Guitar. 1911.
Oil on canvas, 45¾ × 31⅞″. The Museum
of Modern Art, New York. Lillie P.
Bliss Bequest

⌐ of the Cubist style. It is easy to see that Robert Campin (fig. 245) and Van Eyck (fig. 246) have many things in common when compared with Monet (fig. 247) and Degas (fig. 248). The Cubist work of Pablo Picasso (fig. 249) and Georges Braque (fig. 250) is even more alike than the work of the two Flemish painters or the two Impressionists.

But there is another side to style. There are always specific traits in any artist's work which will differentiate him from everyone else. Van Eyck is like Campin, but there are also things about his drawing and painting that are as individual as his fingerprints.

That is obviously true of the two Impressionists. Even the Picasso and the Braque have certain distinctive features that will set them apart for the expert eye. If any of these artists had wished to completely submerge his identity in another's style, he would have been unable to do so. No imitation, no forgery, is ever perfect. For in every individual there are parts of the personality that remain invincibly insulated from external influence or conscious will. This truth is one we must not overlook. But no matter how you view it, the style of a period or group is easier to identify than the style of an individual within a period or group. That is, it's a pretty good bet that you wouldn't mistake a Degas for a Monet the way you might the Braque for the Picasso. But there's *no* chance that you'd mistake either the Monet or the Degas for any of the others.

Just as there is a branch of art history (iconography) which deals with subject matter, there is a branch concerned with form. Its concern is with historical problems, not with art criticism; it hasn't much to do with quality, it focuses on objective description. It is called *theory of style*. And its principal objective is to explain the evolution of styles throughout history. There are a number of theories of stylistic development, all open to serious question and none without the kinds of flaws that would cause any scientific theory

to be discarded. One of the most interesting is Heinrich Wölfflin's.

Wölfflin's Theory of Style and "Instant" Connoisseurship

Before we get into this thing, let me make it clear that Wölfflin's theory is applicable only to a specific period, although he himself at first supposed it applied to most historical epochs. Later he admitted that modern art was not accessible to his theory and also confessed that various factors might influence artistic developments so markedly that they would not appear to correspond to his description. But he was unable to modify the

251
SANDRO BOTTICELLI. *The Birth of Venus.* c. 1480.
Tempera on canvas, 5'8⅞" × 9'1⅞". Uffizi Gallery, Florence

252
PETER PAUL RUBENS. *The Rape of the Daughters of Leucippus.* c. 1616–17.
Oil on canvas, 7′3½″×6′10¼″. Alte Pinakothek, Munich

theory to take account of the variables. If I wished to do so, I could give many examples that would dispute Wölfflin's procedures. Anyone seriously interested in art could do the same.[1] I am *not* presenting his theory here with a view to defending it; I use it merely to reveal the ways in which a general view can overcome individual differences among artists.

Wölfflin devised his system in a brilliant analysis of the art of the sixteenth and seventeenth centuries. His contention was that art during this time span tended to move from one set of characteristics to another, specifically from:

1. the linear to the painterly
2. the parallel surface form to the diagonal depth form
3. closed to open compositional form
4. multiplicity to unity
5. the clear to the relatively unclear

He was at pains to point out that he used the terms *sixteenth century* and *seventeenth century* for the sake of simplicity but that the characteristics of the latter had actually appeared before 1600 and lasted on into the eighteenth century. Probably the terms *High Renaissance* and *Baroque* should be substituted for his centuries. In any case, what he was trying to do was map out a sort of topography of historical developments. He did not argue that all artists in every nation modified their styles in a synchronized fashion. Obviously, some artists are ahead of the times and some behind. His favorite example of High Renaissance painting is Leonardo's *Last Supper,* painted before 1500; and he often uses Tintoretto as an example of seventeenth-century form, although Tintoretto died in 1594. We are dealing here with generalities. But they are generalities with a good deal of substance.

In order to give a very clear picture of what Wölfflin's polarities mean, I shall make an exaggerated comparison between an Early Renaissance masterpiece and one from the full-blown Baroque. Let Botticelli's *The Birth of Venus* (fig. 251) of about 1480 represent the first set of terms and Peter Paul Rubens's *The Rape of the Daughters of Leucippus* (fig. 252), done about 1616, represent the second.

The linear to the painterly: By "linear" Wölfflin means that outlines are relatively clear and that stress is laid on limits of things. By "painterly" he means depreciating the emphasis on outline and emphasizing the larger zones of dark and light. In the Botticelli the limits of things are clear. It would be wrong to say of the Rubens that edges do not exist; but it is certainly true that they are not nearly so clear as in the Botticelli. Rubens gives more power to the large spots of light and dark. Darks merge into darks and lights flow into lights.

The parallel surface form to the diagonal depth form: Obviously, the spatial arrangement in the Botticelli is of objects parallel to the canvas surface. Of course, there are diagonal elements—such as the lines in the shell—but they are not preeminent. What is most striking about the forms is that they are lined up more or less parallel to the front of the work. Rubens's picture contains elements that are parallel to the canvas, surely; but there are major forms that move back into space on diagonals. Consider, for instance, the recession from the nearest daughter's right hand to the head of the man lifting her sister. This movement is diagonal across the canvas and also travels progressively deeper into the picture. In more general terms, the effect of the Botticelli is of a very limited space, quite shallow and flat, whereas the space of the Rubens is correspondingly more three-dimensional. This is true despite the fact that the background in the Botticelli portrays things (such as sky) that we know are as far away in fact as any in the Rubens.

Closed to open compositional form: Venus forms a strong vertical axis for the Botticelli. Even though she is posed in a sinuous manner, she has been oriented to the sides of the picture. In fact, everything in the picture has. Verticals and horizontals dominate despite the presence of a few diagonals. This becomes obvious when we contrast *The Birth of Venus* with *The Rape of the Daughters of Leucippus*. *Open* is, perhaps, not a very good term (*a-tectonic* would be better), but it refers to the fact that in seventeenth-century works the horizontal and vertical elements of the picture edge do not dictate the internal arrangement

of forms to the same extent that they do in
sixteenth-century works. What is most evident
in the Rubens is the diagonal, circular
arrangement of things. Briefly put, the
Botticelli looks deliberate and studied; the
Rubens has a more open, casual look. We
might think of the terms *closed* and *open* here
as we do in describing personalities as closed
or open. By the former we mean constrained,
tense, uptight; by the latter we mean free and
expansive. Too, closed compositions tend
towards symmetrical balance, and open ones
are often quite unsymmetrical.

Multiplicity to unity: The Botticelli is constituted of a collection of distinctly separate
forms. We can separate out the nude or the
two figures representing the Zephyrs and
comprehend them as individual items very
easily. We might even look at Venus's long
hair apart from Venus as a whole. Venus is a
composite of separate pieces; the picture is
the result of multiple parts, each worked out
as a separate entity. In Rubens it is possible,
of course, to speak of a given head or hand or
person separately from the others, but no individual figure or part of a figure has the kind
of independence one experiences in Botticelli.
This can be quickly demonstrated by vignet-
ting Venus and one of the daughters (fig.
253). Venus can exist outside her original
context; the daughter is dependent on her
surroundings. This is what Wölfflin meant by
unity in seventeenth-century art—the greater
dependence of one part upon the others so
that the picture as a whole is a unit.

The clear to the relatively unclear: This development is, like the others, closely connected
with the difference between linearity and
painterliness. But here Wölfflin was trying
to tie together some loose ends. And from his
point of view Botticelli wouldn't fit, really:
Botticelli would be distinguished from the
High Renaissance because he was not striving
for the *absolute* clarity of form that later painters such as Leonardo and Raphael sought.
Wölfflin's example of absolute clarity is

253
Vignettes of a daughter of
Leucippus (above) and Venus
(below)

Leonardo's *Last Supper* (fig. 254), in which
human beings have been reduced to geomet-

254
LEONARDO DA VINCI. *The Last Supper.* 1495–98.
Mural. Sta. Maria delle Grazie, Milan

255
TINTORETTO. *The Last Supper.* 1592–94.
Oil on canvas, 12′ × 18′8″.
S. Giorgio Maggiore, Venice

ric forms, in which the perspective scheme focuses on Christ's head, in which all twenty-six of the people's hands are shown. In Rubens's *The Rape of the Daughters of Leucippus* things are not absolutely clear in this way. Things are loose and swinging, the eye moves freely through the picture, and although five figures appear there are only seven hands.

Leonardo's *Last Supper* might seem too "painterly" for the High Renaissance as Wölfflin defines it. This is due in some measure to its physical deterioration and piecemeal repair, but any Leonardo is less obviously linear than any Botticelli. What Wölfflin points out is that in looking at the *Last Supper* we are conscious of the limits of things despite the haziness of the work. Much High Ren-

Colorplate 12
PAUL CÉZANNE. *Mont Sainte-Victoire.* 1885–87.
Oil on canvas, $25\frac{5}{8} \times 31\frac{7}{8}''$. The Metropolitan Museum of Art, New York.
The H. O. Havemeyer Collection. Bequest of Mrs. H. O. Havemeyer, 1929

Colorplate 13
STUART DAVIS. *Colonial Cubism.* 1954.
Oil on canvas, 45 × 60″. Walker Art Center, Minneapolis

Colorplate 14
FRANK STELLA. *Sinjerli Variation I.* 1968.
Fluorescent acrylic on canvas, diameter 10'.
Harry N. Abrams Family Collection, New York

Colorplate 17
RENZO PIANO and RICHARD ROGERS. Pompidou Center,
Paris. 1976

256
ALBRECHT DÜRER. *Adam and Eve.* 1504.
Engraving, $9\frac{7}{8} \times 7\frac{5}{8}$". Museum of Fine Arts, Boston. Centennial Gift of London Clay

aissance painting from Italy has a dark hazy effect (called *sfumato*) that obscures the clarity of edges. Still, the impression is that the edges exist firmly and tangibly beneath the shadows. Remember, this is a matter of *relative* clarity.

Contrast Leonardo with Tintoretto (fig. 255) in terms of Wölfflin's theory. The limits may be somewhat uncertain in Leonardo, but they are buried in Tintoretto. Furthermore, in Leonardo the parallel form is very evident: the table parallel to the picture plane, the figures in a row behind the table, the wall behind them, the landscape beyond the windows. As we have noted previously, Tintoretto drives the tables and figures deep into the picture, and the diagonal depth form is strikingly evident. Of course, the relationship of the horizontals and verticals to the top and bottom of the picture in Leonardo's *Last Supper* is exemplary of the closed compositional form, while Tintoretto's diagonals and swelling curved movements suggest openness and a looser structure. The Leonardo is made up of separate pieces placed together—a multiple situation in Wölfflin's terms—

257
REMBRANDT VAN RIJN.
Adam and Eve. 1638.
Etching, $6\frac{3}{8} \times 4\frac{5}{8}''$. Rijksmuseum, Amsterdam

258
HANS HOLBEIN THE YOUNGER. *Georg Gisze.*
1532. Oil and tempera on panel, 38×33".
Staatliche Museen, Berlin-Dahlem

259
JAN VERMEER VAN DELFT. *Young Woman with a Water Jug.* c. 1665. Oil on canvas, 18×17".
The Metropolitan Museum of Art, New York. Gift of Henry G. Marquand, 1889

whereas in Tintoretto the figures are less distinct and more dependent for their character on the other things in the picture. Finally, the clarity of the Leonardo has been remarked above. The Tintoretto is not comparable; there, light and color no longer serve merely to define the forms but have a life of their own.

Let us now compare a sixteenth-century German work with a piece from seventeenth-century Holland. Albrecht Dürer's engraving of Adam and Eve (fig. 256) corresponds to all the attributes for High Renaissance work: it is linear, has a parallel surface form, is closed rather than open, multiplicity rules (even the figures are made of separate muscle groups), and the individual forms are absolutely clear.

Rembrandt handled the same theme in an etching (fig. 257). It is made up of drawn lines, but it is not linear; indeed, there are places where the edges of things are not indicated at all. Notice the lighted side of Eve's right leg or the way shade merges with shadow under the serpent's foot. What strikes one in looking at the etching is not the outline of the forms but the dark and light spots in the work. Also one is much more conscious of diagonal spatial properties in the Rembrandt. The coordination between vertical and horizontal elements within the picture and the edges of the plane is not critical to the composition. As for clarity, the forms in Rembrandt's work are coherent rather than crisp and clear because of the way he uses light and shadow.

There were also Dutch artists of the seventeenth century who painted very neat, highly detailed pictures. So let us contrast one such picture with a sixteenth-century painting by Holbein. *Georg Gisze* (fig. 258)

260

261

263

262

264

265

Identifying captions for pictures
are on page 342

266

268

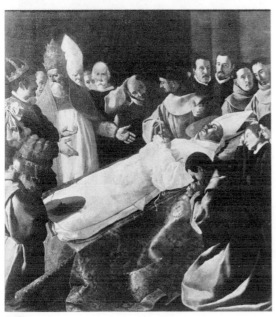

267

269

has a more parallel surface form than Vermeer's *Young Woman with a Water Jug* (fig. 259). It is more linear. It is pretty symmetrical and not so fluid and open-looking; Gisze is a good deal more fixed in his space than the maid is in hers. He is obviously more a sum of individual parts than she, and so it goes throughout the two pictures. Finally, for all of the sparkling clarity of Vermeer's light effects, the objects are not so definite in their appearance as the sharply detailed things in the Holbein.

Now, then, having looked at a few examples of the application of Wölfflin's categories, you should be able to apply them to pictures you know nothing else about. Your "instant connoisseurship" depends on the fact that I am not going out of my way to trick you by including things that don't fit the system. But you may be surprised at how accomplished you are at dating works. Included in figures 260 to 269 are five sixteenth-century works and five seventeenth-century works. Which are which? The answers are on page 342.[2]

I suspect you got most of them right. Granted, if you had not known how many were in each category, you might have picked figure 261 as sixteenth because it is possible to read the figure groupings as parallel to the picture plane and because there are a lot of closed compositional relations to the canvas. But you'll have gotten at least eight out of ten

270

PIETER BRUEGEL THE ELDER. *Peasant Wedding.* c. 1565.
Oil on panel, 44⅞ × 64″. Kunsthistorisches Museum, Vienna

right, which is better than you could have done without the Wölfflin formula. Right? Quite so.

It would have been easy to stymie you. To which century would you assign figure 270? It has a definite linearity, yet the diagonal depth form predominates. There are elements of both the closed and open compositional form. Still, it is made up of individually distinct elements and is clear in the foreground but less so in the distance. It was done in the sixteenth century, as you can see by the caption. Wölfflin called the painter, Pieter Bruegel the Elder, a "transitional painter." He says that Bruegel paved the way for Vermeer but was not yet a Vermeer.

What I am trying to show you is that there are stylistic differences between vast groups of painters that are obvious to anyone who wishes to spend even a little time taking notice of them. In Wölfflin's theory they occur across the centuries regardless of the personal or national differences among the painters. His theory doesn't always work out, but it is true that it describes *most* High Renaissance art in the sixteenth century and *most* Baroque art during the seventeenth. The High Renaissance style of vision is different from the Baroque style of vision. The reason for the emergence of the two modes interests those of us with some concern for the history of ideas, but the point is that you don't have to know anything at all about history to observe the differences in the art; they are revealed in the distinctive forms the pictures take.

Individual Styles Within a Style of Vision

It would not do to neglect the profound differences that exist within a given style of vision. Rembrandt's *Christ at Emmaus* (fig. 271) and Vermeer's *Young Woman with a Water Jug* (fig. 272) were painted seventeen years apart, and both conform to Wölfflin's des-

271
REMBRANDT VAN RIJN. *Christ at Emmaus.* 1648.
Oil on panel, 26¾ × 25½". The Louvre, Paris

272
JAN VERMEER VAN DELFT. *Young Woman with a Water Jug.* c. 1665. Oil on canvas, 18 × 17". The Metropolitan Museum of Art, New York. Gift of Henry G. Marquand, 1889

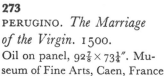

273
PERUGINO. *The Marriage of the Virgin.* 1500.
Oil on panel, 92⅞ × 73¼″. Museum of Fine Arts, Caen, France

scription of seventeenth-century art. But within that general Baroque style of vision these Dutchmen's styles of vision are vastly different. The differences, though, are apparent to anyone. The similarities take a bit of looking for.

Once in awhile we encounter paintings so much alike that a qualitative difference between them seems unlikely. But a little attention to particulars can enlighten us about the way in which individual genius overcomes an imposed style. In the works of Raphael and his teacher Perugino (c. 1450–1523) we have the perfect example. In 1500 Perugino portrayed the marriage of Mary and Joseph (fig.

273). In 1504 Raphael painted his *Marriage of the Virgin* (fig. 274), following the pattern established by his teacher.

At a glance the two works are almost identical. There is a row of figures in the immediate foreground, a courtyard behind them, and a temple beyond the court. A brief study will show that, while the content is the same and the style of vision sixteenth century, the individual styles are really quite different.

The Perugino figures form a much more solid row; they are like a wall. We observe them with the same detachment with which we look upon the temple. The principle of horizontality is ruthlessly carried through by

274
RAPHAEL. *The Marriage of the Virgin.* 1504.
Oil on panel, 67 × 46½″.
Brera Gallery, Milan

Perugino. The figure arrangement, the long panels in the courtyard, the extremely broad temple steps—all stress the horizontal. The temple is a distracting element. It has two porticoes out to the sides. An identical one projects toward us, but we don't realize it's a porch at first. What captures our attention is the doorway in the center of the shaded archway. That door is the most arresting single element in the whole work. The perspective is wrong too. There is one eye level for the temple, another for the figures.

Raphael has overcome most of his teacher's weaknesses. His row of figures is not so absolutely parallel to the picture plane. The young woman on the left stands closer to us than Mary, helping to lead the eye into the picture. Too, the fellow breaking a stick over his knee—symbolic of leaving one family for a new one—matches the girl's diagonal. In the Perugino the same ritual figure is lost among the other members of the foreground group. Raphael's courtyard is calculated to convey depth, and his temple has a coherence Perugino's lacks. Raphael has absorbed the porches into a continuous arcade, and he has decreased the depth of shadow around the door. Moreover, he has given the priest a brocaded belt with a strong vertical accent; it helps connect the temple door to the fore-

275
PIET MONDRIAN.
Composition in White, Black and Red. 1936.
Oil on canvas, 40¼ × 41″. The
Museum of Modern Art, New York.
Gift of the Advisory Committee

276
WASSILY KANDINSKY.
Improvisation Number 30. 1913.
Oil on canvas, 43¼ × 43¾″. The Art
Institute of Chicago. Arthur Jerome
Eddy Memorial Collection

ground figures. Too, the doorway is smaller than the one in Perugino. The courtyard panels are shorter, producing a series of brief diagonals that lead from the figures to the temple steps.

Perugino organized his painting in terms of a family of forms that tend to separate things into horizontal bands. It is a unified composition insofar as the visual pattern is concerned. But Perugino's pattern gets in the way of psychological coherence. Raphael's system of forms is as unified as his teacher's; but it contributes to the representation, it doesn't disrupt it. The different emotional tone of the two works is revealed in small by the postures of the individuals portrayed. In Perugino the people to the left and right of the three central figures form self-contained groups. This is one way of keeping our attention on Joseph, the priest, and Mary. Another is by posing the couple in as symmetrical a manner as possible, even using the same curve for the folds of their robes. (This business of repeating poses is a trademark of Perugino's. You can find background figures on the court whose postures reflect those of figures in the foreground. He uses posture as an abstract, formal element.)

Raphael gives his principals much more individuality in dress as well as in pose. And they are related to the others present by their robes: the folds and hems of their gowns are in line with the folds and hems of other gowns. Still, our attention is drawn back to them again and again because of the strategic positioning of the distant figures on the court, the way in which the divisions in the pavement and the central bank of temple steps create two perfect trapezoids, and the linear developments through the group.

The figures in Raphael, like those in the Perugino, have an eye level separate from the one for the temple. There are also two vanishing points: one in the doorway for the courtyard and temple and one for the figures at the wedding ring Joseph places on Mary's finger.

The ring is directly in line with the vanishing point in the door. Technically, the perspective is incorrect. But it emphasizes that the temple and the marriage ceremony are equally important elements of the scene. The insistence with which both artists try to make this point —the sanctification of love by religious ceremony and the singularity of this particular marriage—is a little obtrusive. The idea is one bound to produce a hint of disunity because our attention is permitted neither to rest on a specific point nor to rove freely over the entire picture. We are torn between the temple and the figures. Nonetheless, of the two treatments Raphael's is by far the more successful. His personal style affords more cohesiveness than Perugino's. His is the more integrated view of the world. Yet when compared to Tintoretto, El Greco, or Rembrandt, the Perugino and Raphael are obviously representative of the same general style of vision.

The Dilemma of Modern Styles

If Perugino and Raphael are alike compared to Tintoretto, then the work of Mondrian (fig. 275) and Kandinsky (fig. 276) is still more alike. Neither Mondrian nor Kandinsky make any pretense of representing visual reality. To the extent that they reject dependence on anything except pure form they are identical. But, of course, they are not at all that much alike in fact. The Mondrian is neat and regulated; the Kandinsky is loose, bold, and emotional. The Kandinsky was painted before World War I and the Mondrian after it. Kandinsky was a Russian living in Germany, Mondrian a Dutchman who developed his style in Paris. But one can find similar distinctions of style among modern paintings done in the same time and place by artists of the same national backgrounds.

One of the painters in Kandinsky's group in Munich was Franz Marc (1880–1916). His *Deer in a Forest, II* (fig. 277) shares the

277
FRANZ MARC. *Deer in a Forest, II.* 1913–14.
Oil on canvas, 43½ × 39½″. Staatliche
Kunsthalle, Karlsruhe, West Germany

278
ERNST LUDWIG KIRCHNER. *The Street.* 1907.
Oil on canvas, 59¼ × 78⅞″. The
Museum of Modern Art, New York

bright colors of Kandinsky's *Improvisation Number 30,* but in other respects the paintings are not much alike. In Dresden, Germany, in the same period Ernst Ludwig Kirchner (1880–1938) painted *The Street* (fig. 278), a work that seems to resemble neither the Marc

279
SALVADOR DALI. *Apparition of a Face and Fruit Dish on a Beach*. 1938. Oil on canvas, 43½ × 57″. Wadsworth Atheneum, Hartford, Connecticut. The Ella Gallup Sumner and Mary Catlin Sumner Collection

280
JOAN MIRÓ. *Person Throwing a Stone at a Bird*. 1926. Oil on canvas, 29 × 36¼″. The Museum of Modern Art, New York

nor the Kandinsky.

Salvador Dali was one of the leaders of the Surrealist movement in painting. His *Apparition of a Face and Fruit Dish on a Beach* (fig. 279) intends to evoke the dream world of the unconscious mind. Spanish painter Joan Miró (born 1893) identified himself with the same trend in modern painting. His *Person Throwing a Stone at a Bird* (fig. 280) appears, however, to have nothing in common with Dali's style.

The apparent contradictions in modern art have been dealt with by an art theoretician, Wilhelm Worringer, who published his doctoral dissertation, *Abstraktion und Einfühlung (Abstraction and Empathy)*, in 1908. An early apologist for modern art, particularly the Expressionistic movements, he attempted to demonstrate the existence of two polarities throughout the history of art. According to Worringer, abstract or geometric art occurs in cultures oppressed by nature and therefore obsessed with spiritualism. Realistic, organic, or empathetic art (according to his terms) flourishes among peoples who have an affinity

for nature and find satisfaction in contemplation of it. Later, in 1912, he argued that the two styles of vision (abstract and empathetic) had generally a geographic identity, with the north of Europe leaning to the spiritualistic form and the south having a predilection for sensualism. In other words northern art is apt to be abstract and/or geometric, while southern art is realistic and organic.

Worringer's system accounts for both Renaissance humanism and Gothic architecture as well as for Mondrian, Kandinsky, and Marc. One can even force it to accommodate the Spaniard Miró, whose shapes are organic and sensual. But others don't seem to fit. Oh, you can make them fit the system, but any system that requires such strain is open to serious doubt.

There are later, rather more complicated explanations of the evolution of art styles throughout history. None of these seem altogether adequate. Certainly, an account of them is unnecessary in an art appreciation text.

9

Modern Art, Its Variety and Unities

If the word *modern* suggests what is up-to-date, then modern art is misnamed. Most authorities date its beginnings with Manet's *Olympia*, and she is now over one hundred years old. *Modern art* is really just a catchall term for the many movements and individual styles that have succeeded Manet's early works. With rare exceptions these styles have been extremely unpopular even when celebrated by umpires of taste—museums, art critics, art collectors, and professors. Modern styles are, by nature, esoteric; that is, understanding of them is limited to a rel-atively small circle. In one sense all art is esoteric. Were that not so, there would be no need to study it and its meanings. But modern art is more puzzling to laymen than traditional forms have been. After all, you can appreciate Raphael's *Madonna of the Beautiful Garden* (fig. 53) or Harnett's *After the Hunt* (fig. 5) for what they represent, while remaining ignorant of the artistry that created them. Doubtless there are a few people who fall in love with Mondrian and Kandinsky at first sight, but they are very rare.

One of the things that makes modern

painting and sculpture hard to grasp is the sheer variety of its styles. The mortality rate of the movements is the most obvious thing about them. Some "ism" emerges, flourishes for a few years, and then drops out of fashion to be replaced by another mode. Sometimes the history of these "isms" seems like nothing so much as a spectator sport played for a special group of bored sophisticates; the champion of today is old-hat tomorrow. It really isn't that simple, but it sometimes seems to be. All those names: Realism, Impressionism, Postimpressionism, Neoimpressionism, Fauvism, Cubism, Expressionism, Surrealism, Futurism, Neoplasticism, Minimalism, and so on. The mind boggles!

In an earlier book of mine it took almost two hundred pages to cover a rather narrow topic—the relation of certain modern artists and movements to developments in scientific theory—even assuming a slight familiarity with the history of modern art on the part of the reader. Obviously, in one chapter of a book designed to introduce people to all art there is no way in the world to explain much about modern art. At the same time, we have already dealt with some major modern works in the earlier chapters, so we can make good use of previous analyses in an overview. Bear in mind, though, that this treatment is very superficial and that distortion of the truth is inevitable in such a survey. All I can hope to do is minimize its effects by warning you beforehand. For those interested in a more complete history of modernity (or, for that matter, of any other period) there are suggested readings at the end of this book.

Neoclassicism

To talk of the art of the nineteenth century, one must begin in the eighteenth. For modern art is a middle-class phenomenon, and it was at the end of the eighteenth century that the middle class finally came into political power. This class had had a decisive influence on taste in art from the time it emerged during the late medieval period. But all through the Renaissance political authority had been in aristocratic hands. And when those of middle-class origin became truly powerful—as the Medici did—they soon gained titles and entered into the line of nobles. There were exceptions to this pattern, the most notable being the Dutch Republic, ruled by an elected group of businessmen; but for the most part feudal rule lingered on in politics even as capitalism was driving it from the economic scene.

After the Treaty of Paris (1763), concluding the Seven Years' War,[1] such centers of aristocratic power as the estates, assemblies, and parliaments were under constant pressure from middle-class and popular radicalism. In 1789 the middle-class and radical elements of France combined to overthrow the government in the name of Liberty, Equality, and Fraternity. Out of the French Revolution was born the First Republic of France.

The First Republic turned out to be a thoroughly middle-class affair. One evidence of this is that not once during the famous Reign of Terror did its leader, Robespierre, challenge the right of private property, the thing which gives any middle class its security and its political clout. One might, then, expect the art of the Revolution to resemble that of the Dutch. After all, the Dutch had the first middle-class republic. Moreover, Dutchlike trends in France (represented by people like Chardin) had persisted throughout the eighteenth century alongside such aristocratic styles as those of Claude Lorrain and Antoine Watteau (1684–1721; see fig. 281). It must seem curious that the Revolution chose for its style a "purified" version of old-fashioned Classicism. But it isn't really odd when you consider the alternatives that were available.

Vermeer's scenes of domestic life, Char-

281
ANTOINE WATTEAU. *A Pilgrimage to Cythera.* 1717.
Oil on canvas, 51 × 76½″. The Louvre, Paris

din's still lifes, and the hundreds and hundreds of similar works by lesser artists all represented the private interests of the middle-class individual. There was no reason for an *official* style to represent that individual's class until the abolition of all feudal privileges occurred. The moment that occasion arose, with the success of the French Revolution, it became obvious that unheroic attitudes could not convey the patriotism and courage of the revolutionaries. Chardin was no more serious or heroic than Watteau. And the revolutionary situation required themes of tremendous gravity. Of the seventeenth- and eighteenth-century styles then current, only Classicism had seriousness to offer.

Were it necessary for us to make up a style that would be in accord with the mood of the Revolution and the propaganda purposes of the First Republic, we could do so quite easily. Seriousness of theme would be a main requirement. The most suitable subjects would surely be drawn from the histories of ancient Greece and Rome. France was surrounded on all sides by hostile monarchies whose rulers argued that Divinity stood on the side of kings. But France could find in democratic Athens and Republican Rome models of civic virtue even older than the royal houses of Europe. As for form, the circumstances required an art distinguished by dignity and solemnity.

282
JACQUES-LOUIS DAVID. *Oath of the Horatii.* 1784.
Oil on canvas, 11 × 14'. The Louvre, Paris

As it happens, we do not have to be content with a description of what the art of the Revolution would have been like. It still exists. And the prescription laid out above is patterned on the canon of Jacques-Louis David (1748–1825), artistic dictator of both the First Republic and the Empire under Napoleon Bonaparte.

In 1785, four years before the Revolution, David had exhibited his *Oath of the Horatii* (fig. 282), the first triumph of his special style. Here the content is serious indeed; three brothers swear to win or die for Rome against Alba. But what set off David's *Neoclassicism* from previous Classical styles was the strict economy of means which characterized its form. His technique is abstemious even when compared to that of seventeenth-century Classicists like Nicolas Poussin (1594–1665; see fig. 261). Everything is broken down into modalities of three. There are three archways, three figure groups, three brothers, three swords, three spatial levels. And any concession to Watteau-like luxuriance has been ruthlessly suppressed. Even his brushwork is flat, in itself uninteresting.

Clarity is the supreme objective of the form, and moral seriousness plus sacrifice the content that it holds. Even before the Revolution the insurgents identified this picture with the goals and ideals of 1789.

David was not the only Neoclassicist. Not by any means. Naturally, there were a few other great painters among the hundreds trained by official schools of art. But he is the foremost, and the purest of them all. He was high in the councils of government, and his ideas virtually dominated the education of artists all the way into the early twentieth century.

I am not the first person to note that David's was a curiously bloodless and dispassionate art, considering the kinds of things with which it was associated. These were the times of the tumbril and the guillotine; public executions and violent death formed an important item of the citizens' diet. David himself consigned lifelong friends to the chopping block with no more reluctance than he'd have thrown away a worn-out brush. And what did he paint all the while? Pictures that are unemotional, spare,

and neat. Impersonal Neoclassicism was, perhaps, the perfect art to "front" for such mass insanity. Even today the major polluters of the environment have the cleanest and most antiseptic-looking homes and offices. But David's times cried out for artistic expressions of deeper feeling. And creative imaginations were not slow to answer.

Romanticism

Romanticism is often defended as a movement that opposed logic and rationality to Pascal's "reasons of the heart," and many people have fallen into the habit of accepting this description as if it were the thing. Just how far most of us have fallen was estimated a number of years ago by Jacques Barzun, who listed eighty separate uses of the term *romantic*.[2] Most of them derive from the idea that Romanticism is irrational. Professor Barzun, however, is of the opinion—an opinion I share—that the Romantics differed from the Classicists mostly in being more comprehensive. Instead of sticking to ancient subject matter of great nobility of purpose, the Ro-

283
THÉODORE GÉRICAULT.
The Raft of the "Medusa."
1818–19.
Oil on canvas, 16′1″ × 23′6″.
The Louvre, Paris

mantics took in the whole world, both the tangible and the supernatural. They dealt with the present as well as the past and with exotic places as much as with familiar myths.

The first painting of real importance in the direction of Romanticism was Théodore Géricault's *The Raft of the "Medusa"* (fig. 283). What it portrays is not something from the Classical past but a contemporary event. On July 2, 1816, the French ship *Medusa* wrecked off the west coast of Africa. One hundred and forty-nine passengers and crewmen were cast adrift on a makeshift raft. By the time they

were rescued only fifteen still lived. The tragedy produced a maritime scandal, and Géricault's picture attracted large numbers of people both in Paris, where, by taking advantage of a loophole, it was slipped into the annual exhibition of official art, and in England, where it was exhibited as a sort of sideshow novelty. The Classicists hated it, but the general public was introduced to a kind of modern painting that took as its models Rubens and Michelangelo instead of Poussin.

The picture was filled with innovations.

284
EUGÈNE DELACROIX. *The Death of Sardanapalus*. 1827.
Oil on canvas, 12'11½" × 16'3". The Louvre, Paris

Surrounded by the waves of the sea, the figures rise in a great wave of humanity at the top of which is a black man. That Géricault used a Negro was no accident; one was among the survivors. That he should be the pinnacle of the group relates to the very origins of Romanticism in the writings of the philosopher Jean-Jacques Rousseau, who contrasted the "noble savage" with corrupt Western civilization, who felt that the European culture of his day thwarted the humanity of man. This notion—that the civilized and reasoned-out is an assassin of the natural, the spiritual, and the human—is a recurrent theme that occurs in different guises throughout recorded history. (We are encountering it again today in "black consciousness," in "organic" food, in the hip subcultures, in all back-to-nature movements, and in the popularity of oriental mysticism.) Romanticism is founded on the assumption that the object of life and art is to grasp *all* directly, spontaneously, and freely.

Romanticism abandoned nothing; it simply incorporated far, far more. It wasn't just a style; it was a genuine intellectual movement, comprising all sorts of styles and many different art forms. The most famous Romantics are the writers Lord Byron, Sir Walter Scott, and Johann Wolfgang von Goethe. *The Death of Sardanapalus* (fig. 284) by the greatest of all Romantic painters, Eugène Delacroix (1798–1863), was based on one of Byron's poems. It concerns an Assyrian potentate who is determined that conquering invaders already at the palace gates shall not enjoy anything he himself prizes. As he is about to immolate himself, he has all his treasures—including his concubines—heaped upon the luxurious funeral pyre. He and all he values are to go up in flames together. Nothing could be less Neoclassical than this subject. It is violent, it is exotic, it is based on contemporary literature rather than the writings of antiquity, and it is painted in a manner altogether different from David's.

Where David sought precision, Delacroix sought power. David's edges are definite and predictable; Delacroix's are more obscure than the Baroque. Where color, for the Neoclassicist, was just added to the drawing as decoration, in Delacroix's painting the color is rich. David's brushwork is as dry and flat as that of the house painter; Delacroix's is lush and textured—it has what painters call a "juicy" look.

The Romantics rediscovered the Middle Ages and the Renaissance. Frequently their subjects were remote in space as well as time. Delacroix visited the Near East to paint Morocco's blazing shores and clamorous marketplaces. Others came to the New World, and still others traveled to Asia, that most ancient world of all. The Romantics tried to capture in paint and poetry the whole of man's experience. Part of that experience is, of course, not dramatic or bizarre in any way at all but simply ordinary day-to-day living.

Realism and Impressionism

Of all the many offshoots of Romanticism, the one that produced the most revulsion was a movement which has come to be known as *Realism*. Its principal exponent was Gustave Courbet (1819–1877), whose *Stone Breakers* (fig. 285) gives you some sense of the style. Courbet was sympathetic to these rough working men in their rude clothing, but, compared to the prettified characters of Neoclassicism or Delacroix's people with their grand passions, Courbet's peasants are vulgar. It was obvious to the middle-class viewers of the day that the painter of such ignoble men must be a socialist. Now political philosophy and compassion for the downtrodden don't have to be connected. But Courbet himself confirmed the opinion, saying that he was "not only a socialist, but also a democrat

285
GUSTAVE COURBET. *The ·
Stone Breakers.* 1849.
Oil on canvas, 5′3″ × 8′6″. State
Picture Gallery, Dresden

and a republican, in short a partisan of the entire revolution, and above all a realist, that is a sincere friend of the real truth." Need I add that the socialists soon began defending Realism as the true art of the age?

Left-wing cartoonist Honoré Daumier shows us, in his serious pictures (fig. 286), the side of Realism that is dependent more on subject matter than on technique. He frequently portrays people of the city who are cut off from the benefits of middle-class urban existence. He is realistic in his willingness to face unpleasant social facts of inequality rather than in his manner of portrayal. Daumier, Courbet, and Naturalist writers like Emile Zola stood on the side of the radicals. From the very outset Realism and the movements it sponsored set themselves in opposition to the official representations of middle-class taste.

Manet's *Olympia* (fig. 287) was as shocking as any Courbet peasant because of the artist's characterization of Titian's Venus as a Parisian whore. Of course, Manet went beyond Courbet's Realism when he diminished chiaroscuro and intensified the role of hue. His painting opened the way for the truly

radical realism of the French *Impressionists,* who, typified by their leader Claude Monet (fig. 288), turned the matter-of-fact technique of the Realists into a registering of exquisite color sensations. Too, Impressionist subjects reveal a quite different sort of taste; they are usually attractive things: landscapes, boulevards, café scenes, ballets, pretty women, picnics, horse races, boating parties, dances, and so on. The colors are pretty and the things portrayed pleasurable or pleasant. Such subjects seem far removed from the vision of Courbet or Daumier. Yet the Impressionists felt that they were rejecting the values of the middle classes. They weren't, really. What they were doing, without knowing it, was opposing the values of the philistine middle class with the more sophisticated tastes of the cultivated elements of that class. In other words, they rejected the kind of "blah" ordinary pictures and ideas that respectable bourgeois society equated with responsible behavior and the good family life. Instead they created pictures that tied in with the more liberal tastes of the fashionable ladies and gentlemen of nineteenth-century Paris. In contemporary slang terms the comparison is rather like this: David's followers represented "straight" middle-class society, while the Impressionists painted for the well-to-do swingers of the late 1800s.

At the outset Impressionism was extremely unpopular with all classes of people, but before the end of the century its practitioners were famous and successful. This is not sur-

prising; their viewpoint was the same as that of the cultivated man-about-town. Except that they weren't all men.

French Impressionism produced two outstanding women painters in Manet's sister-in-law, Berthe Morisot (1841–1895), and the American Mary Cassatt (1845–1926). The former patterned her style after that of

286
HONORÉ DAUMIER.
The Laundress. c. 1861.
Oil on panel, 19¼ × 13″.
The Louvre, Paris

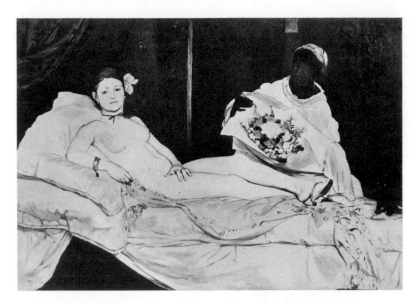

287
EDOUARD MANET.
Olympia. 1863.
Oil on canvas, $51\frac{1}{4} \times 74\frac{3}{4}''$.
The Louvre, Paris

288
CLAUDE MONET.
Haystack at Sunset Near Giverny. 1891.
Oil on canvas, $29\frac{1}{2} \times 37''$.
Museum of Fine Arts, Boston. Juliana Cheney Edwards Collection

Manet's later work (see fig. 289). Cassatt began with a style modeled on that of Degas. She went on to produce a distinctively feminine version of Impressionism—feminine at least in terms of subject matter: nearly always women and little girls (see fig. 290).

Most of its practitioners were not really dedicated to a thing called "Impressionism."

Degas (fig. 291) did not consider himself an Impressionist. He looked upon his own work as a kind of modern Classicism despite the tendency of the color in his pastels to resemble more and more that of Monet and Monet's followers. One genuine Impressionist, Renoir (fig. 292), grew impatient with the casual easiness of the style and combined

289

BERTHE MORISOT.

Woman at Her Toilet.

c. 1875.

Oil on canvas, $23\frac{3}{4} \times 31\frac{3}{4}''$.

The Art Institute of Chicago.

Stickney Fund

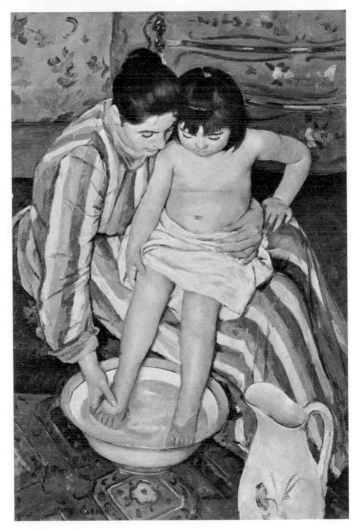

290

MARY CASSATT.

La Toilette. c. 1891.

Oil on canvas, $39 \times 26''$.

The Art Institute of Chicago.

Robert Alexander Waller

Memorial Collection

291
EDGAR DEGAS. *The Tub.*
1886.
Pastel, $23\frac{1}{2} \times 32\frac{1}{3}''$. The Louvre,
Paris

292
PIERRE AUGUSTE RENOIR.
*Le Moulin de la
Galette.* 1876.
Oil on canvas, $51\frac{1}{2} \times 69''$.
The Louvre, Paris

Neo-Renaissance drawing with contemporary color. He is not usually grouped with the Impressionists; usually he is called a Postimpressionist. So is Cézanne.

The term *Postimpressionism* is a clumsy one. It wasn't invented until after 1900. It was first used as the title for an exhibition of recent French paintings being shown in

London. All its inventor, the English critic Roger Fry, meant to accomplish with it was to indicate that all the paintings included in the exhibit came after Impressionism and owed something to it. The term confuses people because it contains artists as diverse as Van Gogh, Cézanne, and Gauguin. The sole value of the label lies in indicating that

293
PAUL CÉZANNE.
Mont Sainte-Victoire.
1885–87.
Oil on canvas, $25\frac{5}{8} \times 31\frac{7}{8}''$.
The Metropolitan Museum
of Art, New York. The
H. O. Havemeyer
Collection. Bequest of Mrs.
H. O. Havemeyer, 1929

294
PAUL CÉZANNE. *The*
Basket of Apples.
1890–94.
Oil on canvas, $25\frac{3}{4} \times 32''$.
The Art Institute
of Chicago.
Helen Birch Bartlett
Memorial Collection

295
GEORGES SEURAT. *A Sunday After-noon on the Island of La Grande Jatte.* 1884–86.
Oil on canvas, 6′9½″ × 10′1¼″. The Art Institute of Chicago. Helen Birch Bartlett Memorial Collection

these men shared the same voyage from nineteenth-century Impressionism to the more extreme movements of the twentieth century.

A more useful way of looking at the history of modern art is to conceive of it as a set of related but contrasting elements, like complementary colors or odd and even numbers. This conception sees everywhere an antecedent contest between Classical precision and Romantic power. There are paired opposites all along the way: David versus Delacroix, Seurat versus Van Gogh, Mondrian versus Kandinsky, Anuszkiewicz versus Pollock. Alongside a tendency towards pure formalism there flows a strong current tending to absolute subjectivity. If one thinks of these tendencies as streams analogous to actual rivers, one must think of them as meandering alongside each other in a common voyage from Impressionism to the present. Sometimes they are parallel. Sometimes they link and pool. Sometimes they are so far apart as to seem entirely unrelated.

The Rationalist-Formalist Current

Of all the followers of the Impressionist method, Paul Cézanne is the most prominent. Although he shared the Impressionists' sentiments about the value of modernity and freedom, he soon became disenchanted with the relative formlessness of their art. His transformation of that art into a personal style which included works as intricate and majestic as *Mont Sainte-Victoire* (fig. 293) and *The Basket of Apples* (fig. 294) is one of the most

296
PABLO PICASSO. *Ma Jolie.* 1911–12.
Oil on canvas, 39⅜ × 25¾″.
The Museum of Modern Art, New York.
Lillie P. Bliss Bequest

297
PABLO PICASSO.
*Les Demoiselles
d'Avignon.* 1907.
Oil on canvas, 96 × 92″.
The Museum of Modern
Art, New York. Lillie P.
Bliss Bequest

298
Guardian figure, from
the Bakota area, Gabon.
19th–20th century.
Wood, covered with brass and copper,
height 30″. Ethnographical Museum
of the University of Zurich

astonishing occurrences in the history of art.
His emphasis on formal structure set him
apart from all the others.

Georges Seurat, too, sought to rationalize
Impressionism. And his work (fig. 295) is
even more concerned with the constructive
aspects of art than Cézanne's. But its peculi-
arity is such that its influence has been somewhat limited, whereas Cézanne's has been
widespread.

The most obvious consequence of Cézanne's example is *Cubism*. Many stages inter-
vened between *Mont Sainte-Victoire* and *Ma*

Jolie (fig. 296), but Picasso's picture is a
direct descendant of the Cézanne. The obses-
sion with structure for its own sake, the concern with overlapping planes, the spatial
ambiguity—all these things were derived
from Cézanne. Of course, Cézanne was not
the only influence on Cubism; African art
was another.

In 1907 Picasso painted the most important
of the works from his so-called Negro Period,
Les Demoiselles d'Avignon (fig. 297). The deri-
vation of the masklike forms on the right is
obvious. But notice, too, that those forms are

299
PIET MONDRIAN.
*Composition in White,
Black and Red.* 1936.
Oil on canvas, 40¼ × 41″.
The Museum of Modern
Art, New York. Gift of the
Advisory Committee

repeated throughout the composition.

Before World War I, African art was extremely popular in Europe, particularly in France. There was, however, no interest to speak of in the cultural sources of the works. What interested Frenchmen was the extraordinary perfection of formal composition exhibited by "uncivilized" tribesmen from Africa. From Picasso's point of view the Bakota sculptor of the guardian figure (fig. 298) was already a modern artist. Some of this sentiment is Romantic identification of the so-called primitive with all that is basic to human life. British novelist D. H. Lawrence, writing of an African statue in *Women in Love*, expresses this strongly:

Her body was long and elegant, her face was crushed tiny like a beetle's, she had rows of round heavy collars, like a column of quoits, on her neck. . . . She knew what he himself did not know. She had thousands of years of purely sensual, purely unspiritual knowledge behind her. . . . Thousands of years ago, that which was imminent in himself must have taken place in these Africans: the goodness, the holiness, the desire for creation and productive happiness must have lapsed, leaving the single impulse for knowledge in one sort, mindless progressive knowledge through the senses.

More important is Picasso's recognition of the genius of black artists whose work he saw in Paris. There is neither time nor space in this little book to go into the continuous influence of African forms on the development of early Cubism. Suffice it to say that the importance of black culture is, in this instance at least, universally recognized and generally accepted.

Ma Jolie is the consequence of many different things. Yet the movement that produced it, Cubism, is the most unique and revolutionary of all modern styles. Nothing before or after it can approach its radicalism. To say so probably sounds odd, even narrow-minded. It isn't, actually.

The Cubist position was that a painting is only a painting just as a building is a building, and that a picture ought to look no more like a house, tree, or person than a house ought to resemble a baker's roll. Once Cubism had come to that, once it had broken with the manufacture of illusions, it freed the painter from what had seemed self-evident boundaries. After that it didn't much matter what a painter did. If his work didn't have to look *like* anything else, the barriers were down, and anything went so far as technique and general approach were concerned. This is one reason for Picasso's incredible variety of styles. *Ma Jolie* was painted in 1911–12, his

Girl Before the Mirror (colorplate 4) in 1932. They are very different at first sight, but the emphasis on pure form is common to both.

Piet Mondrian went further still in the hope of attaining what he called "concrete universal expression." His *Neoplasticism* (see fig. 299) eliminated from painting everything that was not absolutely fundamental: contrast, opposition of directions, variations of scale. The *Suprematist* Kasimir Malevich (1878–1935) went beyond even Mondrian. His notorious *White on White* (fig. 300) reduces painting to the ultimate simplicity of a white square in a white square at an angle. Malevich recognized that the next logical steps would be a blank canvas and then pure space. At various times since 1918 isolated avant-garde artists *have* exhibited plain white

300
KASIMIR MALEVICH.
*Suprematist Composition:
White on White.* c. 1918.
Oil on canvas,
31¼ × 31¼".
The Museum of Modern Art,
New York

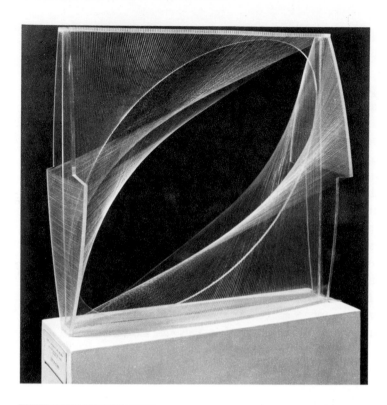

301
NAUM GABO. *Linear Construction, Variation.*
1942–43.
Plastic and nylon thread, $24\frac{1}{2} \times 24\frac{1}{2}''$.
The Phillips Collection,
Washington. D.C.

302
TONY SMITH. *She Who Must Be Obeyed.* 1976.
Painted steel, 20 × 30′.
Labor Department,
Washington, D.C.

303

VINCENT VAN GOGH.

The Starry Night. 1889.
Oil on canvas, 28¾ × 36¼″.
The Museum of Modern
Art, New York. Lillie P.
Bliss Bequest

304

VINCENT VAN GOGH.

The Night Café. 1888.
Oil on canvas, 28½ × 36¼″.
Yale University Art Gallery,
New Haven. Bequest of
Stephen Carlton Clark, B. A.
1903

canvases, and exhibitions of empty rooms have been offered to a dismayed public. But, since unpainted pictures and vacant space are not very marketable as art, the trend has never become an important one.

In the field of sculpture the mood of the Neoplasticists and Suprematists was matched by *Constructivism*. The works of Naum Gabo (1890–1977) are of a precision appropriate to mathematical models and entail the use of then newly invented materials such as nylon and plastic (fig. 301). Like the paintings of Mondrian, they appeal to our sense of exactitude and clarity. Resembling nothing in the natural world, they seem to represent its underlying laws.

Today also there are artists who find this realm of form and logic congenial to their expressive aims. The *Op Art* movement illustrated by colorplate 11 is one example. And there is a form of sculpture that has come to be called *Minimal* or *Primary* which is clearly related to the example of Malevich. The works tend, like *She Who Must Be Obeyed* (fig. 302) by Tony Smith (born 1912), to be massive in scale and unadorned. Frequently, they are slightly disconcerting—seeming to defy the dictates of gravitation or optical law.

Minimalism and Op Art find a sort of marriage in what has been termed "systemic painting," which combines very strict reductiveness with exciting visual effects. Of the artists associated with this trend, Frank Stella (born 1936) is perhaps the best known. His *Sinjerli Variation I* (colorplate 14) is a beautifully precise synthesis of hard geometry and vivid color. Stella's work has become progressively more sculptural in the succeeding decade. In the same way, Minimalist sculpture has tended to become more colorful, and it is frequently impossible to determine whether the pieces are meant to be paintings or sculptures, which, of course, merely demonstrates the futility of categories in the present age.

The Subjective-Expressionist Current

It is possible to demonstrate that the apparent objectivity of Renoir, Cézanne, and Seurat disguises, in every case, a deeply troubled spirit. But their work expresses torment in a very indirect fashion. The work of Vincent van Gogh, the genius of the other side of modern art, conveys feeling in a far more direct way. He reveals some of his feelings in every part of *The Starry Night* (fig. 303), for each brushmark is the track of an impulse directed by emotion. His conviction that truth is a marriage of objectivity with one's subjective reactions is implicit in *The Night Café* (fig. 304) in the identification of the colors of the room with emotional forces. For Van Gogh, things are what they seem, and what they seem is as much the product of one's feelings about the objects as it is of their material reality.

Van Gogh's position is not a sovereign one. There were other late-nineteenth-century artists who held similar views; among the more notable were Paul Gauguin (1848–1903), James Ensor (1860–1949), Henri de Toulouse-Lautrec (1864–1901), and Edvard Munch (1863–1944). All of them were unstable and frequently distraught. They staked everything on art. They were outcasts from respectable society who lived on the fringes of the underworld, among prostitutes, thieves, drug addicts, and derelicts. They turned Impressionism into an art of vehement self-expression; it sometimes seems as though their art was the only thing in the world that made life bearable for them.

Just after the turn of the century, a movement came into existence that translated the despair of the 1880s and nineties into positive terms. Henri Matisse (1869–1954), the leader of the *Fauves*, believed that the sources of joy lie within each man. The goal is to release them. Matisse held an abundant, optimistic view of life and expressed it in a

305

HENRI MATISSE. *Green Stripe (Madame Matisse)*. 1905.
Oil and tempera on canvas, $15\frac{7}{8} \times 12\frac{7}{8}''$. Royal Museum of Fine Arts,
Copenhagen. Rump Collection

306

ERNST LUDWIG KIRCHNER. *The Street.* 1907.
Oil on canvas, 59¼ × 78⅞". The Museum of Modern Art, New York

robust painting style (fig. 305). He and his colleagues—André Derain (1880–1954), Georges Rouault (1871–1958), Maurice Vlaminck (1876–1958), Raoul Dufy (1887–1953), and others—were called *"fauves"* (wild beasts) by a hostile critic, and the name stuck. The paintings looked wild to people of the time, but the ferocity is more that of playful puppies than of dangerous animals. For it is with Fauvism that the radicalism of youth entered into the fine arts for the first time. The conflict between the Establishment and youth was already an old story in European politics, but young artists had never been sufficiently self-assured to create a painting style distinctly their own. (Even the prodigy Picasso derived his early styles from older French and Spanish masters.) Of all the Fauves, only Matisse was much over thirty, and he remained perpetually young in spirit. What Fauvism expressed was joyous, pagan self-affirmation. It was the shout of the young.

It was in Germany, during those years just prior to World War I, that the first movement called *Expressionism* arose. It had two branches, *Die Brücke* (The Bridge) and *Der*

Blaue Reiter (The Blue Rider). The first was founded in Dresden in 1905 by Ernst Ludwig Kirchner. His work (fig. 306) and that of followers such as Emil Nolde (see colorplate 3) had a decidedly representational character and showed the influence of the bright color areas of Van Gogh and Gauguin. The work of these artists is similar to Fauvism in general appearance and character, although it projects a far more pessimistic view of mankind.

Der Blaue Reiter is a more interesting movement. Less derivative of the past, it tended to be abstract, symbolic, and generally more advanced. Moreover, its artists were more varied in style and philosophy. Der Blaue Reiter's locale was Munich, a more sophis-

307

WASSILY KANDINSKY. *Improvisation Number 30.* 1913. Oil on canvas, 43¼ × 43¾″. The Art Institute of Chicago. Arthur Jerome Eddy Memorial Collection

308
PAUL KLEE. *The Twittering Machine.* 1922.
Watercolor, pen and ink, 16¼ × 12″. The Museum of Modern Art, New York

ticated and cosmopolitan city than Dresden, and its artists seem to have had more native talent than those of *Die Brücke*. The leader and principal artist was Wassily Kandinsky, a Russian emigré. In his mature work he seeks to accomplish with paint all that music can express. *Improvisation Number 30* (fig. 307) is fascinating in that it is a genuine improvisation, undertaken without foreknowledge of precisely what would happen. Each part of the canvas has its own peculiar character, and yet all the parts go together. Kandinsky managed to harmonize what would otherwise be chaotic through color, variations in pigment, and lines that trail through color zones, interlace, and cross out one another. If you invert the page, you can discover all

sorts of families of forms which have emerged spontaneously. Kandinsky's work is very lyrical and highly personal. It is not accessible to everyone, certainly. But, then, neither is Brahms, Beethoven, or Bob Dylan.

Another member of Der Blaue Reiter who is of great importance to the history of art was the Swiss painter Paul Klee (1879–1940). His works are very mystical, and often the mysticism is combined with satire. For example, his *The Twittering Machine* (fig. 308) is a symbolic comment on the arrogance of applied science. He is saying that, yes, it is possible to create a machine for duplicating birdsong—here you crank the handle, a sine curve rotates, and the birds jerk up and down, chirping—but see how silly and grotesque

309
FRANZ MARC.
Deer in a Forest, II.
1913–14.
Oil on canvas, 43½ × 39½".
Staatliche Kunsthalle,
Karlsruhe, West Germany

310

MAN RAY. *Indestructible Object (Object to be destroyed)* (1923 replica of destroyed original). Metronome with cutout photograph of eye on pendulum. $8\frac{7}{8} \times 4\frac{3}{8} \times 4\frac{5}{8}$". The Museum of Modern Art, New York. James Thrall Soby Fund

311

MARCEL DUCHAMP. *The Bride Stripped Bare by Her Bachelors, Even (The Large Glass).* 1915–23. Oil and lead wire on glass, $9'1\frac{1}{4}'' \times 5'9\frac{1}{8}''$. Philadelphia Museum of Art. Bequest of Katherine S. Dreier

the machine would be. Klee employs in works of this kind a drawing method calculated to translate his images from the real into the fantastic. They do not resemble things of this world. For instance, it is impossible to tell whether we are looking at the base of the machine from above or below.

The third important member of Der Blaue Reiter was Franz Marc, who died in World War I and never reached the limits of his potential. As *Deer in a Forest, II* (fig. 309)

shows, this artist was influenced by the faceted forms of Cubist art; he used them, however, to very different ends than the Cubists. His was an attempt to, as he said, "animalize" art, to give painting the vitality of nature's throb. His work indicates the degree to which the various kinds of modernisms overlap and coalesce. Here Fauvist color plus Cubistic forms equals Marc's Expressionism.

Sometimes the merging of existing forms into another style is less a matter of artistic

312

SALVADOR DALI. *Apparition of a Face and Fruit Dish on a Beach.* 1938. Oil on canvas, 43½ × 57″. Wadsworth Atheneum, Hartford, Connecticut. The Ella Gallup Sumner and Mary Catlin Sumner Collection

form than of attitude. *Dadaism,* founded in Zurich, Switzerland, in 1916, was such a movement. It was nihilistic, that is, it held that *all* traditional values and beliefs were unfounded, and life without sense or purpose. The poets and artists who participated in the movement were reacting to World War I. They resemble some of the more extreme factions of the counter-culture of the 1960s except that they went far beyond any of these underground groups in ridiculing the hallowed values of Western civilization. Louis Aragon's poem "Suicide" is nothing but the alphabet in its normal order. Other Dadaists

created "poems" by cutting words from newspapers, putting them into a hat, and gluing the words to paper as they were drawn at random from the hat. The poetry was, naturally, nonsensical.[3]

Man Ray's *Indestructible Object* (fig. 310) is an example of a Dadaist "ready-made," ordinary objects put in incongruous combinations or circumstances and treated as art. More famous is the urinal that Marcel Duchamp (1887–1968) signed "R. Mutt" and exhibited as *Fountain.* When Duchamp's *The Bride Stripped Bare by Her Bachelors, Even* (fig. 311) was being shipped to an art show

313
JOAN MIRÓ. *Person Throwing a Stone at a Bird.* 1926. Oil on canvas, 29×36¼". The Museum of Modern Art, New York

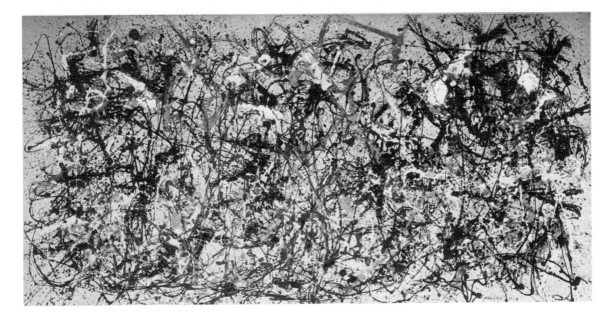

314
JACKSON POLLOCK. *Autumn Rhythm.* 1950.
Oil on canvas, 8′9″ × 17′3″. The Metropolitan Museum of Art, New York.
George A. Hearn Fund, 1957

in 1923, the glass on which it was painted cracked in transit. Duchamp was pleased! He said that the cracks "completed" the painting. His behaviour was perfectly consistent with the idea that all rational activity is absurd.

Dadaism couldn't last. In the first place, the Dadaists were so clever and talented a group that quality and wit distinguished their work even when they were aiming at the ridiculous, Secondly, when anyone decides to contemplate the futility of it all, he's bound to see that it's useless. In 1924, to generate a new kind of order out of the chaos Dada had created, a Dada poet named André Breton (1896–1966) founded *Surrealism.* This movement drew upon Sigmund Freud's psychoanalytic theories, which attribute the greater part of human activity to the motives of the subconscious mind.

Salvador Dali is not the best example of a Surrealist, but he is *the* Surrealist in the public's mind. His *Apparition of a Face and Fruit Dish on a Beach* (fig. 312) can tell us a good deal about Surrealism. The first thing to understand is that the picture does not have a specific, concrete meaning. Like a dream it is subject to a variety of interpretations. (In fact, Dali claims that he is reproducing his dreams and hallucinations with photographic clarity.) For Freud the dreams of men throw open windows on their souls. So do our responses to ambiguous stimuli. You may not be able to say exactly what this picture means to you, but it means *something,* because, in Freudian terms, you "project" your unconscious feelings onto it just as Dali has projected his into it. Dali's art has had much more popular appeal than that of any other modern painter because of the slick rendering it entails. Those techniques of his aren't particularly impressive to art historians and critics because they have all been cribbed from Baroque artists like Caravaggio and Vermeer. What is most remarkable about Dali is his subject matter. It is truly inventive. Who else would come up with a limp watch, the perfect symbol for subjective time, which sometimes crawls and other times races by too fast?

Dali represents a branch of Surrealism that might be called "literalist" because it attempts to mimic dreams and the like in a literal way. Yves Tanguy (1900–1955), René Magritte (1898–1967), and Max Ernst (1891–1976) are others in this group.[4]

There is another major type of Surrealist art which, for lack of a better term, we can call "abstract Surrealism." Paul Klee has sometimes been associated with it, but the best example is the Spaniard Joan Miró.

Miró's *Person Throwing a Stone at a Bird* (fig. 313) is not an accurate reproduction of a mental image, surely. Rather, it is a memory recalled in ideographic form, that is, by way of symbols that stand for ideas and experiences. It has been suggested that what we see here is a record of the occasion described in the title, with only the most impressive elements retained. The stone and its trajectory and the fulcrum of the thrower's arm are extremely evident. The eye, aiming at the bird's bright plume, and the foot to which the thrower has shifted all his weight are stressed. What is not essential has been eliminated.

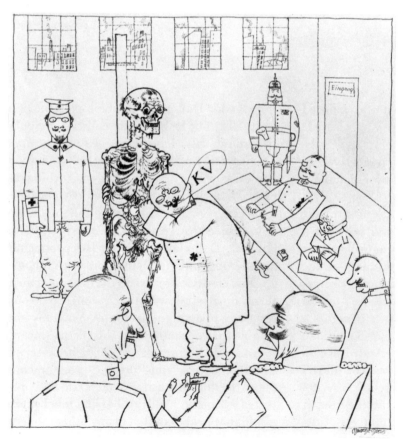

315
GEORGE GROSZ.
Fit for Active Service.
1916–17.
Pen, brush, and India ink, 14⅝ × 13⅜". The Museum of Modern Art, New York. A. Conger Goodyear Fund

316
FERNAND LÉGER.
The Card Players. 1917.
Oil on canvas, 50⅜ × 76″.
Kröller-Müller Museum,
Otterlo, The Netherlands

This interpretation may err in its simplicity. Whatever the case, Miró does insist that his work is not formal in intention. It looks as though it might be, true enough. The shapes have certainly been adjusted with an eye to their compatibility. Miró would say that the arrangement of shapes is just a means to an end and that the picture really has to do with explicit life experiences. The only "abstract Surrealist" whose work resembles Miró's very closely was Hans Arp (1887–1966). Others in this branch include André Masson (born 1896), Arshile Gorky (1904–1948), and Matta Echaurren (born 1912).

The 1950s, particularly in the United States, saw a synthesis of Expressionist and Surrealist trends in a kind of art called *Abstract Expressionism.* Willem de Kooning is one representative. Jackson Pollock (1912–1956) is another. In one sense everything that Pollock did was already contained in the works of Kandinsky. His immense painting *Autumn Rhythm* (fig. 314) is on a far grander scale than anything Kandinsky ever did; but the impulsiveness, the complete nonrepresentationalism, the evocation of mood

through color harmonies, all that is similar. The technique is what's different.

Pollock created his pictures by pouring paint from cans onto a horizontal canvas. To paint a picture in this way strikes many people as completely ridiculous. After all, anyone can pour paint from a can. True. But anyone can make marks with an artist's brush too. It's what you do with the marks that counts. And poured liquids can be controlled, as anyone who has ever poured chocolate syrup over ice cream should know. If you move the stream of syrup slowly, you get a fatter line than if you move it fast. If you move it very fast, you get dotted lines from the broken drips. Move it too fast, and it spatters chocolate all over the table.

Neatness is not a factor in Pollock's art, but control was an important aspect of its creation. His method was not nearly so haphazard and arbitrary as it must seem at first sight. He followed a very deliberate procedure that can be discerned in the final work. He usually began by laying in a background color or colors. Then, on top of this background, he poured paint in a trail that established large,

317
UMBERTO BOCCIONI.
*Unique Forms of
Continuity in Space.* 1913.
Bronze, height 43½″. The
Museum of Modern Art,
New York. Lillie P. Bliss
Bequest

dominant movements that more or less decided the composition of the picture. Next, with another color, a series of subordinate movements were created, usually more intricate ones. From this point on it was a matter of embellishing and articulating the maze of lines and forms growing on the surface.

Autumn Rhythm is not simply a flat picture. Its vortex of thready lines and enmeshed strands of pigment gives one the sense of looking at a tremendously complicated structure existing on a vast, unbounded scale somewhere outside nature. If you think of the works as they originally appeared, lying flat,

so that you are looking down into them, they assume new power and force. The space they contain approaches the conditions of an aerial view shot with vapor trails. The maze is more fascinating than anyone might at first imagine.

Some Synthetic Styles

There are a great many modern styles that do not fall into either of the two mainstreams mapped out so sketchily above. Some of them are the result of a pooling of the two currents.

In Germany, following World War I, a movement called *Die Neue Sachlichkeit* (The New Objectivity) combined Expressionist distortion and Realist attitudes into a style that expressed some of the most horrifying visions art has yet seen. George Grosz (1893–1959) indicted the military-industrial bloc in a series of works of which *Fit for Active Service* (fig. 315) is a good example. Such intensely bitter images typify the movement, whose main artists were Grosz, Otto Dix (born 1891), and Max Beckmann (1884–1950).

French artist Fernand Léger, discharged from the service after he was injured in a gas attack at Verdun, took a curiously positive attitude toward the then-new machinery of war. In *The Card Players* (fig. 316) he has reduced a famous Cézanne into mechanical parts assembled in turn into the forms of soldiers taking their leisure in the trenches. Everything is metallic-looking; even the smoke from the pipe of the player on the right has been turned into a row of shiny plates. Léger said of his war experience: "I was dazzled by the breech of a 75 millimeter gun . . . the magic of light on white metal. This was enough to make me forget the abstract art of 1912–13."

Similar in attitude to Léger were the Italian *Futurists,* whose devotion to the beauty of pistons, power, and motion let them proclaim, as Filippo Marinetti (1876–1944) did, that "a roaring motor-car, which looks as though running on shrapnel, is more beautiful than the *Victory of Samothrace.*" Or, in Umberto Boccioni's words: "The opening and closing of a valve creates a rhythm just as beautiful but infinitely newer than the blinking of an animal eyelid." Boccioni (1882–1916) said that modern sculpture must "give life to objects by making their extension in space palpable, systematic, and plastic." His *Unique Forms of Continuity in Space* (fig. 317) attempts to fix in a frozen pattern all the positions of the various elements of a human form in motion. It has a kind of ter-

rifying power, this heavy, striding monster. It is probably the greatest of all Futurist works.

There are also, of course, myriad individual painters and sculptors whose mannerisms and preferences do not really fit well into any single movement or composite of movements. Ivan le Lorraine Albright's pictures (fig. 122) resemble Realism in some ways, Surrealism in others, and The New Objectivity in still others. Pop artists like Roy Lichtenstein (fig. 239) and their associated workers—for instance, Larry Rivers (fig. 240), Jasper Johns (colorplate 7), and Edward Kienholz (fig. 6) —have derived a great deal from both the rationalistic and Expressionistic currents. Richard Lindner (fig. 92) stands somewhere between the Pop artists and the Surrealists. Mark Rothko (colorplate 2) incorporated into his style both Abstract Expressionism and the superrational directions signalized by Mondrian and Malevich.

Lest this brief survey give you the impression that only the names here listed are of importance, I should mention that I have not even scratched the surface. In the realm of fantasy the painter Marc Chagall is at least as important as Klee or Miró. Without Giorgio de Chirico's paintings for a prototype, the kind of Surrealism practiced by Dali and Tanguy would not exist. Rouault is as outstanding as Matisse. A list of important modern artists not mentioned elsewhere in this book would include the painters Bonnard, Modigliani, Kokoschka, Soutine, Schwitters, Tchelitchew, Gris, and Feininger. It would contain such sculptors as Brancusi, Giacometti, Nicholson, Moore, Calder, Pevsner, Duchamp-Villon, David Smith, and many, many others. (Even as I type these lists, I think of artists I have omitted who are more important than some included: for example, the painters Dubuffet and Bacon and sculptors Lipchitz and Paolozzi. And—oh well.) All I have tried to do in this chapter is give you a chronological, historical outline in which

318
CHRISTO. *Wrapped Coast, Little Bay, Australia.* 1969.
Surface area of project 1,000,000 square feet

to place the artists we have already discussed. It is, however, also a good place to include a group of artists whose work has been ignored elsewhere in these pages.

Conceptual Art

Possibly the so-called conceptual artists do not belong in any book so concerned with material objects as this one is. For these people do not create paintings or sculptures, prints or pottery; instead, they attempt to evoke from viewers new conceptions of the world in which we live. And those conceptions are what they hold to be art. Many works falling into the category of *Conceptual Art* have much more in common with theater and dance than with painting or sculpture. Indeed, some of the "pieces" are made up exclusively of words in the form of lists, strict descriptions, quotations, and enigmatic (often shallow) aphorisms. That the art produced thereby is itself purely ideational—having no more material attributes than a mathematical proof—is seen as the most important thing about it.

Frequently, conceptual artworks have

expressed a very distinct ideology. Since ordinary artists produce things that can be purchased, their art easily fits into the value scheme of ordinary commercial activity. By eliminating the possibility of anyone actually possessing their art, some conceptualists hoped to overcome the prevailing commercialism of the art world. They failed, of course.[5] Still, the activity of those who disavow art objects has been salutary in opening up new possibilities for creative expression within the arts, especially by way of cooperative ventures by avant-garde workers in such distinctive disciplines as music, theater, dance, cinema, and electronics. As it happens, however, most of what these people do is without visual interest. The exceptions, though, are of considerable importance.

Christo (born Christo Javacheff, 1935) is, at least marginally, a conceptual artist. But his creations are not only visible, they make truly remarkable additions to the landscape. Christo's largest undertaking was the wrapping of a mile of the Australian coast in one million square feet of polyethylene plastic. The result (see fig. 318) actually modifies the appearance of the cliffs, lending to them a precipitousness of line and a consistency of color which hints at drawing almost as much as it does at sculpture or architecture. Thus, in concealing the landscape, Christo reveals new aspects of a shoreline to any moderately interested observer. The sheer logistics of such an enterprise are themselves impressive. The scope of the planning, the marshaling of financial support, the enlistment and direction of literally hundreds of voluntary participants is inevitably dramatic and inspiring. But the results are singular. Whether Christo's vast packagings of whole buildings and landmarks, canyon-spanning curtains, and colorfully "aimless" fences are sufficiently artistic to justify the cost paid out for their extremely brief existences is, of course, arguable. But his creations do constitute a foundation for extensions of creative possibilities in the visual arts.

10

Media and Methods

Some Media in Two Dimensions

Many of the words used in discussions of art are vague because they were drawn from common language. *Form*, *style*, *color*, and *line* are all in very general use and so have meanings other than the special ones we have given them in the vocabulary of art. This was not formerly true of the word *media*, but in recent years it has come to be the case. Nowadays, everyone speaks of "the media." What they refer to are the media of mass communication: radio, television, newspapers, magazines, motion pictures, and so forth. *Media* is the plural form of *medium*. We have the medium of radio, the television medium, and broadcasting media. In the fine arts we are concerned with painting media, sculptural media, printing media, and, within painting, sculpture, and printmaking, the oil medium, the medium of cast bronze, and the medium of the block print.

The medium an artist chooses for a given work has an important bearing on how the work is going to look, and not all media lend themselves to the same expressive ends. Monet's haystack pictures would not be effective cast in bronze, that's obvious. But neither would they be as effective in tempera or watercolor as they are in oil. To understand this is to go a long way toward an appreciation of an artist's work and, therefore, some discussion of media is in order. Again, the size of this book will not permit more than a cursory look at a few of the more prominent two- and three-dimensional media. But one can get a notion of how material considerations affect artistic decisions from examining just a few media and works. Additional information can be obtained from the books listed in the bibliography at the end of this book.

PAINTING MEDIA

In the discussion of pigments in chapter five I mentioned that paints differ according to the medium or vehicle[1] into which the pigment is mixed. It would be possible to add water to the pigment powders and paint a picture with them. But the pigment would not adhere to the paper or canvas; as soon as the water evaporated, the pigments would dust off. To have a painting it is necessary that the pigments stick to the surface, and this, in its simplest terms, is what a medium causes to happen. A medium binds the pigment particles together and to the picture surface.

Tempera One of the best media for binding pigment is egg yolk. Yes, just plain egg yolk. If you've ever tried to clean breakfast dishes which have been left sitting for a couple of days, you know how hard dried egg can be. The pigments that Botticelli used to paint *The Birth of Venus* (fig. 319) were ground in whole egg, and the name for that medium is *egg tempera*. The term means simply that the pigment has been "tempered" by egg. (What they call "tempera" in grade schools is not real tempera; it's a cheap distemper in which the binder is a glue.) Normally, we speak of egg tempera as "tempera."

Tempera paint has some very desirable characteristics for an art material. The major one is that it is highly permanent; colors

319
SANDRO BOTTICELLI.
The Birth of Venus.
c. 1480.
Tempera on canvas,
5'8⅞" × 9'1⅞". Uffizi
Gallery, Florence

ground in it don't change appearance much over a long period of time. But there are also problems connected with its use. It is very viscous—sticky—and it dries instantly. This means that the artist cannot blend tones together smoothly; his picture must be made up of short little strokes, all of which are separate. The Botticelli doesn't look this way in the reproduction because the painting is large and reproductions are small. But if you look at the original from up close, you can observe that it is built of very, very tiny individual brushstrokes.

Another factor tempera painters must take into account is a slight transparency of the medium. It is in the nature of the relation between the pigment and the egg that a completely opaque color cannot be achieved. This means that correction of errors is pretty much out of the question. Consequently, tempera paintings are carefully planned and executed according to a prescribed routine:

1.   Tempera paintings are usually done on wooden panels. *The Birth of Venus* was done on linen, but it is an exception. Most of Botticelli's works were done on wood. For a large painting such as his *Madonna of the Pomegranate* (fig. 52) several planks of Italian poplar or German limewood were joined together virtually without a seam. The wood used for the panel must be completely dry, and it will have been seasoned for a year or more. It is then sanded to a perfect smoothness.

2.   The panel is prepared to receive the picture by covering it with several coats of a mixture of plaster of Paris and glue called *gesso*. The successive layers are sanded alternately rough and smooth so that each layer is bonded to the one before and after it. When sufficient thickness has been applied, the surface is sanded to a degree of smoothness such that the finished product looks like a sheet of ivory.

3.   The next step is to make on paper a fine, detailed drawing the exact size the final work is to be. Such a drawing is called a *cartoon* (the

source of our term for frivolous drawings) and is made up from various preparatory sketches and diagrams the artist has created in the course of conceiving the picture. The cartoon is transferred to the panel in the following manner: Tiny holes are pricked through the outlines of the shapes. Then the cartoon is placed on the panel, and the artist shakes charcoal dust through the holes onto the gesso. The resulting tiny dots can be connected up with a line.

4.   The entire work is painted in one color—normally earth green, a dull but highly permanent green made from earth. The shadows will be dark green, the penumbra pale green, and the lights clear white. This *underpainting* is exact but is monochromatic (all of one hue).

5.   The artist then builds his picture up in a series of layers. Initially they are very light and transparent, and they grow stronger as the final outside layer is approached. Highlights are most opaque, shadows most transparent. Certain colors are excluded from the palette because eggs contain albumen and albumen contains sulfur, which tends to darken certain pigments.

The effect of the completed tempera painting is one of neatness and delicacy. Because of the semitransparency of the medium and because the gesso base is white, tempera paintings have a certain kind of luminosity and glow denied other media. Still, it is a tedious medium in which to work, and it is rarely used today. Among Americans, though, one of the best known of all modern works is a tempera painting, *Christina's World* (fig. 320) by Andrew Wyeth (born 1914).

At first *Christina's World* resembles a Surrealistic work, but the image is based on fact, not fancy. Christina Olsen was a crippled neighbor of Wyeth's in Cushing, Maine, and she used to crawl about her property in just this way. The poignance of his friend's circumstance touched Wyeth, and in the painting he has turned it into a symbol of each person's solitude. In order to do so, he eliminated a few critical items from the landscape. For instance, there is a grove of trees up to

320
ANDREW WYETH. *Christina's World.* 1948.
Tempera on gesso panel, 32¼ × 47¾". The Museum of Modern Art, New York

the left of the house, rising against the crest of the hill. Vast emptiness suited the theme of the work, so he left out the trees.

Oil paints Robert Campin, painter of the Mérode altarpiece (fig. 207), seems to have been the first person to add vegetable oil to his egg yolk and pigment. Since oil dries very slowly, this had the advantage of making the paint somewhat easier to handle. Jan van Eyck and Hubert van Eyck developed Campin's gimmick into an elaborate painting technique which substituted a clear, quick-drying varnish-oil mixture for the egg-oil medium.

Jan van Eyck's *Giovanni Arnolfini and His Bride* (fig. 321) was done in almost exactly the way that tempera paintings are. The principal difference was the vehicle for the pigment. But what a difference! Even quick-drying varnishes take many hours to harden, and it is possible to manipulate the layers of transparent pigment (called *glazes*) so that brushstrokes are practically nonexistent. Precise degrees of transparency or opacity can be secured. It is relatively simple to make corrections when painting with oils. The range from dark to light is much greater than with tempera. Since the oil does not affect the color of the pigments, no hues have to be omitted. Moreover, the range of technical effects that can be obtained is far, far greater

321
JAN VAN EYCK.
*Giovanni Arnolfini and
His Bride.* 1434.
Oil on panel, $32\frac{1}{4} \times 23\frac{1}{2}''$.
The National Gallery,
London

with oil than with tempera.

Most of the paintings in this book were done in oil. Van Eyck, Titian, Vermeer, Monet, Mondrian, Kandinsky, et al., all worked with oils. Yet how dissimilar were the effects they obtained. Oil paint can be transparent or opaque, can be applied thinly or thickly, can be used to secure precise edges or bold splashes, depending on the preference of the painter. Small wonder that of all painting media oil has been the most popular among artists.

Nothing is without its handicaps, however. Oil color is not quite so permanent as tempera, even though the range of hues and values is far greater. And, while it is relatively easy to correct errors because oil as typically used is opaque and light colors will cover darks, there is at least one factor which limits the painter's freedom. In painting with oils you must always put fat over lean, never lean over fat. This is workshop jargon for indicating that it is not possible to paint a less oily pigment over an oily one. Oh, it's possible to apply it, but the paint will craze and peel off. Oil painters take care to proceed in such a manner that all the paint is of the same oiliness throughout or that successive layers are progressively oilier.

At first, oil paintings were done on wooden panels covered with gesso, just like tempera paintings. But in the early sixteenth century in Italy panels were replaced by canvas stretched over wooden frames. The use of canvas has continued down to the present day. Canvas is lighter than wood, and it is easier to weave large canvases than it is to build immense panels.

Titian's *Venus of Urbino* (fig. 322) is a fine example of oil on canvas. The technique Titian followed was essentially as outlined below:

1. Linen canvas is stretched taut over a frame of wood. Then the canvas is rendered impervious to oil (which eventually rots fabrics) by coating it with a hide glue of some sort.

2. Various kinds of grounds other than brittle gesso may be applied. The simplest is white lead with enough oil (10 or 15 percent) to make it plastic. Applied to the canvas with a trowel or thinned with something "lean" (such as spirits of turpentine) so it can be painted on, the white lead forms the base for the picture. Since it is much leaner than any usable oil pigment, it will pose no problems for the artist.

3. The entire surface is stained gray, brown, or dull green with an *imprimatura* of earth color thinned in spirits of turpentine or some other nonoily solvent.

4. Monochromatic underpainting is worked out onto the imprimatura according to the method the artist prefers. It might be as detailed as a tempera cartoon, or it might be sketched onto the canvas rather loosely and then worked up by trial and error. In any case, Titian would have painted the major elements of his *Venus of Urbino* in a monochrome.

5. Hues of varying intensity and value are then glazed over the underpainting. The oil-varnish glazes let the values show through but add the richness of color to the work.

6. Finally, various details and highlights are added to complete the work. Some of the paint

322
TITIAN. *Venus of Urbino.*
1538.
Oil on canvas, 47 × 65".
Uffizi Gallery, Florence

323
JOHN CONSTABLE. *The Hay Wain*. 1821.
Oil on canvas, 51¼ × 73″. The National Gallery, London

is applied opaquely, some of it is *scumbled*. To scumble means to drag the brush lightly across previous brushstrokes or canvas to produce a broken, speckled effect.

The technique described here (but using varying formulas for grounds, underpainting, and glazes) constituted the technical procedure in oil painting from the High Renaissance all the way up to the middle of the nineteenth century. Some artists still make use of the same methods today. They provide the painter with well-established and time-tested means of control without rigidity.

Whatever one can say in favor of the Venetian oil technique, it too has strict limita-

tions. Constable's *Hay Wain* (fig. 323), Monet's haystacks, or Van Gogh's *The Starry Night* could not have been created using Titian's system. All these paintings are done in what we call *alla prima*. In this technique the final colors and relationships are already present in the first attack on the canvas. This is the way most laymen think most pictures are painted, and it is the way amateurs always try to paint. But it was only after 1800 that many oils were done in this way. The *Hay Wain* had a seminal role in the change from the traditional working up of a painting from monochrome through successive layers of color to the more direct way of painting a picture.

Constable, more than any previous artist,

was intrigued by the transitory effects of nature. A close friend of William Wordsworth, he attempted to capture in his paintings all that is spontaneous and naturally poetic in the British landscape. No classical technique could have given us all those flickering reflections on the water or hinted at the flutter of leaves in a summer breeze as successfully as Constable's scumbled color over scumbled pigment. Delacroix recognized the merit of the method when he first saw the *Hay Wain* and incorporated some of its technique into his own work. Realists and Impressionists followed suit. But the Impressionists had the advantage of materials which were not at Constable's disposal.

Today oil paints are sold in tubes. The first year that they were so dispensed was 1841. Prior to that the colors were sold in flat tins or, more commonly, in powders which the artist ground into his medium. Commercially produced oil pigments sold in tubes have some special properties. For one thing, they are far more transportable packed in tubes than in the other forms. This portability made it possible for Monet to go out and paint directly from nature rather than from sketches and memory. The haystack series, among others, is contingent on such direct observation of nature. A second feature of tube colors is that they tend to be thicker than pigments mixed by hand. Tube color is about the consistency of toothpaste; a ribbon of it laid on straight from the tube will stick to the canvas and not run off. Also, brushstrokes can have an extremely high impasto. Van Gogh used his oils in both these ways.

Another factor that had an important bearing on the work of the Impressionists and so-called Postimpressionists was the invention of new chemical pigments. Some of these, like the malachite green that turned Van Gogh's billiard table brown, were disastrous for painting. But many of the new colors were tremendously important for artists like Monet who wished to capture every nuance of nature's hues. Between 1826 and 1861 artificial ultramarine blue, cadmium yellow, mauve, cobalt yellow, and magenta all appeared.

Polymer paints Contemporary artists are beginning to move away from oil paint and to favor synthetic media, of which the most common is polyvinyl acetate. Polymer pigments look much like oils but have tremendous advantages for many artists. They are similar in many ways to their house-paint brethren, the so-called latex paints. They are water-compatible, that is, they can be thinned with water and the brushes can be cleaned with water. But once they have dried, water will not dissolve them. Neither will anything else except special solvents designed to remove house paint and furniture varnish. You can, therefore, paint layer upon layer of polymer pigments without fear of dissolving the lower layers or worrying about them bleeding through. The paints can be applied as thickly as oil paint, or as thinly, but the painter can ignore any consideration of fatness or leanness. The consequent range of effects is incredible, but the medium lends itself particularly to clean, hard-edge abstractions such as *Yellow Arc* (fig. 324) by Michael Smith.

Whereas it may take days or weeks for oil paint to dry enough to overpaint, with polymer-tempered pigments it is a matter of minutes or, at most, two hours. Most writers on art consider the quick-drying quality of the polymers to be an advantage, and for most modern styles it is. However, for anyone who works in a style that requires a good deal of blending and carefully articulated modeling, the polymers dry too quickly. The producers of the various brands have marketed agents which slow the drying time of their paints, but I have not yet found one that works really well—at least not as of this writing.

Acrylic paints Another group of synthetics use acrylic resins as a binder. These paints

324
MICHAEL SMITH.
Yellow Arc. 1968.
Synthetic polymer paint on
canvas, 30 × 28″. Collection
Robert Kutak, Omaha,
Nebraska

are oil-compatible and can be thinned with water, linseed oil, or turpentine. The use of oil will slightly slow the drying time. Without the addition of oil these paints behave much like the polymers. Too, the acrylics can be dissolved with turpentine long after they have dried. This means it is possible to "erase" portions of a painting and rework it.

The artist Paul Jenkins (born 1923) has done a number of extraordinary works with acrylic-resin pigments in a way that takes advantage of the relative quickness with which they dry, their clarity, and their range of opacities. In his beautiful *Phenomena Graced by Three* (colorplate 15) the delicate zones of color were not painted on but floated and poured on before the canvas was stretch-

ed. His ability to control the effects thus achieved is nothing short of uncanny.

Both polymers and acrylics have been tested for durability by exposure to every possible factor except unlimited time. They are far more resistant to climatic conditions, light, and heat than oils or egg tempera. They do not darken as much as oils. And they are generally tougher, more flexible, and less easily damaged.

Watercolor There are several kinds of water-compatible paints—tempera, polymer, acrylic, gouache—but the best-known is transparent watercolor. Transparent watercolor pigment is available to artists either in tubes or in dried cakes which are soluble in water. The binder in this medium is gum arabic, a water-soluble gum which comes from the acacia tree. The painting surface is ordinarily a handmade paper with a prominent texture.

Two of the world's greatest watercolorists, Winslow Homer (1836–1910) and John Marin (1870–1953), happened to have been Americans. Homer's *Hurricane, The Bahamas* (fig. 325) exploits every characteristic of the medium. The palm fronds bending in a high wind are captured in a few swift brushstrokes, the buildings noted in a sketchy way that helps convey an impression that the air itself is blurred by the speed of the wind. The sky is overcast and glaring. No white paint has been employed—the latticework behind the red flag was produced by scraping with a knife. Since the major aims of the watercolorist are the attainment of transparency and spontaneity, white paint is almost never used. Traditionalists would consider it cheating. Light value is achieved by letting paper show through. This means that Homer always had to start with lights and work toward darks;

in working with watercolor this is even more essential than with tempera.

People whose only experience with watercolor was in childhood are always amazed that watercolorists can control the paint. Laymen expect that the paper will lump up and the colors all run together and get muddy. It does require skill to prevent those things, but professional artists' materials help. Good watercolor paper is very heavy and is taped onto a drawing board or tacked to a canvas stretcher while dripping wet. When it shrinks, it stretches as flat and firm as a drumhead. Watercolorists use quite expensive sable brushes which can produce either bold strokes or extremely fine ones, depending on how they're handled. And, of course, professional artists' pigments are much more intense than children's play sets.

John Marin was an "original." Back in the 1930s he was wearing his hair to his shoulders. No one hassled him about it, though. He was too great an artist, an Expressionist in a peculiarly American way. Some consider him the greatest twentieth-century American artist,

325
WINSLOW HOMER. *Hurricane, The Bahamas.* 1898. Watercolor, 14½ × 21″. The Metropolitan Museum of Art, New York

largely because he used the watercolor medium with unprecedented strength and vigor. *Marin Island, Maine* (fig. 326) speaks to the viewer in a kind of shorthand signifying trees, rocks, and rills—a shorthand that does not depart from the realities that inspired the picture. Marin's watercolors are abstract in the ordinary sense that he has left out a lot of nonessentials. They are also abstract in the sense that they are concerned with the play of

formal elements in and of themselves. Note the way in which the great sweep in the sky is mirrored in the island and the water. The rough texture of the paper and the transparency of the paint contribute to an extremely effective image of Marin's private island.

Fresco painting   All the paintings we have discussed thus far fall under the general head-

326
JOHN MARIN. *Marin Island, Maine.* 1915.
Watercolor, 15¾ × 19″. Philadelphia Museum of Fine Arts.
A. E. Gallatin Collection

ing of panel pictures. This term applies even though most of them are on canvas and two on paper. The point is that they are not *murals* —paintings done on walls.

Most of the great mural paintings which have been done throughout history are either mosaics, formed of bits of glass and stone, or are frescoes. Because fresco is a bit more difficult to understand without knowing something of the process, I have chosen to deal with it here.

Fresco is an Italian word which means "fresh." There are two kinds of fresco, *fresco secco* (dry fresco) and *buon fresco* (good fresco). The former is done on a dry wall with a medium closely resembling egg tempera.[2] The latter is what normally goes by the name *fresco;* it involves painting into wet lime plaster with pigment mixed into limewater. The layer of calcium carbonate formed by the limewater binds the pigment to the plaster wall, and the mutual wetness of the pigment and the surface causes the color to dye the wall. This makes for a highly permanent decoration, as long-lived as the building itself. Permanence is the main advantage of fresco and is, of course, its own recommendation.

Michelangelo's *Creation of Adam* (fig. 327), like all the other works on the ceiling of the Sistine Chapel in the Vatican, is an example of fresco painting. Since plaster cannot be rewet, once it is dry, the fresco artist never applies more plaster to his surface than he knows he can finish in a single day. Consequently, we can find places in this fresco where plaster joints occur. There is a seam where Adam's neck fits onto his body and another at the line between the torso and the legs. Adam is about twelve feet long, and it took Michelangelo three sessions to complete him.

Because of the bleaching effect of the plaster, fresco color is never very intense. Some pigments are excluded because of the chemical incompatibility between them and lime. Too, in fresco even more than in tempera, correction is impossible. To have effected a change in Adam's nose, Michelangelo would have had to remove all the plaster containing the head and begin anew. Here, too, elaborate cartoons and precise preparatory studies were necessary before the artist undertook the actual painting.

Frescoes are still done for large buildings, but the method has not changed in hundreds of years except for the introduction of colors that Michelangelo did not possess.

PRINTMAKING

No matter how well-to-do you happen to be, an original Rembrandt oil painting is probably beyond your means. Today such a work would cost you at least a million dollars, most likely. But if you wish to save up for awhile, you might be able to pick up a good etching from the hand of the same master for only a few hundred dollars. At an auction in St. Louis a few years ago I bought one from the Pulitzer estate for $200 that is superior in quality to the impression owned by the Rijksmuseum in Amsterdam. My etching is just as much an "original Rembrandt" as an oil painting but not nearly so precious because it is but one of a number of copies. It has the qualities of great art but isn't as rare a thing as a one-of-a-kind painting. That is the main purpose of printmaking—to produce multiple originals of genuine quality.

In order to make what I'm talking about perfectly clear, it is wise to distinguish between *prints* and *reproductions*. Artistically speaking, a print has the following characteristics: The printing surface was made by the artist himself. It is printed by him or under his direct supervision. The processes involved are done by hand. In modern times a specified, limited number of individual pictures are made from a given plate or block

327
MICHELANGELO. *The Creation of Adam.* 1508–12.
Fresco. Sistine Chapel, Vatican, Rome

which is then defaced or destroyed so that more cannot be printed.

A reproduction is produced by photomechanical methods, not by hand, and the relations between the artist and the printer are incidental or nonexistent. A so-called print of Andrew Wyeth's *Christina's World* is not a genuine artist's print; it is a color reproduction. Wyeth had nothing to do with it. Some reproductions are of very high quality; some are poor. Some reproductions of artists' prints are *so* fine that they can be palmed off on the inexpert as original etchings, woodcuts, and lithographs; in that case the reproduction is a mechanically produced facsimile—a counterfeit. Sometimes one sees ads for a "limited edition of color prints of" what is clearly a reproduction of a painting. The limits of such an edition will, as likely as not be a thousand or more. Legally it is "limited," and narrowly defined it is a print (after all, a press prints it); but from a printmaker's point of view anything over a hundred is a very large edition. And the reproduction of a painting is worth no more than any other gift shop item. Of course, it may be worth every penny to you as a decor item; a good reproduction of the Wyeth is higher on the scale of aesthetic value than the tenth-rate original oil paintings turned out by hacks for department stores.[3] All I wish to make clear here is that a reproduction and a print are not in the same category.

Degas's *Self-Portrait* (fig. 328) is an etching. What we are looking at here is a black-and-white reproduction of the print. The reproduction was made from a photograph of an impression of the print owned by the National Gallery of Art in Washington, D.C. There are other impressions of the same print in other collections here and abroad. The *print* is the picture Degas's etched copperplate produced. An *impression* is any individual picture made from the etched plate. An *edition* is the total number of impressions Degas printed from the plate. If you buy a print from a contemporary artist, it should have the following information in pencil on the lower margin: title, edition number, artist's signature, and year.

The edition number is important. It will read "16–100" or "24–50" or "34–34" or something. This means that you are examining the sixteenth of one hundred impressions or the twenty-fourth of fifty impressions or the last of thirty-four. The artist will also have "pulled" (that is, printed) a few impressions for himself which are not in the numbered edition. Normally these will be labeled "artist's proof" and will be marked with a Roman numeral to identify the order in which they fall. Early impressions and artist's proofs are supposed to be worth more than later impressions, but in an edition of less than one hundred there are not apt to be any real qualitative differences.

Prints fall into four general categories: relief, intaglio, planographic, and stencil.

Relief prints   The principle of relief printing is easy to grasp because it is so familiar. You have made thousands of them. When you

328
EDGAR DEGAS.
Self-Portrait. 1855.
Etching, $9 \times 5\frac{5}{8}''$. National
Gallery of Art, Washington,
D.C. Lessing Rosenwald
Collection

leave a wet footprint on a poolside, you are relief-printing your sole in water onto concrete or tile. Unless you have abnormally flat feet, only the toes, ball, heel, and a tiny part of the outside edge of the foot come into contact with the surface. These are the parts of the sole that are in relief. The arch, the spaces between the toes, and the area between the toes and ball of the foot are recessed; they don't touch the surface, so they don't print.

That's all the term *relief printing* means: that the image is printed by carrying ink to the paper from a raised surface. Fingerprinting is another commonplace example. Stamp pads ink the relief surface of the rubber stamp. Typewriter keys strike the ribbon with the relief part of the key and make the mark. Printers' type is another example.

Relief prints can be made from so many substances that it is useless to enumerate them. In grade school halves of potatoes are sometimes used to make relief-print designs. Linoleum is used by children and artists as well. There are many, many possibilities.

Among artists the most common forms of relief printing are *woodcut* and *wood engraving*. The basic difference between the two is that woodcuts are carved into the plank grain of the wood and wood engravings into the end grain (See figure 329). Since it is difficult to secure smooth, unchecked end grain of any

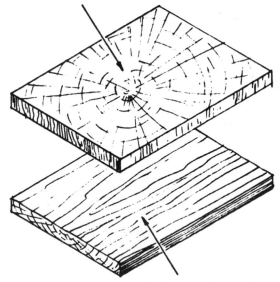

end grain for wood engraving

plank grain for woodcut

329
Woodgrain and relief prints

size, wood engravings are seldom over a few inches wide. At the same time, because end grain does not pose problems of cutting with, against, or across the grain, it permits much more intricate designs than plank grain. Not that woodcuts are necessarily crude. *The Anatomist* (fig. 330) by Leonard Baskin (born 1922), is anything but that. The same thing, however, could be done on a far smaller scale as wood engraving.

Figure 331 is a graphic demonstration of the relief process as it is carried out in woodcut. (A) This is the image the artist wishes to print. Notice that the rectangle is to the left of the circle. When the printmaker draws the design onto the plank (B), he will reverse the image because all relief prints come out backward. (C) He then chisels away all the areas he wants to come out as white when the block is printed. All the relief forms are carved wider at their bases to prevent chipping. (D) With a soft rubber or gelatin roller called a *brayer* the artist inks the block with oil-base printers' ink. (E) A soft thin rice paper is best for printing. Placed on top of the block, it is rubbed with a wooden spoon or similar implement so that the moist ink is transmitted from the relief surface to the paper. (F) An impression is pulled. The block is reinked for the next impression, the rubbing   d. and so on, until an edition is com

Blocks can also be printed mer presses, but hand rubbing is pref. artists for a number of reasons. Althougn some, hand rubbing offers more control, since the printer can see just enough through the rice paper to tell what is properly printed and what is not. Also, in order to be printed on a press properly, a wood block should be absolutely true, which is not necessary with rubbing. Finally, it is possible to print woodcuts of much larger dimensions by rubbing because the size of block is not limited by the size of the press.

In Baskin's print whatever is white was

carved out, and whatever is black was left standing. The areas that appear to be gray in our reproduction are red in the original print. They could have been blue or green or yellow or any color, since they depend for their hue upon the ink the printer chooses. I do not know whether the anatomist's chart was cut into the same block as the anatomist and inked a different color or cut into a different block and printed separately in red on the same sheet of paper. But most color woodcuts involve separate blocks. By combining several blocks so that their successive impressions overlap on the same piece of paper, it is possible to secure secondary and tertiary hues, as shown in colorplate 16. Such effects can be obtained because the inks can be made transparent by the addition of a clear base. Of course, relationships far more subtle and complex than the diagram suggests can be obtained by a practiced printer. But this is the idea. And it is the procedure followed in the other kinds of printmaking too; normally, a separate color means another block, plate, stone, or screen. Colorplate 16 is of a block print.

One kind of relief printing deserves special mention. Since 1960 *collagraphy*, originated by Glen Alps, has become extremely popular among printmakers. In this technique, pieces of cardboard and of materials such as lace and cloth are glued to a rigid surface (masonite, hardboard, or metal). The resulting collage (which sometimes includes "found objects") is then inked and printed on an etching or lithography press. Delicate and striking textural effects can be obtained by lacquering the materials; indeed, the design is sometimes created with lacquer brushstrokes alone. Advantages of collagraphy are that it permits the artist to achieve large-scale relationships with relative ease, it produces color fields that are very flat and powerful in their impact, and it lends itself to combination with intaglio and lithographic printing.

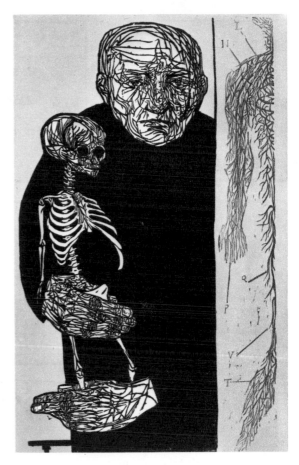

330
LEONARD BASKIN.
The Anatomist. 1952.
Woodcut, 18¾ × 11". The Museum of Modern Art, New York. Gift of the Junior Council

Intaglio prints Intaglio printmaking is exactly the opposite of relief printmaking. Rather than printing from a raised surface, the intaglio method prints from recessions. Line engraving, etching, and drypoint are the most common forms of intaglio. Ordinarily they are done on plates of metal, but it is possible to use other materials, for example Plexiglas or Formica. American currency is printed from steel-plate line engravings by an intaglio process called *gravure*. Most fine-

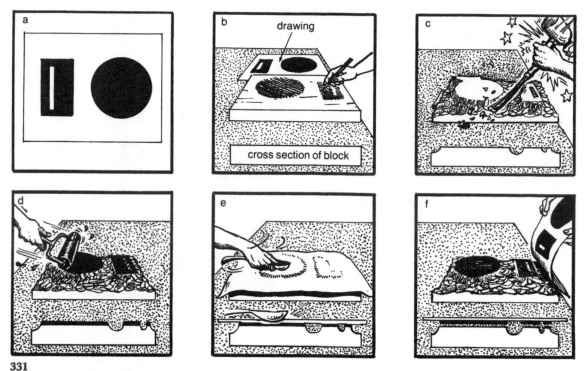

331
The relief-printing process

arts prints are done on copper.

A *line engraving* entails incising grooves directly into the metal with sharp steel tools called *burins*. Burins are of various shapes and sizes, but the kind shown in figure 332 is typical; it is a lozenge-shaped steel rod bent at an angle of about 30° so that the worker's hand clears the plate. To cut through metal with this instrument requires considerable muscular control, since continuous pressure must be exerted and the burin cannot be tilted or rocked during cutting. Line engraving is a difficult and demanding medium, but the resulting line has a vigor, clarity, and intensity no other kind of mark can match. Dürer's *Adam and Eve* (fig. 333) is a splendid example.

Figure 334 shows the process in serial form. (A) One begins with a polished copperplate about one-sixteenth of an inch thick (that is, 16 gauge), completely flat and beveled on all four edges. (B) Sitting facing the direction of the cutting motion, the engraver pushes the burin through the metal. The burin is never turned; all curved lines are made by pivoting the plate. Burin grooves are clean, clear, sharp V-shaped troughs. The deeper they are, the heavier and darker the line they will print. No mark is too fine to print; the merest scratch will show. One of the characteristics of an engraved line is that it can be made to fatten and taper. Cross-hatching can suggest powerful volumes by taking advantage of this capacity. Very broad lines in engraving are really the consequence of many smaller cuts made right against one another. This effect can easily be seen in the engraving by H. G. Adam (fig. 335). As one cuts, a spiral of metal shaped like a watch spring curls up ahead of the burin. These burrs are razor sharp and must be removed as the

332
Burin

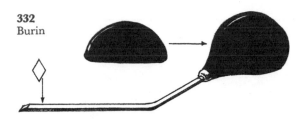

engraver proceeds.

As you can see, line engraving is a mode of expression that requires a good deal of practice and tremendous patience. Many artists do not care for the effects it produces, preferring a more spontaneous medium. Others simply have neither the time nor the will to master the peculiar skills required. For these another method of intaglio is available.

Etchings are far, far easier to produce than engravings. That is why so many painters of the past have chosen this medium instead of some other graphic-arts technique. The Degas (fig. 328) is an etching. We have seen two Rembrandt etchings thus far, his *The Descent from the Cross: By Torchlight* (fig. 136) and *Adam and Eve* (fig. 257). Picasso's *The Frugal Repast* (fig. 336) is also an etching. What these artists have done, in effect, is substitute acid for pressure to create the intaglio

333
ALBRECHT DÜRER.
Adam and Eve. 1504.
Engraving, $9\frac{7}{8} \times 7\frac{5}{8}$″. Museum of Fine Arts, Boston. Centennial Gift of London Clay

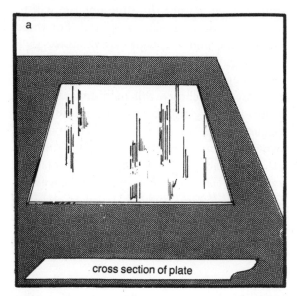

cross section of plate

broad line

334
Engraving

recesses in their plates.

Figure 337 shows you in part A the kind of design the artist wishes to produce in an etching. (Notice that both the circles and the lines are partly thin and partly thick and that in one place thick lines cross thinner ones.) As in engraving, the deeper the recess, the darker the line. (B) A copperplate identical to the kind used in engraving is covered with a waxy substance called *etching ground* which is impervious to acid. (C) The lines are scratched through the wax with a sharp needle so as to lay the metal bare. (D) The artist immerses the plate in a solution containing a mordant, for instance, nitric acid. The acid eats the exposed copper away—it "etches" the plate. The longer the plate stays in the solution, the deeper the acid eats. (E) To produce the contrast between thin lines and thick ones the etcher removes the plate from the etching solution and paints over the parts he wishes to remain lighter. This is called *stopping out*. Usually one uses an acid-resistant varnish for this purpose because

it is easier to control than ground. (Varnish is no good to use for ground because it is too brittle for the needle to cut cleanly.) (F) When the plate is reimmersed in the etching solution, the parts covered by the varnish remain as they were, but the acid continues to eat away at the exposed areas. To achieve the thin lines crossed by heavy ones, the etcher cleans the plate with solvents, regrounds the surface, and draws through the new ground over the old lines. Then he simply reetches the plate for as long as he needs to produce the effect. This is easy enough to do because etching ground is applied in a very, very thin layer and the existing troughs are readily visible. Rembrandt was a master of the technique. Some of his shaded areas contain five or six different line weights.

It is also possible to secure black and gray tonal areas in etching by using *aquatint*, a technique that involves dusting the plate with rosin powder, fixing it to the surface by heating the plate, and etching areas of the plate so that the surface becomes sandpapery

335

H.G. ADAM. *Anse de la Torche, No. 12.* Engraving, 18 × 33½″. The Brooklyn Museum, New York

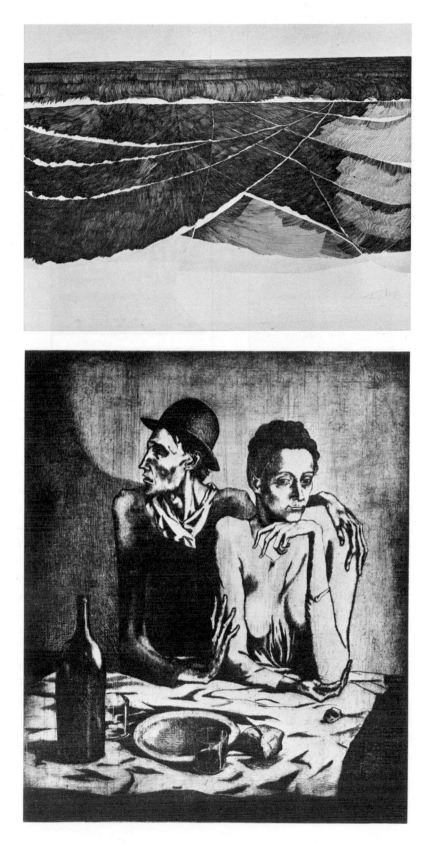

336

PABLO PICASSO. *The Frugal Repast.* 1904. Etching, 18¼ × 14¼″. The Museum of Modern Art, New York. Gift of Abby Aldrich Rockefeller

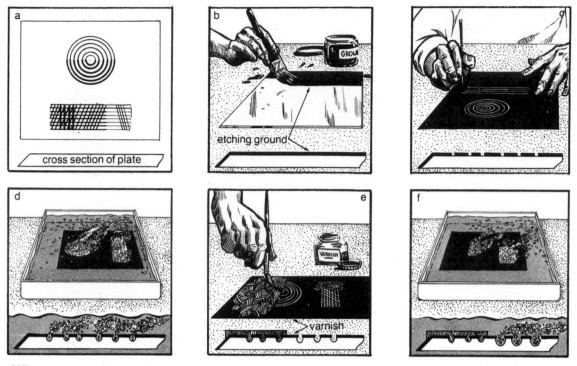

337
The etching process

in texture. There is a method of securing exact duplications of the textures of fingerprints, lace, feathers, and other similarly delicate substances by putting petroleum jelly or tallow into etching ground so that it remains soft. The texture is pressed into this *soft ground*. When it is removed, some of the ground pulls away, leaving an impression. Then the plate is etched as it would be in line etching. There is also a primitive form of engraving called *drypoint*. Here, an etching needle is used to scratch the surface of the metal. The scratching causes furrows of metal to rise up on either side of the groove, and their roughness produces a furry-looking line when printed. All the methods—engraving, etching, aquatint, soft ground, and drypoint —might be used in a single plate.

What puzzles most people about intaglio printmaking is the printing itself. How do you get an image from the recesses? You do it by the process shown in figure 338. (A) The plate is completely covered with sticky printers' ink. The ink is driven into the grooves with a felt-covered tool called a *dauber*. (B) The printer wipes the ink from the surface while leaving the ink in the recesses. He begins wiping with coarse, open-weave material such as mosquito netting or tarlatan (starched cheesecloth) and then moves to muslin and/or the edge of his hand. Wiping requires a certain amount of skill, and different people do it in different ways. The idea is to clean the surface and not the lines. (C) The plate, then, rests face up on an etching press, which is essentially a steel bed between gear-driven steel rollers. (D) The artist places on top of the plate a sheet of heavy printing paper, moistened to the point where it is limp, blotted so that no truly wet spots remain. On the paper he places three soft felt blankets. (E) The press bed rides between the rollers as the artist turns the star-wheel spokes. The top roller squeezes the blankets onto the paper and the paper onto the plate under tremendous pressure. Because the dampened paper is pliable and the felt is soft, the pressure drives the paper down into the grooves. (F) The paper has been *embossed*. If it had been run through the press on top of an uninked plate, it would be white on white embossing; since the grooves were filled with black ink, they are now black. Sepia ink produces sepia lines; green, green lines; and so forth. This same printing technique is used in engraving, etching, and all other intaglio processes. Unfortunately for indolent artists, the complete process of inking must be repeated for each impression.

Embossing and intaglio go together. You don't get one without the other. An original intaglio print will also reveal the impression of the plate itself as an indentation in the paper. (The reason we bevel the plate is to prevent the sharp edge from slicing through the paper and also cutting the felt blankets.) Today intaglio prints are framed with a cardboard mat so that a margin of paper shows between the plate impression and the mat. On the bottom margin the artist's signature, the date, the edition number, and the title will appear in pencil. The same procedure is also used when matting other kinds of prints, but with intaglio the relation of the mat to the edge of the impression is much more evident.

Planographic prints   There is only one kind of planographic printing in the fine arts,

338
Intaglio printing

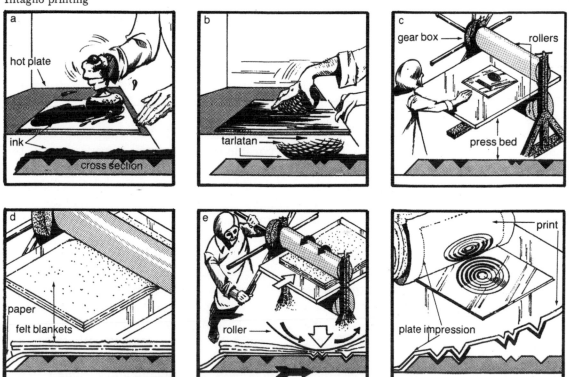

339

HONORÉ DAUMIER. *Les Témoins (The Witnesses at the Door of the Council of War).* 19th century. Lithograph, 10 × 8¾". The Metropolitan Museum of Art, New York. Schiff Fund, 1922

lithography. Planographic means that the print results from an image that is neither above nor below the surface but on it. The surface involved was originally, and usually still is, the smooth face of a block of Bavarian limestone, hence the name litho (stone)-graphy (drawing or writing). Plates of zinc and aluminum can also be used. Unlike other printmaking media, which are mechanical in nature, lithography is chemical. It depends upon the fact that oil and water will not mix.

Lithographs are easily mistaken for ink or crayon drawings because they are drawn with *tusche,* a water-soluble grease that comes in both liquid and crayon form. Honoré Daumier's lithograph *Les Témoins* (fig. 339) exemplifies the power of the medium. Compared with relief or intaglio, it is a relatively swift process and far more direct. Neither a

wood block nor an engraved plate look much like the black-and-white thing printed from them. They are indirect. A woodcut is a carving. When you draw lines to be etched, they appear as bright copper trails against the dark brownish hue of the ground. But in lithography the drawing you make on the stone closely resembles the image it will print, except that it is reversed.

The lithographic process (fig. 340) begins with a perfectly flat slab of limestone (A) which has been given a slight tooth by grinding with carborundum powder. We are going to produce an image like the one at upper left.[4] (B) For solid areas tusche in liquid form can be painted on or drawn on with a pen. The material is a grease, but it behaves more or less like ink. It can be thinned with water to give watercolor-like effects. (C) For graduated areas tusche in the form of a solid crayon is used. There are different grades of crayons, each producing a progressively darker mark. (D) Etching the stone is a complicated process involving rosin and whiting (talc) as well as acid, but the basic substance used is the etch itself. This is much milder than anything used in intaglio etching. It is a syrupy mixture of water, gum arabic, and nitric acid. To one and a half ounces of gum arabic solution the artist will add somewhere between fifteen and fifty drops of acid. The exact amount is impossible to say, because stones vary and because temperature, humidity, and the age of the acid all affect the outcome. The lithographer tests his etch on the margin of the stone, and when it foams in a certain way he knows he has what he needs. Delicate crayon work or tusche watercolor variations require a stronger etch than solid spots of tusche. The gum solution is painted onto the stone and left overnight. What happens is complicated, but the upshot of it is this: When the gum arabic comes into contact with the tusche areas, it makes them insoluble in water. The acid bites the limestone just enough to make it slightly more porous than before and, therefore, more capable of absorbing water. (E) The next step is apt to terrify the novice, especially if he has spent days and days slaving over an intricate drawing on his stone. With water and turpentine the artist *washes out* the image. It vanishes! (Well, if you look closely, you can see a kind of yellowish stain where the drawing was, but that's all.) At this point the stone is ready to be printed.

The black color of tusche ink and crayons has nothing to do with the darkness of the print; it is nothing but lampblack put into the tusche so that the artist can see what he's doing. The real difference between a dark lithographic crayon and a light one is that the dark one contains more grease. Similarly, when you add water to tusche ink to make a pale gray, what you actually have done is reduced the amount of grease. Grease is all that counts. And one dares not touch the stone with his hand as he is working because even the cleanest hand exudes a bit of natural oil. This oil, though invisible, will show up as

a gray dirty spot when the stone is printed. Any grease that gets onto the stone before it is etched will eventually print.

Printing the stone (fig. 341) depends upon the antipathy of greasy areas for water and of wet areas for grease. (A) The limestone is wet down with water. The open stone areas absorb the water, but it beads up on the areas where tusche had been applied. (B) A previously inked roller the size of an extremely large rolling pin but covered with soft leather or rubber is passed over the wet stone. Since the bare stone areas are wet, the ink, which is greasy, will not adhere to them. But in greasy areas the roller pushes the drops of water out of the way, and the oily ink is attracted to the oily surface. As if by magic, the original drawing reappears on the stone. (C) A lithographic press has a movable bed like an etching press but has a *scraper bar* instead of a roller. The stone, which is kept moist all through printing, rests on the bed. As in intaglio printing, the paper is damp. The paper goes onto the stone, a blotter or two on top of

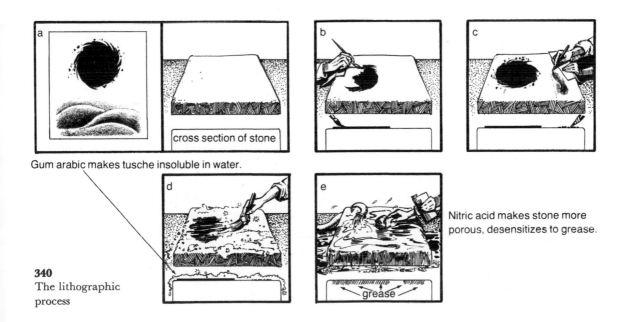

Gum arabic makes tusche insoluble in water.

Nitric acid makes stone more porous, desensitizes to grease.

340
The lithographic process

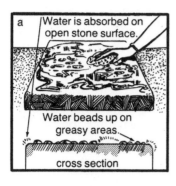

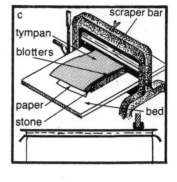

341
Lithographic printing

that, and a piece of red fiberboard called a *tympan* on top of that. (D) The scraper bar, which has been lubricated with mutton tallow, clamps down onto the similarly well-greased tympan, pressing the paper down hard onto the stone. (E) The printer cranks the press handle, driving the bed along under the scraper bar. The bed, of course, carries the stone along with it, and the pressure of the bar squeezes the image onto the paper. (F) Then the stone is rewet, reinked, another sheet of paper applied, and the whole business run back through in the other direction. This is continued until the edition is completed.

Lithographic stones may be used over and over because the tusche and etch affect only the uppermost surface of the stone. When an edition has been run, the stone is ground down with carborundum sufficiently to remove the inked image entirely, and another lithograph can be drawn on the same stone.

Some printmakers, for example Robert Nelson, combine intaglio, relief, and lithographic methods in the same design (see fig. 342).

Stencil prints (serigraphs) A stencil is anything that blocks out areas so they will not be touched by something else. The most common kinds are those used to do lettering. *Serigraphy* (literally, silk-writing), or silk-screen, is the most sophisticated of the stencil processes known to the fine arts. It is an extremely flexible medium, capable of hard-edge effects of high impact (fig. 343) or of an extremely subtle and delicate imagery rivaling painting (fig. 344). For those who do not like to work in reverse, serigraphy is ideal because stencil processes do not require you to reverse your conception.

The technique, as you can see from figure 345, is a simple one. (A) One begins with a wooden frame over which silk has been very tightly stretched. Silk comes in two weights—standard (x) and heavy (xx)—and is available in coarse (6) to extremely fine (20), that is, from six strands per square inch to twenty per square inch. In my opinion the best silk for average screen-printing use is 14xx. Once the silk is on the frame, any area which contacts wood is taped with brown wrapping tape and waterproofed with shellac. (B) All parts of the screen that are not to print are blocked out. There are a number of ways of doing this. Some involve materials that stick to the silk, some entail painting in with glues or lacquers, and some involve "resist" techniques which permit you to put in thin lines or brushstrokes and to use crayon textures. The main point is that because the stencil is being prepared on a silk surface it is possible to block out areas in the center of an open space. (C) The printmaker pours into his screen ink containing materials which slow the drying of the pigment and make it flow smoothly. Silk-screen ink comes in a fantastic range of colors (including Day-Glos) and can be oil base, water base, or lacquer. In serigraphy, fast-drying oil inks are customary. (D) A *squeegee* (a hard rubber blade inserted in a wooden handle) is used to draw the ink across the screen. As the artist pulls it toward him, he presses it down and squeezes the ink through the mesh of the silk onto the paper beneath the frame. (E) The ink goes through the openings in the silk where the stencil is vacant but not where it is solid. When the paper is removed, the texture of the silk will not be visible because the ink is fluid enough to flow around the tiny threads. The printed area is very flat and solid. The printer inserts another sheet of paper, pulls the squeegee in the other direction to produce another print,

and so on and on until the run is finished. Once a color has been used up, the screen is cleaned and the stencil removed with solvent, which will either completely dissolve the block-out material or will loosen it but will not affect the silk or the shellacked tape. Successive colors are run on the paper by repeating the process described above. By strategic overlapping with the use of transparent bases in the ink, and through controlled printing techniques, it is possible to obtain very elaborate relationships.

PHOTOMECHANICAL REPRODUCTION
All the pictures in this book were reproduced by photomechanical printing processes. That

342
ROBERT NELSON. *"Wagner"*. 1971.
Lithograph and relief printing, 41 × 27½".
Southern Illinois University, Edwardsville

343
MICHAEL SMITH. *Arc I.*
1967.
Serigraph, 14⅞ x 14¾″.
Private collection

344
JOHN ADKINS RICHARDSON.
Road to Xanadu. 1963.
Serigraph, 11¾ × 14¾″.
Private collection

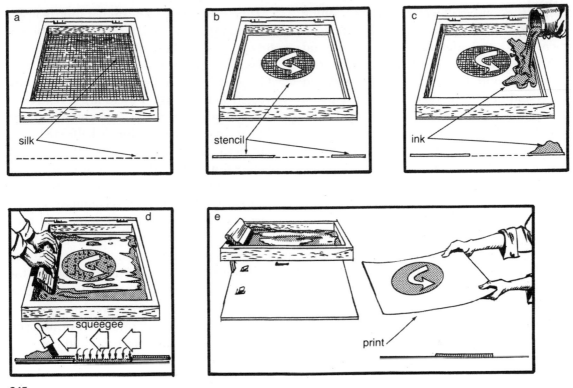

345
Serigraph printing

is, the works of art were photographed onto photosensitive plates which were then chemically prepared for printing by machinery. The processes correspond to those in the fine arts and, indeed, derive from the hand processes of the artist. There are relief, planographic, intaglio, and stencil forms.

Relief (letterpress) Letterpress is the kind of printing with which most people are familiar. Raised type, having been inked, imparts the image to a sheet of paper. Most newspapers are printed by this process. Pictures reproduced for letterpress are of two types: linecut and halftone.

Linecuts are made from drawings that are of one value only—like the diagrams I have drawn to illustrate the printing processes.

Sometimes my diagrams contain what appear to be grays, but if you look closely at the reproductions, you will see that the grays are really made up of tiny black dots very close together. Such a dot pattern is called *benday tint* and is available in many patterns and forms. In linecut the drawing is photographed onto a glass plate to produce a negative. Normally, the negative will be smaller than the original drawing; most comic strips, for instance, are drawn three or four times the size you see them. The negative is placed on a sheet of zinc that has been coated with a photosensitive solution and is exposed to a very strong arc light. The black of the negative (white in the drawing) blocks out the light; the clear area on the negative (black in the drawing) permits light to pass through. The light hardens the coating on the zinc so that it is insoluble in water. Careful washing removes the unexposed areas. The plate is then inked and dusted with a fine ground called *dragon's blood* which is very similar to etching ground. It clings only to the hardened areas and not to the remainder of the plate. The piece of zinc is immersed in an acid bath, and the parts not covered with ground are etched away. The plate is then mounted on a wooden block to bring it up to the same height as type and is printed exactly like type. What it prints, of course, is a small duplicate of the original drawing.[5]

The same procedure is used for the reproduction of continuous-tone photographs, that is, for things like the pictures of paintings and prints in this book. All photographs are reproduced by this process, called *halftone*. The difference between halftone and linecut is that in halftone two sheets of plate glass covered with lines are involved. The lines are engraved diagonally and are filled in with black pigment. When the two plates are placed face to face with the lines at right angles, a grid or *screen* is formed. The negative is photographed onto the zinc plate through the screen. Because the plate is able to "see" only in terms of the highest possible contrast, it reads light areas as made of large dots and dark ones as small dots. (Remember, all this is in negative.) The ultimate consequence is that when the zinc has been prepared as it is for a linecut a lot of little dots stand up in relief; there are many dots close together where the image is to be black and very few where it is to be light. If you look at a newspaper, you will see that reproductions of the photographs answer to this description. Newspapers use very coarse halftone screens for their halftones. Magazines use finer ones. The dots can become so fine that you cannot see them with the naked eye.

The magnified section of a color reproduction (colorplate 10) reveals the way in which halftone dots can be united into a color image.

Offset lithography   The preparation of negatives and plates for the mechanical version of lithography is about the same as for letterpress; it is the printing process that differs. The plate is a thin sheet of zinc or aluminum treated so that certain areas are receptive to ink and others to water, exactly as in stone lithography. Once the line or halftone image has been fixed in the plate, the plate is wrapped around a drum on an offset press. When the press is turned on, the plate on the drum turns. As it turns, it is contacted first by a set of rollers that wet it with water and then by a set of rollers that apply the ink. The plate next contacts another drum, this one wrapped in a rubber blanket. The inky image on the plate is "offset" onto the blanket, and the roller prints it onto the paper.

Offset lithography permits finer printing on rougher paper than letterpress and has such other advantages as speed and longer lasting plates. Practically all magazines, brochures, and illustrated books are printed by this method. The images are not, however, quite as clean and sharp as in good letterpress work.

Intaglio (gravure)   Gravure plates are prepared in much the same way as letterpress ones, except that the areas to carry the ink are etched away instead of the areas that are to remain white. In doing halftones with gravure, the printer actually achieves real half tones—that is, genuine value changes. For the halftone dots in gravure are all the same size, differing in depth. Deep zones print darker than shallow ones. It is a much more subtle system than linecut or lithography. Gravure plates are cylindrical, like offset ones; but the printing is done directly from the plate onto the paper. A flat bar called a *doctor blade* scrapes away the surface ink leaving deposits in the recessed areas only. Better grades of paper are required for gravure than for either letterpress or offset lithography.

Stencil (silk-screen) Serigraphy is really just a fancy name for a medium that originated as a commercial process and was taken over by artists in the 1930s. It is used for making placards and posters, for applying machine printing to glass, for printing fabrics and other things. Window decals are often silk-screened. The slogans on sweatshirts are printed by silk-screen.

Photoscreening accomplishes with silk-screen what linecut and halftone do with letterpress. A photosensitive film replaces the other stencil materials, and the work proceeds from there. The major limitation is that the halftone dots must be enormously large because they can never be smaller than the mesh of the silk. Mechanized squeegee arms permit tireless repetition of the printing job.

Some Media in Three Dimensions

SCULPTURE

I have tended, thus far, to give very short shrift to the sculptural arts because they are three-dimensional and an illustration in a book cannot do them the kind of justice it can a picture. In two dimensions genuine formal analysis of sculpture is impossible; even with a multitude of views of something existing in the round we fail. Motion-picture films which show continuously shifting viewpoints similar to those experienced by the human observer do not capture the full qualities of solid objects. Moreover, tactile values are important to the character of a sculpture. Some works cry out to be touched, caressed, fondled. And people do touch them; they do it so much, in fact, that museums try to discourage the practice. It increases cleaning costs and, in some cases, adds unwanted polish to stone and bronze. Also, pieces can actually be worn away in spots where they're always touched, as in the famous right foot of St. Peter in the Vatican statue.

Still, even though pictures can't really do the job, it would be wrong to overlook media that contain some of mankind's noblest conceptions of human form and spatial organization. Basically, there are four kinds of sculpture: (1) those that are carved, (2) those that are built, (3) those which have been cast, and (4) so-called found sculpture.

Carved (subtractive) sculpture There is nothing difficult to understand about carved sculpture; it involves nothing more than, as Michelangelo said, "knocking away the waste material." Conceptually the procedure is obvious; doing it is another story. Whittling a small figure from a stick is quite different from hewing some great log down into a statue. And the creation of a thing like Praxiteles' *Hermes and Dionysus* (fig. 83) or Michelangelo's *David* (fig. 227) out of a monolith is a tremendously impressive feat.

Most of the great carvings of the world are in stone. Some are of igneous rock (granite, basalt, diorite, obsidian), formed from molten minerals that have cooled. Others are of sedimentary rocks (sandstone, gritstone, limestone), formed by deposits of sediment in successive layers. Still others are made from metamorphic rocks (marble, steatite, slate), rocks which have begun as igneous or sedimentary stone and then undergone heat, pressure, and chemical changes that have transformed them. Igneous rocks tend to be very obdurate. Hard to carve but long lasting, they were a favorite of the Egyptians. The sedimentary rocks range from those that are extremely durable to those that are highly impermanent. Of these rocks, limestone is the favorite sculptural material because it is relatively permanent, is easy to work, and can take a very fine polish. But the rock which has unsurpassable properties for sculpture is marble, a metamorphic rock. Marble is greatly varied in color range, from pure cream and white to blazing polychrome, and it is, sculp-

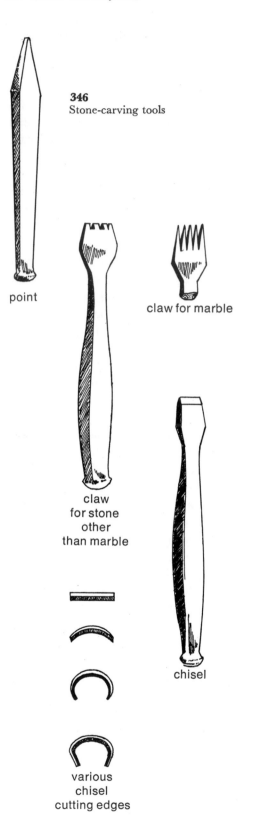

346
Stone-carving tools

point

claw for marble

claw
for stone
other
than marble

chisel

various
chisel
cutting edges

tors say, a pleasure to carve.

Freshly quarried stone is best for carving because exposure to the elements would cause it to form a hard outer skin and make it difficult or impossible to carve. Any block of stone a sculptor is to use must be free of flaws and should be set up according to the structure of the bed from which it came. For a standing figure like *David* a tall block would be used; for a reclining figure, a long low one.

The sculptor in stone who wants to make a very large statue begins his work by making a small version of the statue in clay, wax, or plaster of Paris. This model is called a *maquette* or a *bozzetto*. The proportions of the maquette are carried over to the block mechanically. This can be done either by using a *pointing machine* (a sort of three-dimensional pantograph) or with *enlarging frames*. Enlarging frames are two open boxes constructed around the maquette and the stone, built to exactly the same proportion and with constant vertical and horizontal members and a movable plumb line. In use, the plumb and a horizontal pointer are set at a given spot on the maquette, and the stone carved to the same ratio. Michelangelo used a variation of this in his work. He made a maquette for the *David* and placed it in a vessel similar to the shape of the block. The container had a hole in the bottom which was stopped with a plug. He filled it with an opaque fluid and let the liquid out at different times during the carving. The liquid around the maquette dropped to a level corresponding to a predetermined height on the stone and revealed the exact section to be carved.

The removal of waste material from the block is accomplished by hammering a steel tool into the stone with a mallet of wood or iron. All the differently shaped tools (fig. 346) come in various sizes. The "roughing out" of the block is done with a tool called a *point*. The point is just what its name suggests, a sharp-tipped rod. Its purpose is to explode away the stone. Usually the sculptor carves with points to within about half an inch of the final surface. He then switches to the *claw,* so-called because of its teeth. Claws used for marble have longer teeth of a harder temper than those used on other kinds of stones. At this stage the sculptor carves his image more precisely into the stone, achieving a kind of three-dimensional cross-hatching. Chisels are used in diminishing sizes to make the final statement. The surface of the work is then refined with rasps, files, and abrasives.

Different kinds of stones dictate special procedures. Granite, for example, is too hard to be modeled with a claw, and so an instrument called a *granite ax* is used. A tool called

a *boucharde*—a hammer with teeth not unlike those of a meat mallet—can be used to bruise stone away; it is used on marble and limestone as well as granite. Before the invention of steel, sculptors approached the stone by abrading it with other stones, iron hammers, and chisels. This is the way Praxiteles and other ancient sculptors worked. Indeed, the technique dates back to prehistoric ages when Paleolithic men pounded stone against stone to fashion spearheads and axes. It is a very slow process, pounding the surface of stone to dust, but it has the effect of stroking and smoothing the forms into their final state and lends a sensuousness to the carving that other methods do not attain. Michelangelo gains

347
MARY MISS. *Four Horizons* (detail). 1976.
Steel, concrete, and crushed rock, 140′ across, 8′ deep. Artpark, Lewiston, New York. Courtesy the Artist and Max Protech Gallery

348

DAN ANDERSON. *Mad Dog Fern Stand.*
1978.
Earthenware and mixed media, height 16″.
Private collection

power and clarity denied Praxiteles but sacrifices some of the Greek's surface appeal.

You perhaps have noticed that David's leg rests against a stump. This sort of leg rest— usually a stump but sometimes an animal, child, kneeling figure, stone, or other object— is found in nearly any stone statue of a standing figure with legs that are not attached to a background. It is not an aesthetic device; it is a structural one. Stone is strong but it is brittle. Marble has so little tensile strength that the thin ankles of the *David* could not possibly carry his massive weight without assistance. The stump was introduced to increase the diameter of the support. In *Hermes and Dionysus* the same function is performed by the falling drapery.

Perhaps the most basic kind of subtractive sculpture is a relatively recent kind that in the past would not have been considered at all artistic. This is *earth sculpture*, which uses the earth and its terrain for a medium. The most essential act the sculptor performs is

arranging for the earth to be removed and re-formed, sometimes to exist as an artifact in its own right, sometimes to permit the addition of sustaining walls, ornamental structures, or other elements. Often "earthworks" have the dull and indifferent character of an ordinary excavation. But some are quite striking in their presence. For example, *Four Horizons* (fig. 347) by Mary Miss (born 1944) is based on a compass directed to the four quarters and has, in its curious autonomy, the look of some mysteriously puissant emplacement set upon the land by alien forces. At the same time, it summons up thoughts of ritual, ancient rites, and final causes.

Built (additive) sculpture Carving takes away material, building adds it on. Naum Gabo's *Linear Construction, Variation* (fig. 301) is an accumulation of plastic forms and nylon thread; it is a construction, and a construction entails addition of part to part. Similarly, the Bakota guardian figure (fig. 298) was constructed of elements which had themselves to undergo subtraction in order to fit together but which find their final form only in combination. Tony Smith's *She Who Must Be Obeyed* (fig. 302) was made of wood, joined and painted. Later it was fabricated in steel by welding, another form of building. These are very obvious forms of built sculpture because they involve putting separate components together to form a whole. The most common type of built sculpture, however, is terra-cotta sculpture (the kind shown in figure 348). It is of earthenware, a rather soft and porous clay fired at relatively low temperatures (1740–2130° F.) in an oven called a kiln.

Clay is the residue of decomposed granite. A sticky substance, it clings to itself because of the peculiar shape of the particles: they are not granular, like particles of sand, but flakelike, which is why they tend to adhere to each other. This makes clay malleable when wet and indurate when dry, an ideal material for the sculptor. Wet clay is usually built, wad by wad, into a piece; it can also be shaped into solid blocks and carved, or thinned into the liquid form called *slip* and cast in plaster molds.

In its raw form clay is highly fragile, but when it is fired it becomes quite hard. In drying and firing, clay shrinks considerably. One way to keep shrinkage to a minimum and decrease the possibility of cracking is to introduce into the clay body a material called "grog" (fired clay which has been ground). Another way is to fire the body very slowly—as is done in making bricks. To prevent uneven shrinkage sculptors usually hollow out the piece from the bottom, leaving an equal amount of clay on all sides. Dan Anderson's earthenware piece was built up hollow like a bowl or pitcher. Then it was decorated.

Frank Gallo's (born 1933) girls (fig. 349) are a different type of built sculpture. They are made of *epoxy resin* formed in molds of plaster and then pieced into amazingly voluptuous forms. Although the process entails the use of molds, it differs from conventional casting in that the material is not poured into the mold but is itself built up from fiber strips saturated with resin. The same technique produced a less appealing set of figures in Duane Hanson's *Tourists* (fig. 228).

Among the most intriguing built sculptures are Louise Nevelson's (born 1900) wood constructions (fig. 350), made up of odds and ends of woodwork, old boxes, and scraps from the carpenter's shop. They are peculiarly evocative, considering the unpretentious materials that have been used in their construction.

Somewhat related, in terms of the unexpected use of materials and methods previously associated with minor endeavors, are works by those artists who weave various

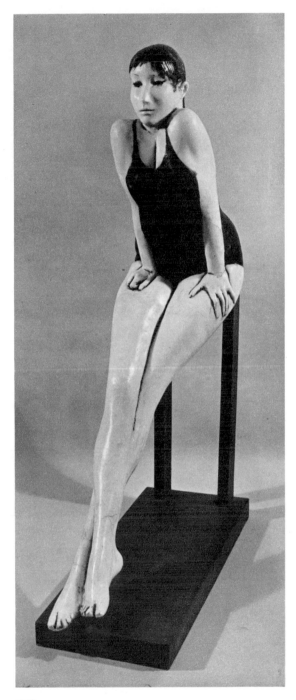

349
FRANK GALLO. *The Swimmer.* 1964.
Polyester resin, $65 \times 16 \times 41\frac{1}{4}''$.
Whitney Museum of American Art,
New York. Gift of the Friends of the
Whitney and the artist

350
LOUISE NEVELSON. *Sky Cathedral.* 1958.
Painted wood, 11′3½″ × 10′¼″ × 1′6″. The Museum of Modern Art, New York.
Gift of Mr. and Mrs. Ben Mildwoff

kinds of fibers into fabrics. Within the last twenty years fiber artists such as Arturo Sandoval (born 1942) have begun to exploit the ancient practical craft of weaving for distinctly artistic purposes. Sandoval's pieces are extraordinarily inventive and rich, particularly those that have a distinctively sculptural aspect (see fig. 351). He incorporates into his work such materials as microfilm, paper, battery cables, and mylar as well as the more conventional natural fibers of old-fashioned fabric design.

Cast (replacement) sculpture Sculpture can be cast from any material that can be transformed from a plastic, molten, or fluid state into a solid state and still hold together. Casting always involves the creation of a mold, that is, a negative form from which a positive cast may be taken. If you fill a bowl with fruit gelatin (Jello) in liquid form and let it harden, then tip the bowl over to release the jellied dessert, you have made a casting. The bowl was the negative mold and the molded dessert the positive form, the casting. The same kind of thing can be done with plaster of Paris in place of gelatin or (given a silica bowl) with molten bronze.

A small thing made of solid bronze poses no problems, but a moderately large bronze statue does. For a work as large as or larger than Boccioni's *Unique Forms of Continuity in Space* (fig. 317) it is normal to cast the piece so that its inside is hollow. To do so is more economical, since less metal is used. It also produces a lighter sculpture. And hollow structures are actually stronger than solid ones. Since bronze castings shrink when they cool, solid ones run a greater chance of cracking than hollow ones.

The most flexible method for producing hollow castings of metal is the *cire-perdue*, or *lost-wax*, method. The Boccioni was done by this process, and so was the twelfth-century head by an Ife tribesman in Nigeria (fig. 60).

351
ARTURO ALONZO SANDOVAL. *Pond.* 1977. Woven battery cable with patina, 5′ × 9′ × 2″. Private collection

352
AUGUSTE RODIN. *The Walking Man.* 1905. Bronze, height 87⅞″. Courtesy of Mr. B. Gerald Cantor, New York and Beverly Hills

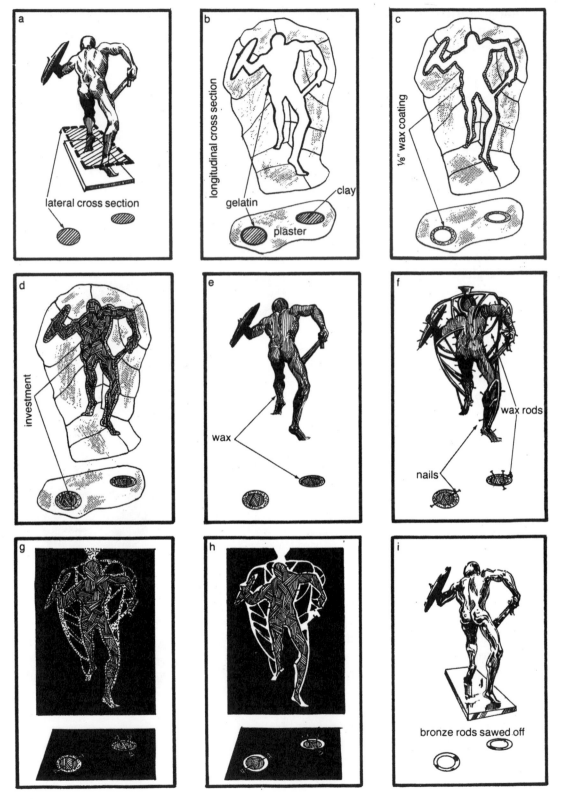

a — lateral cross section

b — longitudinal cross section — gelatin — plaster — clay

c — ⅛″ wax coating

d — investment

e — wax

f — wax rods — nails

g

h

i — bronze rods sawed off

353
Lost-wax process

One of the great masters of lost-wax bronzes was Auguste Rodin (1840–1917), whose *Walking Man* is reproduced here (fig. 352).

Close examination of the *Walking Man* would reveal many marks and impressions that suggest direct modeling as if in clay. This is because a bronze casting is made from a sculptural model of wax or clay that is exactly the size and precise character the artist wants the finished work to be.

The lost wax process is depicted in figure 353. The lower diagrams are of the cross section indicated by the dotted line. (A) The clay model is (B) completely covered with flexible gelatin, which can be cut apart and removed without losing any of the details. It is supported by a plaster jacket. (C) The gelatin mold is taken off and then coated on the inside with wax to the normal thickness of a bronze statue—about an eighth of an inch. (D) The mold is filled with an investment material made of plaster of Paris and silica. (E) Having removed the mold, we are left with a perfect wax casting identical in size and contour to the clay model and filled with a core of investment material. (F) Rods of wax are applied to the casting. These rods will carry off melted wax during baking and eventually will provide channels for molten bronze to enter and for air to escape. Iron nails, driven through the wax into the investment core, protrude from the cast. (G) In preparation for baking, the cast is covered with an outer mold of plaster-silica material. It surrounds the rods and nails. (H) The whole thing is put into a kiln and heated to 1500°F. This melts and burns out all the wax in the form. What is left is the core, separated from the mold by a space an eighth of an inch wide and held in place by the nails. This is the space formerly filled by the wax, hence the term *lost* wax. (I) Molten bronze is poured into the *casting gate,* a large opening at the top of the mold, and fills the cavity. When the bronze has cooled and hardened, the outer

mold and inner core are removed, leaving a bronze replica of the wax form complete with the rods and gates. (Accomplishing this in such a way that a number of casts can be made from the same mold and core becomes complicated, but the problems of the foundryman need not concern us here.) The gating structure of rods is cut from the cast with a hacksaw, and then the surface of the work is finished: the holes left by the anchor nails are plugged, the rough edges are reworked, and some areas are accented by the use of files and punches (this last is called *chasing*). If it has been necessary to saw parts of the cast apart in order to remove the core, these parts will be joined together. Today, with modern electronic equipment, it is possible to weld and braze bronze joints. But it is simpler to follow the procedure of antiquity—joining by pounding with a hammer. Bronze is sufficiently malleable to do this without betraying the seam.

After a bronze is finished, the sculptor may wish to enhance it with color. If left alone, the metal will in time acquire the *patina,* or thin layer of corrosion, that gives it its characteristic green or dark brown color, but the natural process of oxidation can be hastened by brazing and the application of organic acids. Obviously, there are many other possibilities. The sculpture can be painted with enamels, materials can be applied to its surface, colored lights can be set to play on it. But sculptors have usually preferred the natural effect over the artificial.

A contemporary artist/jeweler, E. Austin Goodwin (born 1930), creates fantastical sculpture on a minute scale through a variation of the lost-wax process. His extraordinary chess pieces (fig. 354) were formed in wax from which one-piece molds were made. The wax having been melted out, sterling silver was forced into the cavity by *centrifugal casting*—a procedure in which the mold itself is spun at a very high rate of speed while locked onto the end of a steel arm so that molten metal is, quite literally, hurled into the mold space, filling every cranny. Each of these chess pieces is unique since the individual molds were destroyed once casting had been completed.

In the photographs one views each team as an opponent would at the outset of the game; pawns forming the first line, then (left to right) rook, knight, bishop, king and queen, bishop, knight, rook. The positions of queen and king are, of course, transposed in the white-and-black lineups so that, like the other pieces, they face one another across the field of play. Each queen is crowned with a ruby, and both kings wear semiprecious stones in their collars. The pawns, says Goodwin, are hybrids invented by him—the black ones predominantly animal-fish-reptile combinations, the white mostly bird-animal mixtures. The rooks are storybook Bavarian castles, the knights centaurs, the queens sphinxes, the kings dragons, and the bishops "Hindu juggernauts, complete with devout pilgrims being crushed underwheel." Overall, the black team has a more sinister, ominous, and imposing character than the white, which is intended to seem comparatively benign.

Goodwin's work is an example of the conscientious, yet lighthearted way a contemporary craftsperson may approach a time-worn task. Given the solemnity with which European culture surrounds the ritual of chess, these chessmen seem almost frivolous despite the preciosity of their materials. Still, beneath the superficial appearance lurks a profound awareness of the fundamental nature of the game and of the functions of the individual pieces; thus, the queen is the most powerful piece and also the most richly decorated, the knights are tosspot centurions of both four-footed and two-hoofed varieties, and the kings (whose capture is the object of the game) are rather stupid-looking dragons whose evasive maneuvers are limited to clumsy staggers from square to square, one at a time. The nature of the game and the character of those who play it are revealed in subtler ways than may at first seem evident. In a special way, too, the pieces resemble the game itself; they are characterized by an introspectiveness that shouts for attention in a whisper.

Found sculpture Sometimes, in a junkyard, attic, or at the beach, one discovers things never intended to be artistic which nonetheless have all the characteristics of a work of art when seen with artistry in mind. For example, figure 355 is an iron object I call *Miss America* because of the long legs, absurdly high torso, and tiny head. It might very well be a welded-steel statue by a modern artist with a satirical turn of mind. But it isn't; it's a nineteenth-century tennis-net tightener. An artist I know had it welded onto a metal plate and gave it to me as a tasteful jest. It is an example of *found art*. One of the simplest and most exquisite of these "works" I've ever seen was a chrome-plated camshaft set vertically on an ebony base.

Duchamp's urinal called *Fountain* and Man Ray's *Indestructible Object* (fig. 12) are found art with an ideological purpose. Kienholz's tableau (fig. 6) is not really found art so much as a *combine*, a combination of common items presented to us as artistically meaningful.

ARCHITECTURE

Of all the fine arts, architecture is the most complicated, the most comprehensive, and the most expensive. It reveals the values of different periods and places to a far greater degree than any other art because it usually represents the major artistic investment of a society. Consider the contrast between a fourteenth-century European town and contemporary Manhattan.

In the Middle Ages the cathedral was the

354

E. AUSTIN GOODWIN. *Chess set.* 1978.
Silver, onyx, limba wood, and jewels,
$1\frac{3}{4} \times 3\frac{1}{4}''$ tall. Private collection

most prominent building in a town. It
loomed more than a hundred feet above the
marketplace. From almost any point its
spires, its buttresses, its walls dominated the
scene. It rose up among small buildings like
a great island of power, a carnate symbol of
the authority of the Church as a worldly institution, an institution to which all men
looked for spiritual succor in times of fear and
on whose charity they sometimes could rely
in times of famine. The cathedral commanded
the town in a quite literal way, too. Its spires
served as lookout posts in time of war. In
peace the music of its bells filled the air
throughout the day. (The word *belfry* is
derived from the Middle English word
berfray, a watchtower used in warfare to gain
a higher lookout. Since the church towers

were used for the same purpose, they were
sometimes called berfrys. Over the years the
pronunciation of the word changed to
belfry. The change from *r* to *l* is common, and
the association with bells made it all the more
likely in this case.) The cathedral made it
quite obvious that in the year of our Lord
(anno Domini) 1325 the Church was the most
powerful institution on earth.

In the vicinity of Rockefeller Center in
Manhattan are a couple of cathedrals built
in imitation of the Gothic and every bit as
large. Poor little things; they look tiny and
forlorn against the backdrop of gigantic
towers of commerce and pleasure. A two-
hundred-foot church spire is a mere trifle
compared with one of those skyscrapers. The
RCA Building is 850 feet tall. And it is by no

355
MARTHA HOLDEN.
Miss America. 1963.
Found object welded to base.
Private collection

Classical architecture In surveys of the history of architecture one normally begins with the Egyptians. But few of their motifs have real currency today. This is not true of the architecture of the ancient Greeks and Romans. Their building styles and elements were revived during the Renaissance, and many of the forms you see in American and European public buildings are imitations of ancient Classical prototypes.

Early in Greek history the three *orders* (fig. 356) of Greek architecture emerged. An order is a specific type of base, column, and entablature forming the unit of a style. The diagram describes the principal elements and subelements that constitute the orders. These proportions, however, are not in scale from one to another. For instance, a Doric column is typically much thicker than the other two, which have comparatively slender shafts. (See the glossary for more precise definitions of the elements.)

The Greeks considered the *Doric* order a masculine form and the lighter *Ionic* a feminine style. The *Corinthian* was not popular among Greeks even though it was their invention; a Classical building containing Corinthian columns is almost surely Roman.

The finest example of the Doric order occurs in a building constructed about 2500 years ago on a hill in Athens called the Acropolis. The Parthenon (fig. 357) has been a noble ruin only since 1687. At that time the Turks, who ruled Greece, were warring with the Republic of Venice. A Venetian bomb set off gunpowder stored in the ancient temple, and the resulting explosion destroyed the central portion of the building. Later, between 1801 and 1803, the British ambassador to Turkey, Lord Elgin, arranged to have most of the sculpture removed and taken to England where it now resides in the British Museum. (At the time, and in some quarters still, Lord Elgin's actions were considered criminal despite the fact that he sold the statues to the

means the largest building in New York City. Obviously, the society that builds such architecture is not terribly devout; at any rate, religion does not play anything like the role it did in fourteenth-century Europe. Now the Church looks to the State for protection, and men stake their hopes on economics and technology, not on the will of God. This is clearly evidenced in the scale of the buildings themselves. It is a gross contrast, but a very real one.

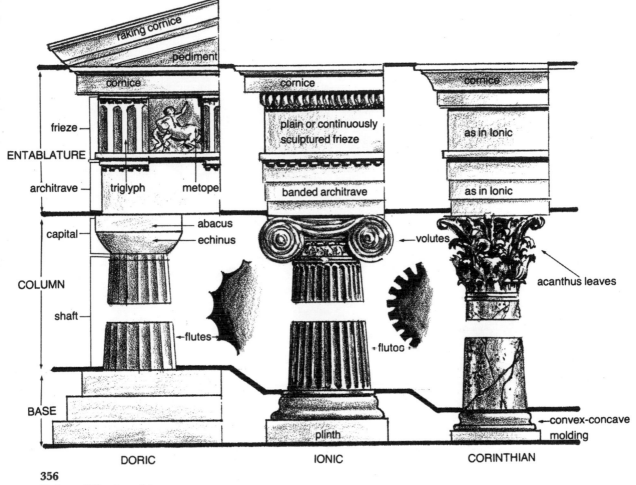

356
Orders of Greek architecture

British government at a great financial loss to himself. In his day the statues were being ignored and would probably have fallen to ruin. He seems to have acted out of highly civilized motives and, in fact, we probably owe their existence to him.) The fragments are now popularly known as the Elgin Marbles. Despite these subtractions, the building remains one of the great edifices of the world.

The Parthenon is an example of *post-and-lintel* construction. That is, posts hold up horizontal beams (lintels), and the roof is laid over and across the support system. The engineering system is a simple one, and it has severe limitations, the most obvious of which is that posts cannot be far apart because stone has so little tensile strength that a long stone beam will break.

What is impressive about the Parthenon is not the engineering but the refinements its architects introduced. Because long horizontal lines in buildings give an impression of drooping, İctinus and Callicrates contrived to put a faint upward curve in all the steps, cornices, and other prolonged horizontals. Since a completely straight column appears to be concave, the Parthenon's columns were carved with a convex bulge. Such a curve is

357
ICTINUS AND CALLICRATES. The Parthenon, Acropolis,
Athens. 448–432 B.C.

called *entasis*. Too, a structure which is per-
pendicular to the ground often looks as
though it is leaning forward. This illusion was
neutralized in the Parthenon by tilting its
front slightly backward. Because a column
which is silhouetted against a bright background seems smaller than one which is not,
the four corner columns—the ones most often
seen against the sky—were made a little
larger than the others. Finally, the architects
have overcome a problem common to long
colonnades, namely, that when all the spaces
between columns actually are equal they do
not appear equal. That is an effect of perspective distortion. It is negated in the

Parthenon by making the spaces widest in the
center and progressively smaller toward the
ends of the colonnade. The deviations involved in the use of entasis, bowing, tilting,
and varied intercolumnation are about two
and a half inches at most. This isn't enough
to disturb an onlooker, but the prestige of the
temple shows that these devices were effective. In the earlier part of the twentieth century the Parthenon was reconstructed as ac-
curately as possible in the city of Nashville,
Tennessee (fig. 358). The reconstruction
gives us a good notion of what the original
building looked like.

Where the Greeks strove for perfection and

refinement in their buildings, the Romans preferred majesty. One of the best techniques for achieving scale in building is a device called the *arch*. Arches are based on the fact that if two things of equal weight lean against each other, both will stand. In a structure like a Roman aqueduct (fig. 359) the stones that make any single arch are literally falling toward the center of the arch. The keystone at the center of the top of the curve forms the resting place where all the stones lean together. The stones on the bottom don't pop out because of the equal counterthrust of the arches on either side or (at the ends of the arcade) by the sheer mass of stone. One of the advantages of the system is that no more stone is needed to support an arch at the end of a million arches than is needed to support one arch alone. If you could build an arcade like the Segovia aqueduct clear around the globe so that it met itself, it would be self-supporting. In fact, cylindrical arcades are precisely that.

Roman aqueducts are a perfect example of what the term *imperialism* really means. These structures transported water from distant points into the centers of the cities of the Roman Empire. In a day when water was really precious and was jealously guarded, the peoples conquered by Rome's legions had as much water as they could possibly use. Some of the aqueducts are over thirty miles long. They are artificial streams, carrying water by gravity downgrade from the source to the urban terminus. If you think seriously about this kind of project for a moment, you will see what an impressive feat of engineering, surveying, and masonry construction an aqueduct is. Building an aqueduct is far more difficult than building a pyramid (really just a regularized pile of rock) or a Greek temple. It is not surprising that the Romans were able to Latinize most of the known world. Not only were they courageous warriors and masterful strategists, they were also superb administrators, great public relations men, and be-

358

HART AND HART. The Nashville Parthenon, Nashville, Tennessee (second replica). 1920

359
Roman aqueduct.
Segovia, Spain

neficent rulers. Their conquered subjects came to be dependent on them. Rome, of course, had markets for its goods and resources to exploit for its industry.

In the capital city itself the Romans built a palace to all the gods, the Pantheon (fig. 360). It involves a different kind of arch, the dome, and a material the Romans used magnificently, concrete. (Many people think concrete is a recent invention, but it is not. What *is* fairly new is steel-reinforced concrete.) The Romans accomplished a good deal with their

variety, which used pieces of cut stone for reinforcement. Many of the great buildings of Rome—the Colosseum, the Basilica of Constantine, the Baths of Caracalla—are built of it.

Medieval architecture   A dome is a form of *vaulting*, the spanning of space with arched roofs. The simplest form of vault is the *barrel vault* (fig. 361), nothing more than one arch set against another until there is a tunnel of arches. When you run two barrel vaults through each other at right angles, you have a *groin vault* (fig. 362). Such a vault is stronger than a barrel vault and also permits openings out to all four sides.

Vaulting made it possible for the Church to construct the vast cathedrals that dominated the towns of the Middle Ages. These were designed to accommodate large crowds of local worshipers and pilgrims and huge cadres of clerics and monks who performed the rituals and manned the choirs.

There are two large divisions of architectural church style in the Middle Ages. The *Romanesque* style obtains from about 1000 to 1150. The *Gothic* style was prevalent from about 1150 to 1500. The dates are general boundaries, of course, and the individual buildings differ tremendously from place to place. The Romanesque is more varied than the Gothic; it is comparable to the Romance languages—Italian, French, Spanish, and Portuguese—which deviate from the common Latin of their origins. In broad outline, though, the churches of the medieval period have the same floor plan and functional divisions.

The typical floor plan of a church (fig. 363) throughout the Middle Ages is in the form of a Latin cross. The arms of the cross

360
The Pantheon,
Rome. 118–125 A.D.

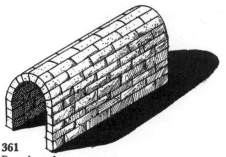

361
Barrel vault

362
Groin vault

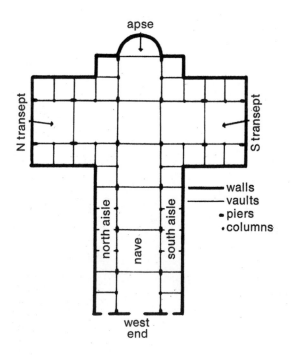

apse

N transept

S transept

walls
vaults
piers
columns

north aisle

nave

south aisle

west
end

363
Floorplan of a medieval church

form *transepts,* and the main body is the *nave,* the principal open area of the interior. On either side of the nave is at least one *aisle.* Christian cathedrals are always oriented to the compass points so that the worshipers look to the East (toward Jerusalem). The altar is at the eastern end of the nave, and beyond it is an exedra called the *apse.* West ends vary considerably from one part of Europe to another, but they frequently contain two bell towers, or at least a heavy block of building, to serve as an accent for the entrance.

A cross section (fig. 364) of the building usually has the parts shown here. There may be more aisles, and the proportions may differ, but the pattern is pretty much standard. The *clerestory* is a section of the building which rises clear of the roofs of the other parts, and whose walls contain windows which admit light into the nave. The *triforium galleries* run along the top of the aisles and accommodated the overflow traffic on special occasions.

St.-Sernin, a Romanesque church in Toulouse, France (fig. 365), was built over a forty-year span on either side of 1100. Looking down on the building from the air, one can observe that it has most of the characteristics of our plan and cross section. A central spire rises from the place where the nave and transepts cross. The contour of the aisle roof and nave is obvious against the block of the west entrance. There are small apses off the main apse; these are chapels. The aerial view shows us a characteristic of most Romanesque churches: they are composed of clear geometric masses—cylinders, cubes, hemispheres, and planes—linked together into a coherent whole. The walls of the building are very heavy so that they can support the masonry structure that rises aloft.

There is no clerestory in St.-Sernin, and its barrel-vaulted nave is not completely satisfactory as a ceiling, so we shall turn elsewhere for a more typical Romanesque interior. St.-Etienne's (fig. 366) designers vaulted their

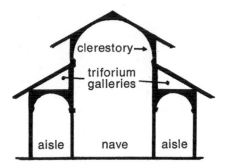

364

Transverse section of a
medieval church

roof with a series of domical vaults, each divided into six sections by ribs. For every dome vault in the nave ceiling there are two small ones in the aisle. In St.-Etienne heavy piers hold up the aisle domes and also carry the main weight of the nave. In some Romanesque churches the supporting piers alternate with single columns that support aisle domes and reinforce the transverse ribs of the nave domes. Either of the systems makes it possible for builders to include a gallery above the aisles and also to retain the clerestory. At St.-Etienne domical vaults arch up on all four sides, so the sides along the wall can serve as windows for the nave. The relative lightness of St.-Etienne was the Romanesque inspiration to the Gothic that succeeded it.

Every true Gothic church has *pointed arches*. These alone don't make it Gothic; some Romanesque buildings also use the pointed arch. But this kind of arch (fig. 367) has attributes which lent it to the aims of the Gothic builders. First, it has less lateral thrust than a round arch. Secondly, the height of a pointed arch is not determined by its width as is that of a round arch. If you want to make a round arch 50 percent higher than another round arch, it must also be made twice as

365
St.-Sernin,
Toulouse, France. 1080–1120

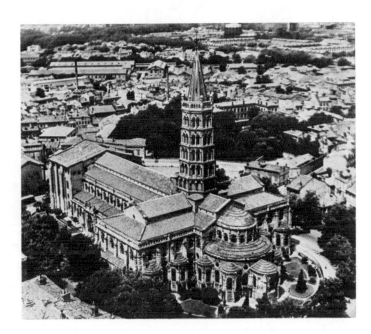

366
St.-Etienne,
Caen, France. 1068–1120

wide. To make a pointed arch higher one has only to change the curve of the sides. Such flexibility is the essence of the Gothic. For Gothic architecture is really a particular kind of engineering system. Its major features are the pointed arch and the *flying buttress.*

Notre Dame in Paris is, I imagine, the most famous of all Gothic cathedrals. Its west facade (fig. 368) reveals the divisions within. The central portal corresponds to the nave, and the other two to the aisles. The great *rose window* above the middle portal overlooks the nave. Looking at the building from the southeast (fig. 369), one sees how the towers on the west side blocked our view of the gallery roof, the clerestory, the transepts, and the nave roof. They also prevented us from seeing those queer arms sticking out all over the place; they run down both walls and around the apse. They are flying buttresses, and their function is to absorb the thrust of the stone ceiling of the nave. A glance at a transverse section (fig. 370) will show how the system operates. The shading represents what is closed in, the interior. The aisle wall is supported by *pier buttresses;* the nave is carried by the flying buttress, really a detached arch which conveys lateral thrust over to the pier.

Notre Dame's interior (fig. 371) is loftier and lighter than Romanesque interiors. The vaulting of the nave is similar to the vaulting in St.-Etienne; but the pointed arches that divide the bays permit the crown of the vaults to be level rather than domical, and they free more space for clerestory windows. In fact, the exterior walls of Gothic buildings are practically nothing but windows. Romanesque walls had to be thick to support the weight of the vaults. Notre Dame's buttressing would provide support even if the walls were all pulled away. This fact enabled Gothic masons to incorporate vast amounts of stained glass into their churches. Stained glass has a tendency to absorb light, and the buildings are actually rather dark despite the stupen-

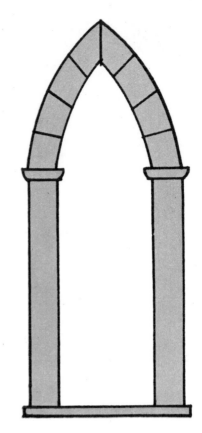

367
Pointed arch

dous amount of window surface. But the windows themselves are like magic jewels, and the shafts of rainbow light that fall onto the stone columns and paint bare floors with radiance transform cold buildings into holy places.

Renaissance architecture For centuries the Gothic system of construction remained the loftiest attainment of architectural engineering. No major technical advances beyond it were made until modern times. Still, it would be a mistake to assume that all of the stylistic variations that occurred between the emergence of the Renaissance and the opening of the industrial age were of a purely

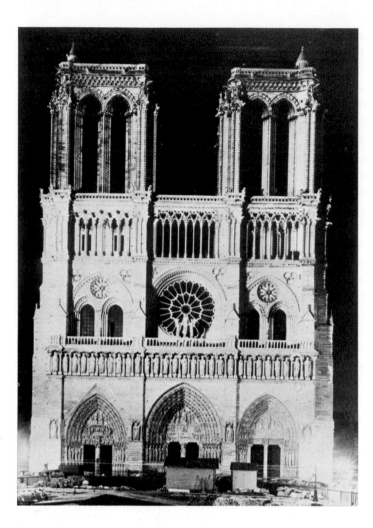

368
Notre Dame,
Paris. 1163–1200.
West facade

369
Notre Dame,
Paris. View from the
southeast

cosmetic nature. Consider, for instance, the dominant feature of the city of Florence, Italy—the great dome of its cathedral (fig. 372). Its construction posed a singularly difficult problem, and the architect solved it with the kind of ingenuity we might expect from the same mind that devised the Renaissance system of scientific perspective.

Filippo Brunelleschi (1377?–1446) surmounted the limitations of his medieval training when he devised a way to cap a medieval structure with the widest dome built since the Pantheon's and the highest one built up to that time. To accomplish this feat he had to invent a special machine to hoist stone, a unique scaffold to support the working masons, and even an unprecedented method of laying brick and masonry. The main difficulty to be overcome, however, was the sheer thrust of the dome at its base. The Pantheon dome had been cast of concrete; like an inverted teacup it bears directly down upon the supporting walls of the temple. But the Florentine dome is of brick and masonry. The tendency of the stones in such a dome is exactly the same as in any kind of arch; falling toward the center, they push outward at the sides. Yet, in Florence the dome, about 150 feet across and 308 feet tall, appears to rest effortlessly, unbuttressed upon its octagonal base. How can that be? What holds in the sides? They are restrained by a girdle. Beneath the superficial covering visible to the eye is hidden a structural system of separate stone arches leashed together by a girdle of heavy, chain-linked, oaken beams. These contain the thrust of the stone in the same way that iron bands strap barrel staves together to make a container that is both strong and self-supporting.

The cathedral dome is thus a clear example of newness set upon the foundations of the past. The building itself dates from the fourteenth century, and the octagonal opening for the dome was finished about 1405.

Everything up to that point was strictly medieval in character. Only the *campanile*, or bell tower, might be considered a partial exception; it seems somewhat independent of the building to which it is connected. Designed by Giotto, it has a geometric clarity of parts that at first resembles the Romanesque. But like Brunelleschi's dome, the campanile anticipates the coming age in its logical clarity and self-sufficiency. Its individual parts have a distinctive, autonomous character, much like the parts of a

370

Transverse section
of a Gothic church

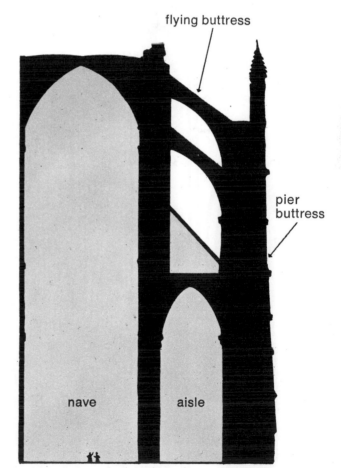

371
Notre Dame, Paris. Nave

372

FILIPPO BRUNELLESCHI. Dome, Florence
Cathedral. 1420–36

373

FILIPPO BRUNELLESCHI. Pazzi Chapel,
Sta. Croce, Florence. Begun 1430–33

painting from the late fifteenth or early sixteenth century. Masaccio, Botticelli, and
Leonardo sought just such clarity in their
pictures. They and their patrons shared a
taste for natural appearances wedded to
abstract design, but they also felt that the
harmonies of a simple, clear geometry dis-
closed the pattern of the hidden orderliness
of God's universe.

That conviction sprang, most probably,
from a passionate interest in ancient Greece
that had emerged in Florence during the end
of the fourteenth century. As a matter of
fact, the term *Renaissance* is ordinarily taken
literally to mean a renascence (or rebirth)
of the Classical humanism of ancient Greece
and Rome. Such an interest in things Classi-

cal came to be called *Humanism* largely
because of a medieval distinction between
Divine Letters (writings on religion) and
Humane Letters (writing concerned with
worldly affairs). Mainly, Renaissance *Humanism* was a Christian expression of Plato's
(427?–347? B.C.) confidence in the essential
rationality of existence.[6]

Since Roman ruins stood everywhere in
Italy and some ancient buildings and roads
were still in use, it is not surprising that the
association of Classical design and humanist
reason should have found expression in paintings, sculptures, and buildings taking their
inspiration from the ancient world.

Brunelleschi's later buildings reveal a progressively greater commitment to Classical

374
ANDREA PALLADIO. San Giorgio Maggiore,
Venice. Designed 1565. Facade

models. In his Pazzi Chapel (fig. 373), for instance, there are Corinthian columns, an entablature, a central plan similar to that of the Pantheon, and even such Classical refinements as making the height of the supported wall the same as the width of the intercolumniations.

The life history and work of a man like Brunelleschi show just how arbitrary are academic distinctions such as medieval, Renaissance, or Modern. Actually, each age is part of a continuous stream of developments, some of which anticipate the future, some of which perpetuate the past. The Renaissance was full of architects designing Gothic buildings, painters emulating Giotto instead of Masaccio, and most people were no more conscious of being part of a rebirth of Classical thought than the reader is aware of being the representative of some massive historical tendency. Yet, there did emerge during the period an influential new culture with a distinctive literature, music, art, and architecture.

By 1570 Andrea Palladio (1518–1580) was able to compile his version of Renaissance architecture in a set of four books, the *Quattro Libri*, which conveyed the Palladian vision to the entire Western world. His words and drawings contained within these volumes made Palladio what one critic has called "the most influential architect in history."[7] The title is well given. From Palladio's style came Thomas Jefferson's Monticello and the University of Virginia; he was the inspiration for the master of London's skyline, Sir Christopher Wren, designer of St. Paul's; nearly all of the elegant mansions of England and America during the seventeenth and eighteenth centuries have their ancestry in Palladian designs.

His most famous work is a Venetian church, San Giorgio Maggiore (fig. 374). This facade would by itself serve to make Palladio's place in history, in at least a small way. You may have noticed that other church architects—for example, the designers of St.-Sernin (fig. 365) and Notre Dame (fig. 368)—concealed the rather queer shape dictated by the cross section (fig. 364) behind the massive walls and towers of the west entrances. In terms of aesthetic unity these disguises were never entirely satisfactory even though they were, as individual things, quite beautiful. Palladio devised a unique and astonishingly plausible solution to this formal

375
ANDREA PALLADIO. San Giorgio Maggiore, Venice. Interior

376
CLAUDE PERRAULT. East Front of the Louvre,
Paris. 1667–70

problem. Rather than screen out the gap between the central nave and the side aisles, he accepted and intensified it by imposing upon a wide-set temple form, ornamented with pilasters, a lofty, slender temple supported by engaged columns. This is an ideal synthesis of Classical Roman elements with the medieval arrangement dictated by function and tradition. It would seem to have been the definitive answer to the problem and yet it is unusual among Palladian inventions in that it has never been repeated and has but rarely served as a point of departure for similar schemes. Perhaps it appeared so late that, unlike earlier treatments, it could not be construed as anything except the work of one man's mind and, thus,

made any derivations appear to be mere copies.

The interior of San Giorgio Maggiore (fig. 375) has the measured grace one associates with Palladio and those inspired by him. It is rather pristine, virtually without adornment. The massive pilasters, engaged columns, and gigantic piers comprise a majestic parade of flat, round, and blocked forms.

Baroque and Rococo architecture Heinrich Wölfflin felt that architecture, no less than painting and sculpture, responded to his descriptive polarities—that the buildings of the Renaissance were linear, clear, and multiple while Baroque structures were painterly (that is, dominated by light and movement), unclear, and unified. His system works less well when applied to buildings rather than to pictures, perhaps, but there is quite a good deal to be said in favor of it. Yet, even Wölfflin's categories could not really absorb the varieties of style present during the seventeenth and eighteenth centuries.

The most common way of describing the architecture of the *Baroque* period is to say that it is "ornate." But this is true of the architecture of the period only to the extent that it is accurate to say of Baroque paintings that they are "flamboyant" in the manner of Rubens or Tintoretto. Poussin's work is usually not; neither is that of most of the Dutch. Similarly, there are several kinds of Baroque architectural styles. Some buildings, like the east facade of the Louvre (fig. 376), are more restrained than Palladio's; some are heavily laden with ornamental embellishments. Thus, Carlo Rainaldi (1611–1691), in his Sta. Maria in Campitelli (fig. 377), piles columns and pilasters atop clusters of columns and pilasters to support segments of entablatures, cornices, raking cornices, and arches. The interior shows a similar profusion of detail. A palace by Guarino Guarini (1624–1683), illustrated in figure 378, is less heavily garnished but exhibits its own kind of enrichment of the facade in the undulation of the wall surface itself. Guarini was fascinated by geometric intricacies, and some of his designs are of such ingenuity that they are almost fatiguing to behold. For instance, the supporting elements of a chapel dome in Turin (fig. 379) take the form of hexagons inscribed within one another at lateral shifts of 30°.

Elaboration of standard components and exaggeration of the stylistic features of earlier styles were very much in the mood of the Baroque period. The Italians tended toward fanciful extravagance; the French preferred dignity on a majestic scale. But, whether the approach was plain or fancy, the main characteristic of the Baroque was grandiosity of conception, and the great buildings of this age often overawe us with effects that are mainly visual rather than structural.

Nowhere is that trait more evident than in the pilgrimage church of Vierzehnheiligen (The Fourteen Saints) near Bamberg, Germany. The exterior gives no real hint of the fanciful complication of the interior (fig. 380). Within, every surface is polychrome, all of them seem to float and flow together, and nothing looks altogether solidified. The architect, Balthasar Neumann (1687–1753), turned the realities of a large-scale building into a fairyland of the imagination.

Some authorities describe Neumann's work as *Rococo*. No distinction in the entire history of art is less clearly drawn than the one made

377

CARLO RAINALDI. Sta. Maria in Campitelli, Rome. 1663–67. Facade

378

GUARINO GUARINI.
Palazzo Carignano,
Turin. Begun 1679

379

GUARINO GUARINI.
Dome, Chapel of the
Holy Shroud, Cathedral,
Turin. 1668–94

between Baroque and Rococo. This is not to say that it is a meaningless discrimination. Rococo connotes frivolity and a fragility of effect. Usually, the term can be applied with greatest usefulness to fashionable French interiors of the eighteenth century. One of the finest examples is the Salon de la Princesse in the Hôtel de Soubise (fig. 381) in Paris.[8] Here, the grave pomposity of the Baroque gives way to a more lighthearted decor. Classical orders have been supplanted by pictorial diversions. Everything is framed or accented by elaborately delicate plaster moldings. Wood is rarely plain; nearly everywhere it is covered by molded plaster, smooth white paint, or pseudo-Classical representations of antique heroes and heroines acting out their mythological roles. Most often, the buildings containing such rooms were themselves restrained. The houses and their owners were alike; they clothed an exquisite hedonism in garments of conspicuous refinement.

Nineteenth-century architecture The central fact of the nineteenth century is the Indus-

trial Revolution. Factory-produced bricks, iron posts, and steel beams could be carried anywhere by trains and steamships. Inevitably, the availability of such structural materials in the profusion that mass production made possible was going to make for portentous changes in the nature of buildings and in the ways they were concentrated together. But, for the first part of the century, this would not have seemed the case. Ar-

380
BALTHASAR NEUMANN.
Vierzehnheiligen.
Near Bamberg. 1743–74.
Interior

381
GERMAIN BOFFRAND.
Salon de la Princesse,
Hôtel de Soubise,
Paris. Begun 1732

382
CHARLES GARNIER. Opéra,
Paris. 1861–74

383

GUSTAVE EIFFEL.
Eiffel Tower,
Paris. 1889

384

HECTOR GUIMARD.
Métro entrance,
Paris. 1900

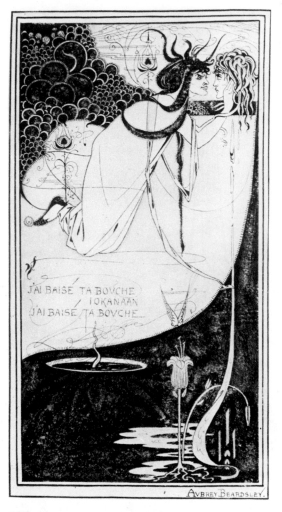

JAI BAISE TA BOVCHE
IOKANAAN
JAI BAISE TA BOVCHE

AVBREY BEARDSLEY.

385

AUBREY BEARDSLEY. *Salome.* 1893.
India ink and watercolor, $10\frac{7}{8} \times 5\frac{3}{4}''$.
Princeton University Library, Princeton, N. J.

Renaissance facades, and a great many anomalous designs date from this time. But there were also some glorious achievements.

Paris is surely among the most beautiful and picturesque of all cities. Its stately thoroughfares and mighty monuments date, for the most part, from the reign of Napoleon III, whose principal engineer, Baron Georges-Eugène Haussmann (1809–1891), rebuilt Paris with one eye on beauty and imperialist showmanship while the other was firmly fixed on the military usefulness of wide, well-lit boulevards and open squares. Baron Haussmann's Paris lent itself to dominance by artillery and massed troops with a clear field of fire, unlike the narrow streets of earlier times where a group of ten good revolutionaries could resist a hundred of the ruler's mercenaries simply by restricting the front to the width of an alleyway.

The focus of the Paris that Haussmann created was to be the Opéra (fig. 382), designed by Charles Garnier (1825–1898). Although this structure is of wrought iron, its visible surfaces are multicolored marbles, onyx, bronze, and other traditional materials. The facade is an opulent overlay of motifs culled from French and Italian palaces of the Renaissance. The very splendor of their profusion has been described as "barely tolerable" by a noted Renaissance specialist. He goes on to say of the Grand Staircase, possibly the most famous of all staircases, that its richness "becomes offensive to modern eyes."[9] His is a discriminating vision and the sensibility is a polished one. For us more ordinary people, however, the Opéra is the most illustrious of all theaters, a veritable measuring stick for what we mean by "magnificent." Of course, she's a bit of an old fraud, what with all of those columns and beams and neo-Baroque arches supporting nothing at all while they themselves are held up by a skeleton of iron. But what of it? The final effect is very grand and not at all

chitects—by then professionally trained in schools dedicated to the purpose—had the whole history of styles at their disposal and new materials with which to achieve constructions unfeasible in the ages when those styles first emerged. Nineteenth-century designers did not hesitate to conceal ironwork behind Gothic pinnacles, Ionic columns, or

incoherent. Still, one can understand Empress Eugénie's dismay over the sheer ostentation of the place. Certainly it appeals to some moderns largely because it gratifies our fantasies as to what grandeur really is. Appropriately, perhaps, it is a theatrical spectacle writ large. It is also a marvelously functional opera house; the architectural historian Nikolaus Pevsner has called it "glorious."[10] But no one could call the surface treatment straightforward or honest.

On the other hand, the structure that *has* become the focal point of modern Paris is altogether candid. The Eiffel Tower (fig. 383) is nothing more than a spire of exposed ironwork. Built for the Paris Exposition of 1889, the tower was designed by Gustave Eiffel (1832–1923), already celebrated as a designer of railway stations, bridges, and viaducts. Inspired by the pylons he had created for daring bridges over deep gorges and vast rivers in Europe, Africa, and Indo-China, his tower is 300 meters (984') high and, when built, was the tallest structure in the world.

That the tower should be as uncompromising as it is in expressing the purely engineering side of building is rather surprising. Eiffel himself was not advanced or radical in his artistic tastes; his home was filled with routinely uninspired, conservative art objects. His main purpose for the tower was to show that the French tricolor at its peak flew higher than the flag of any other nation. He would have liked to disguise his structural steel with a veneer of tradition, but as it turned out, the only concession made to decorative effect was in the purely ornamental arches

386

CHARLES MACKINTOSH. Glasgow School of Art. 1896–1910

387

LOUIS SULLIVAN. Wainwright Building, St. Louis, Missouri. 1890–91

388

LOUIS SULLIVAN. Ornamental panel from
the Schiller Building. 1892.
Terra cotta, 26½ × 26½″. Collection
Southern Illinois University at Edwardsville

that link the four great piers. For there were
some overwhelmingly practical reasons for
revealing the construction itself, the principal
one being the propaganda purpose of the
great exhibition. The French, having lost the
Franco-Prussian War of 1870–71 and having
suffered the economic consequences thereof,
were attempting to regain their share of the
world's business. Both the Eiffel Tower and
the great Hall of Machines by the architect
Dutert and the engineer Contamin were rad-
ically advanced, employing prefabricated
steel components assembled on the site to
create a situation in which the tallest structure in the world looked down upon a building whose span of 380 feet was unprecedented. These two huge structures dominated
the fair and advertised to the world that
France was in the technological forefront
of the Industrial Revolution despite the

damages she had suffered in the war.

At first the tower was very unpopular. To
the representatives of good taste it was considered a disgrace, an affront to the beautiful
city of Baron Haussmann. But by 1910 it
had become a beloved symbol of the unique-
ness of the ancient town and modern
metropolis whose very name suggested everything that was up-to-date and progressive.

Paris got the entrances to its subway
stations (fig. 384) a little more than a decade
after the tower. These take a very different
approach to the use of metal. Here, functional components of wrought iron have been
treated in a fanciful, decorative way to suggest that the Métro gives access to some
exotic, magical underworld. The designer,
Hector Guimard (1867–1942), was the leading exponent in France of a trend or movement called *Art Nouveau*. The term includes
all sorts of different stylistic approaches. Tif-
fany glass is considered exemplary of the
style, but so are the book illustrations of
Aubrey Beardsley (1872–1898) and the bold
geometry of buildings by the Scotsman
Charles Mackintosh (1868–1928). What ties
them all together is a common repulse of
strictly traditional forms. Normally, this took
an approach similar to that of Guimard;
sinuously wrought metals and interlaced lines
of a feverish movement entwine around flat,
unbroken areas or encircle an open space.
Where one might have expected plain
wrought iron, lilies and budding plants
burst forth. In just the opposite way Art
Nouveau illustrator Beardsley took a figure
like Salomé (fig. 385), who is usually treated
in a highly organic and sexually provocative
manner, and reduced nature to an exquisitely refined family of black-and-white
partitions.

Beardsley's deliberately "weird" approach
to his subject was motivated by the cult of
"decadence" subscribed to by Beardsley and
the author of *Salomé*, Oscar Wilde. Whatever

389
MIES VAN DER ROHE AND PHILIP JOHNSON.
Seagram Building,
New York. Designed 1958

in life the ordinary person might consider perverse or unnatural seemed inherently artistic to this segment of Art Nouveau. Mackintosh, quite contrary to this, was conventional in his personal life. Indeed, his buildings—though they sometimes appear extraordinarily modern—were often inspired by the traditional forms of baronial manor houses in his native Scotland. His Glasgow School of Art (fig. 386) took its lead from the baronial style but was given a unique, untraditional character by virtue of the elegantly elongated bay windows. Mackintosh also designed as much of the interiors of his buildings as possible; in this one, shelving, cabinetry, tables, and even the chairs were his creations. They tend to have the same economy of line and form as the exterior of the building, repeating throughout the attenuated proportions of the soaring window lines.

In one way or another, the Opéra, the Eiffel Tower, and Art Nouveau signify the forces setting the direction for modern architecture. That may seem an odd thing to say about the Opéra, but the mere fact that its ornate facade is draped upon a substructure of iron ties it to such advanced buildings as the Wainwright Building (fig. 387) in St. Louis, Missouri, designed by the American, Louis Sullivan.

If modern skyscrapers have a father, he is Louis Sullivan (1856–1924), and he owes his paternity to the existence of steel. Without steel beams the construction of a skyscraper would be unthinkable. Forged steel has higher compressive strength than stone and vastly more tensile strength than wood or iron. The Wainwright Building may seem quite conventional to modern eyes. It isn't even very tall. Its ten stories hardly compare with the soaring Eiffel Tower. But it represents a milestone in the development of high-rise architecture. The building itself is a cage of steel which reveals its gridlike cells in the verticals and horizontals of the window units. These are clad in vertical strips of brick and horizontal panels of terra-cotta embellished with one of the many Art Nouveau designs of Sullivan's own creation (fig. 388). Into this one building, then, are compressed all of the advanced trends in nineteenth-century building design: a steel skeleton revealed externally and neatly clad with the clean stylizations of Art Nouveau. The clarity of this late-nineteenth-century structure was further purified by twentieth-century architects working in what came to be called the *International Style*, an architectural movement that emphasized the properties of steel and strove to make buildings reveal them.

Twentieth-century architecture   Mies van der Rohe (1886–1969) was the outstanding spokesman for the International Style. His Seagram Building (fig. 389) is essentially a steel cage supporting floors and partitions to make rooms and corridors. The exterior is a light skin of bronze and amber-colored glass.

Skyscrapers worthy of the name did not appear first in New York City but were built initially in Chicago during the enormous building boom that followed the fire of 1871. One of the great architects of modern times, Frank Lloyd Wright (1869–1959), was a product of that boom. In 1936 he built a private home, the Kaufmann House (fig. 390), called *Falling Water* because it straddles a waterfall. One of the great home designs of all time, it is of interest here because it involves the use of steel-reinforced concrete and a structured system called *cantilever*. A cantilever is a horizontal beam extending out from a supporting post and carrying a load. Here the terraces are cantilevered. A central block of building houses utilities and chimneys and acts to anchor the horizontal extensions. Many skyscrapers and apartment houses utilize this system, which was first employed in steel bridges, cranes, and railway terminals.

390
FRANK LLOYD WRIGHT. Falling Water,
Bear Run, Pennsylvania. 1936

Another towering figure of modern architecture was inspired by a European exhibition of Wright plans. This creator, a Swiss named Charles-Edouard Jeanneret (1887–1965), adopted the pseudonym Le Corbusier (the name of his maternal grandmother). Le Corbusier built his first masterpiece of domestic architecture in France several years before Wright built Falling Water. The Villa Savoye (fig. 391) is as urbanely detached from Nature as Wright's house is integrated with her. Le Corbusier conceived of the home as a shelter from which nature could be viewed

and taken advantage of. The interior of the dwelling is far more complicated than it appears. The upper level is a box containing the living area. But part of it is open to the sky. Rooms lead onto a terrace that is sheltered by walls. These walls are penetrated by openings that extend the window lines. What you see in the photograph is the box that surrounds the irregular and beautifully articulated interior, an interior of several levels tied together and attached to the terraces by a series of ramps. The cylinders rising above the box form a tower housing the staircase

391
LE CORBUSIER. Villa Savoye,
Poissy, France. 1928–30

and act as a windbreak for the roof garden. Set well back beneath the overhang are the garage and the service functions.

Both Wright and Le Corbusier have designed major projects known to all the world —to cite only two, Wright's Guggenheim Museum and Le Corbusier's plan for the new capital of the Punjab at Chandigarh, India. In Chandigarh Le Corbusier got a chance to undertake an entire architectural environment—something both he and Wright had always wanted to do. Both had distinctive theories of how the vast populations of the world should be housed. Their differences in attitude are interesting to consider.

Wright, a son of the wide-open Midwest at the turn of the century, had the point of view of an American Romantic; he disliked cities and believed in the dispersal of the population through an open landscape of farms and unblemished nature. It is an appealing dream, one that the suburbanites seek and never find. Wright felt that by clever use of land and strategic placement of service centers and commercial complexes modern man could have the best of the rural and the industrial. This antagonism to population density is just what one would expect from the naturist who designed Falling Water.

Le Corbusier was a sophisticated European

intellectual. His ideal was to house people in tremendous buildings separated by parks and boulevards, canals and thoroughfares. He once proposed a solution to the traffic-population density problem which involved highways that would run on top of continuous apartment buildings of typically Le Corbusieran scale.

Whether cities are going to disappear or whether they will survive in some new form is still controversial. One thing is clear; the present form of the city is incapable of supporting life in a humane fashion. Even the wealthiest apartment dwellers are assailed by poisoned air, horrendous noise, and unsafe streets. Most thinkers today tend to incline in the direction Le Corbusier indicated—dense concentrations of people and unspoiled intervals between them.

One thinker and designer who has devoted considerable attention to the problems of survival on the planet Earth is R. Buckminster Fuller (born 1895). Fuller feels that all architecture of the past is obsolete; he would say that every building we have so far discussed is inappropriate for man's future existence on the Spaceship Earth. He was trained not as an architect but as an engineer, and his ideal structures from the past are not buildings, but plant stalks, crystals, tension bridges, sailing ships, and airplanes. Strength, efficiency, and lightness dominate his designs, the most famous of which is the *geodesic dome*. A geodesic is the shortest distance between two points on a mathematically derived surface such as a plane (where the geodesic is a straight line) or sphere (where the geodesic is the arc of a great circle, that is, a circle that is the intersection of the surface of a sphere with a plane passing through the center of the sphere). The largest of Fuller's domes is the one used in the United States Pavilion at Montreal's EXPO 67 (fig. 392). The dome is constructed of steel pipe and transparent acrylic panels. It is 200 feet

tall and 250 feet across. Altogether, the metal pipes weigh 720 tons. Yet, in terms of total space contained, this averages out to four ounces per cubic foot, an absolutely astonishing figure. No other man-made shelter comes close to the efficiency of the geodesic dome. These domes, built of triangular sections, can be constructed of anything from cardboard to steel and are being appropriated by all kinds of counter-culturists in both communes and private hideaways. They are tremendously strong—the tetrahedron, a pyramid composed of equilateral triangles, is the strongest structure known—and there seems no limit to the size that can be attained. Considering their advantages and spaciousness, the domes are dirt cheap. Fuller has proposed a two-mile-wide dome for New York City and is now designing a floating, two-hundred-story, tetrahedron-shaped city near Tokyo.

Another person who thinks on a grandiose scale is Paolo Soleri (born 1920), whose design for "Arcosanti" (fig. 393), a complete living-work environment in Arizona, locks three thousand souls into a commune that is really a vast building of interlocking concrete modules. It is with preservation of the surrounding wilderness in mind that Soleri proposes such dense concentrations of people; the landscape would be left as it has been for centuries. Soleri recognizes that people need privacy as well as a habitable natural environment beyond the walls. Presumably this is designed into the hivelike complex.

Similar concentrations of people have been living in Habitat (fig. 394), the massive experimental housing project built for EXPO 67. It looks weird, but its inhabitants like it. This pileup of one- and two-story apartments consists of precast modular boxes which were fitted together by an assembly-line technique. What is particularly intriguing about Habitat is that this machine-made stack of blocks makes buildings with hand-laid brick seem mechanistic. For Habitat is more like a Medi-

392
BUCKMINSTER FULLER.
United States Pavilion,
EXPO 67, Montreal. 1967

393
PAOLO SOLERI.
Project for "Arcosanti"

terranean seacoast village than an apartment house. The ingenious Israeli architect Moshe Safdie (born 1938) designed the cubicles so that they can be coupled together in a number of ways, then opened up and partitioned off to make individual interiors more distinctive than is customary in ordinary apartments. Moreover, each apartment is sealed off from the others, having its own entrance from "sidewalks" that form a network of streets through the cluster. And each apartment has its own private terrace.

As an experiment in low-cost, high-density housing, Habitat was expensive—even more so than anticipated, because the special crane designed to position the cubicles turned out

to be inadequate, and a second had to be built. The complex cost fifteen million dollars to construct. But now that the crane exists and the other bugs are out, it could be duplicated for about five million dollars. In fact, the duplicate would be of higher quality; interior finish in the original was skimped in the interest of keeping down ever-rising costs. Too, the more units such a complex contains, the less cost there is per unit.

The idea of using prefabricated apartment units that can be "plugged" into larger matrices had occurred to Le Corbusier too. He had, in point of fact, experimented with them, inserting identical apartments into a concrete grid. Buckminster Fuller's Tokyo project also

394
SAFDIE, DAVID, BAROTT, AND BOULVA. Habitat, EXPO 67, Montreal. 1967

conceives of the living units as segmental—indeed, he envisions each unit and any stable collection of them as portable.

Which of these ideas will dominate the city of the future is impossible to say. Quite likely all of them will be synthesized and used by lesser men. Their hope will be to house the masses of the world humanely while avoiding the desecration of land produced by the suburban sprawl with its commuter highways and dreary shopping plazas. To do so is within the technological reach of mankind; what is needed is the will.

Even the most concerned among us may lack the will to take up residence in domes, bell jars, hives, or hoppers. And we are quite discouraged to be told that it is imperative for us to reconstruct human society and—as a preliminary—pull down all that time and experience have built up. Moreover, we *should* be upset by such assertions because the very newest order it is possible to achieve, no matter how bold its experiments, must be as continuous with the past and the present as the new generations of human beings are continuous with those that went before. The American novelist, William Faulkner, once said: "The past is never dead. In fact, it isn't even past." If that is true, it is equally true that the greatest promise in city planning lies in the direction of preservation and re-adaptation of existing structures.

Observe a street (fig. 395) in New Harmony, Indiana. It is as depressing and ordinary as any other. Rehabilitated, Main Street has become a model of urban renewal (fig. 396). But isolated successes of this sort are heavily outnumbered by failed attempts to revitalize some area or other. Various private interests and outmoded regulations combine to make a monstrous opponent to rehabilitation. Only infrequently does government authority or citizens' outrage overcome commercial interests. In at least one instance, that of Houston, Texas, the

absence of any except the most rudimentary and essential building and zoning regulations would seem to have eliminated many of the problems usual in American cities. In most of our metropolises, however, the problems are terrifyingly large, real, and worsening. It will take more than neglect to cure what threaten to become terminal afflictions.

In general, most of us can easily agree that rehabilitation is preferable to destruction. Deciding what is to be saved, how, where, and when is not so easy to do; getting whole groups of people to concur with a given recommendation is nearly impossible. Usually, the situation is muddled and the solution controversial. Again, we can turn to Paris for an example. I am thinking of a remarkable building, the Pompidou Center (colorplate 17) located in the so-called Plateau Beaubourg just north of the Seine River.

Georges Pompidou (1911–1974), President of France from 1969 to 1974, was one of those leaders who was more enamored of progress than tradition. Like the French of 1889, he wished to restore his nation to her earlier level of economic distinction. But he became a veritable assassin of the obsolete and a nearsighted, if not blind, champion of modernity. Thus, distressed by the horrendous traffic jams of Paris, he set out to replace the picturesque quais of the Seine with automobile expressways. That aim was accomplished on the Right Bank, which now resembles any of a dozen anonymous riverside drives along streams coursing through the industrial cities of the United States. The Left Bank seems secure in its picturesque dignity; transformation of it was blocked by Valéry Giscard d'Estaing, Pompidou's successor.

In light of Pompidou's zealous promotion of newness, it is hardly surprising that his name should be associated with an extremely radical piece of museum architecture. He had expressed a passionate interest in es-

395

Main Street,
New Harmony, Indiana. 1973.
Courtesy of Historic New Harmony, Inc.

396
Main Street (restored),
New Harmony, Indiana. 1977.
Courtesy of Historic New Harmony, Inc.

tablishing in Paris a "cultural center that is both a museum and a center of creation, where the plastic arts would be side by side with music, cinema, books, and audiovisual research." This idea struck fire. It was heavily promoted in the press and supported by various groups interested in returning Paris to the cultural prominence she had enjoyed before World War II. After several false starts, the project was undertaken. A site had

been available for about forty years in the form of five acres of land that had been cleared for an urban-renewal project in 1930. That project had been aborted; the Plateau Beaubourg sat empty. It has now been filled with the most aggressively modern of all cultural centers. Designed by Renzo Piano (born 1937), an Italian, and the English architect, Richard Rogers (born 1933), the Pompidou is a vast affair (166 meters long,

60 wide, and 42 tall) that has been compared in appearance to an oil refinery, a distillery, and a hundred other things, none of them associated in the public mind with beauty or good taste. Even in this, perhaps, the Center is heir to all that Eiffel had begun.

In structure the building is exoskeletal. That is, the supporting trusses are on the exterior of the walls rather than hidden behind them. So, too, are the ducts and pipes that, in most buildings, would be concealed by partitions, walls, and ceilings. The eastern face of the Pompidou Center exposes them in polychromed distinction. Air-conditioning ducts are blue, waterpipes green, elevators red, and so on. The effect is startling. But keeping the structure and functional entrails of the Center on the perimeter provided a tremendous amount of unimpeded space within the 17,000 square meters the windows enclose. Contained therein are the following: 1) The National Museum of Modern Art, formerly housed on Chaillot Hill at the Avenue du Président Wilson; 2) Paris's first genuinely *public* library (The world-famous Bibliothèque Nationale is a library for serious scholars, and other well-known collections are for use by students.); 3) The Center for Industrial Design, providing displays of everything from architecture and furniture to posters and commercial pottery; 4) IRCAM (Institute for Research and Coordination in Acoustics and Music), a subterranean complex of studios and laboratories directed by internationally renowned composer-conductor, Pierre Boulez; 5) Multipurpose halls for theater, musical performances, cinema, and public lectures; 6) A poetry gallery; 7) A children's studio for introduction to art; 8) A permanent exhibit featuring the reconstructed studio of pioneer modern sculptor, Constantin Brancusi (1876–1957); 9) A sculptural maze by contemporary French sculptor, Jean Tinguely (born 1925); 10) A bar and restaurant.

These things, along with a miscellany of offices and so on, comprise the Center. They are embraced by a scaffold-like cage containing such notable innovations as roll-down metal shutters that drop automatically when the interior temperature rises from solar gain or from a fire. In case a fire does occur, the shutters serve to protect the external structure and also the adjacent buildings. Many visitors who care not at all for the appearance of the glass-enclosed escalators running up the side of the building (fig. 397) are favorably impressed with the way these function, for they permit one to enter the building at whatever level he wishes. In terms of convenience and efficiency the Pompidou Center is a splendid exploit.

As for the style of the architecture, opinions will vary. And if this book has done even a part of its work, you should be well aware of just how arbitrary and changeable such likes and dislikes can be. Certainly, the Pompidou Center is presently in the same situation the Eiffel Tower once was; it is anathema to conservative taste. But it has turned out to be unexpectedly popular to visit and shows every likelihood of eventually becoming an object of civic pride. Indeed, the structure has already inspired a more-or-less spontaneous renewal of the area around it. Decaying buildings have been refurbished, restored, and redecorated. There are now pedestrian walks, and new shops abound. The street sellers of the city are drawn to the zone. And tens of thousands of people have been attracted to an area that was what Americans call "blighted." Today the atmosphere is festive, and the Beaubourg neighborhoods are becoming increasingly prosperous.

On this optimistic note we close. The end to which this book was designed to lead—feeling able to enjoy art at its best, whether it is truly classic in aspect or avant-garde in attitude—is a rather modest objective. For

397
RENZO PIANO and RICHARD ROGER.
Pompidou Center,
Paris. 1976

to be unintimidated by art and the pomposities sometimes set up alongside it is only a beginning. I hope that what I have done toward achieving that start can never become a hindrance to further growth. Still, no matter how helpful you have found the book, to put too much value on these particular words, examples, and values would be unfair to yourself, embarrassing to me, and unjust to the field of art. There are other ways, perhaps better ways, of looking at art.

And there are vast ranges of expression untouched by *Art: The Way It Is*. One of the ways art "is" is being too rich for description in any one volume. For that reason a bibliography is included and also a glossary of terms general in the field of art. By making use of these, one may develop a far more discriminating, yet elastic sense for art. My responsibility is at an end; from here on where you go and how you proceed is up to you and those you choose to lead you. Good luck.

Notes to the Text

1. Who's Putting on Whom?

1. Erwin Panofsky, *Meaning in the Visual Arts* (Garden City, N.Y.: Anchor Books, 1955), p. 19.
2. René Huyghe, *Ideas and Images in World Art,* trans. Norbert Guterman (New York: Abrams, 1959), p. 9.
3. Somewhere Vladimir Nabokov, a celebrated lepidopterist and the author of significant novels in three languages, mentions that he has never been able to master the art of refolding a road map.
4. It is not trashy in the sense of being obscene, however, although this charge has been brought against it. The figures in the rear seat are as incomplete as the automobile body; if we did not associate motor vehicles with instruments of illicit pleasure, the tableau would not be suggestive.
5. For those who haven't read this tale, it concerns a pompous ruler who is "conned" by two characters who claim that they weave a beauteous fabric which is invisible to anyone who does not deserve his position. In fact, they weave nothing, but only pretend to—the sovereign's garment is purely imaginary. But since no one—least of all an emperor—wishes to be thought undeserving of his job, all his subjects pretend that they can see the new clothes. Indeed, they vie with each other in praising the quality of the material. The entire adult population is unstinting in its admiration of the emperor's new clothes. It is only when an innocent and unpretentious child cries out that the emperor has no clothes on that the hoax is revealed.
6. The numbers are arranged alphabetically by their names, the last number being called zero. As for the mysterious OTTFF-SSENT, these are the initials of the names of the cardinal numbers from one to ten.
7. Wassily Kandinsky, *Concerning the Spiritual in Art,* trans. Francis Golffing, Michael Harrison, and Ferdinand Ostertag (New

York: Wittenborn, Schultz, 1947), p. 40.

2. Image Creation and Convention

1. The impression that the reflection is larger than it measures is due to the belief that one's image is on the plane of the mirror. Actually, it is twice that distance. As Dr. Henry Knoll, senior scientist at Bausch & Lomb's Soflens Division, diagrams it:

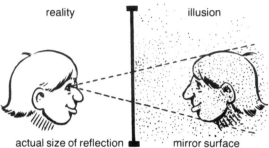

2. The Byzantine Empire was the eastern half of the later Roman Empire, given a separate identity in A.D. 395, and containing all of Greece and Turkey and large portions of adjacent lands. The site of its capital, Constantinople, was an ancient Greek town named Byzantium, and we use the adjective *Byzantine* to describe the entire culture. The empire was dissolved in 1453 when the Ottoman Turks conquered it, changing the name Constantinople to Istanbul.
3. In this connection it might be remarked that a wage is not the same as a profit. You profit only if you invest less than you get back.
4. That is to say, American "Indians."

3. Line and Form

1. These marks are sometimes referred to as draftsman's lines. Unfortunately, this terminology confuses most people because to them a "draftsman" is someone who prepares plans and diagrams using mechanical drawing instruments. This use of the term *draftsman,* however, is a very special one. It is comparable to the use of the term *driver* at a racetrack. If you were at Indianapolis or Sebring for the races and a track official asked you if you were a driver, you would say "no" because you would realize that he wanted to know whether or not you were entered as the driver of a racing car. But if I were to see you on the street and ask whether you were a driver, you'd probably say "yes." To artists a draftsman is anyone who draws well, and someone like Degas or Picasso is characterized as a fine draftsman. Thus, a draftsman's line is the kind of mark produced by a drawing implement such as a pen or pencil.

2. Kenneth Clark, *The Nude* (Garden City, N.Y.: Anchor Books, 1959), pp. 172–73.
3. I am not making reference here to the absence of pubic hair, something about which people often wonder but rarely ask. The deletion is a tradition stemming from cosmetic practices of the courtesans of ancient Greece, who removed all body hair for hygienic purposes by painting themselves with hot wax and then stripping it away once it had dried, a technique still employed by some women in Middle Eastern countries today. In any event, the sculptors imitated the effect in ancient times and later artists imitated them. By the nineteenth century, however, timidity about the carnal nature of people caused the same procedure to be applied to paintings and statues of males, something the ancients had not done.

4. Light and Shade

1. It is true, of course, that white men have made use of the identification of black with evil and white with purity. In fact, describing the skin of the lighter races as "white" is itself this sort of thing; no human skin is genuinely white, not even an albino's. Still, blackness does not always have negative connotations. There are, after all, raven-haired beauties as well as tall, dark, handsome men. Most formal evening wear is black. For many years most automobiles were black. And every

businessman wants to be "in the black."

5. Color

1. See, however, note 3 to this chapter.
2. It is typical to say (as I did in the first edition of this book) that red "absorbs all the white light except red." But, in fact, a spectrophotometer reveals that a red absorbs only a fraction of non-red light at the same time it reflects back nearly all of the red. I am indebted to Charles C. Fuller for bringing this to my attention.
3. Most authorities would view this as a weakening of the intensity of the red, but I prefer not to think of it in this way because we so often refer to "bright pinks" or to a "dull rose." A bright, intense red will make a bright, intense pink; a dull red will make a dull pink.
4. I was once seated behind two middle-aged ladies at the movies. Suddenly during a travelogue feature one turned to the other and said, "Ain't it too bad life's not in Technicolor?" I thought this very sad, since it indicated something about the way most people see. Technicolor or Koda-chrome intensifies certain hue levels and dark-light contrasts. Everything looks lush. But it eliminates far more than it captures. Still, most of the population is conditioned to see in the coarsest possible way.
5. Hermann von Helmholtz, *Treatise on Physiological Optics,* ed. James P. C. Southall (New York: The Optical Society of America, 1925), III, 6–7.
6. Quoted by John Rewald in *Post-Impressionism from Van Gogh to Gauguin* (New York: Museum of Modern Art, 1956), p. 83.
7. See Larry T. Reynolds, "A Note on the Perpetuation of a 'Scientific' Fiction," *Sociometry,* XXIX (March, 1966), 85–88.

6. Space

1. The first record of perspective theory appears in a little book published after Masaccio's death. It is Leonbattista Alberti's *Della pittura,* the most influential of all early Renaissance treatises on art. It first appeared in Latin in 1435 under the title *De pictura* and in the following year was rewritten in Italian by the author, who dedicated it to Brunelleschi.
2. Helmholtz, *op. cit.,* pp. 8–9.
3. The term *frontality* is a somewhat vague one in art circles. When applied to modern works, it means what is suggested here. But it is also used to describe figurative statuary that has a definite front and back, and distinct left and right sides. Egyptian statuary is frontal, Bernini's is not. In a related way we describe such static figurative painting styles as the Egyptian and Byzantine as frontal. Consciousness of surfaces to the front of the work is the distinctive feature of all these usages.
4. It is not my intention to argue such difficult matters in a book intended for neophytes. Those with a special interest in philosophy, the history of science, or the history of art are directed to chapter five of my book *Modern Art and Scientific Thought* (Urbana: University of Illinois Press, 1971), pp. 104–27.

7. Formal Composition

1. The letters in the Greek word for fish, $IX\Theta Y\Sigma$, are also the initial letters of the words in the statement $I\eta\theta o\upsilon\varsigma\ X\rho\iota\sigma\tau o\varsigma\ \Theta\epsilon o\upsilon\ Y\iota o\varsigma\ \Sigma\omega\tau\epsilon\rho$, which means "Jesus Christ, Son of the Redeeming God."
2. Meyer Schapiro, *Cézanne* (New York: Abrams, 1952), p. 90.
3. *Mona* is a contraction of the Italian word *madonna* and means "my lady." Lisa, of course, is short for Elizabeth.
4. Albert Boime, "Roy Lichtenstein and the Comic Strip," *Art Journal,* XXVIII (Winter, 1968–69), 158.

8. Styles of Vision

1. In 1938 Paul Frankl published an immense

work, *Das System der Kunstwissenschaft (A System of Aesthetics)*, which attempted to retain what seemed valid in Wölfflin's theory while overcoming its difficulties. Frankl's theory depends on the assumption that art, at its extremes, represents things as either in a state of Being—having a firm, fixed existence (Raphael)—or in a state of Becoming (Rembrandt). Within each of these categories are three stages: preclassic, classic, and postclassic; and the preclassic and postclassic within them have alternative directions. It is a far more complicated and subtle theory than Wölfflin's.

2. Fig. 260, 16th century; fig. 261, 17th; fig. 262, 17th; fig. 263, 16th; fig. 264, 17th; fig. 265, 16th; fig. 266, 16th; fig. 267, 17th; fig. 268, 16th; fig. 269, 17th.
Fig. 260: Raphael. *School of Athens.* 1510–11. Fresco, Stanza della Signatura, The Vatican, Rome. Fig. 261: Nicolas Poussin. *The Rape of the Sabine Women.* c. 1636–37. Oil on canvas, 60 7/8 × 82 5/8". The Metropolitan Museum of Art, New York. Harris Brisbane Dick Fund, 1946. Fig. 262: Peter Paul Rubens. *The Raising of the Cross.* Triptych. 1610–11. Oil on panel, 15'2" × 11'2". Cathedral, Antwerp. Fig. 263: Giorgione. *Enthroned Madonna with St. Liberalis and St. Francis.* c. 1500–1505. Oil on panel, 78 3/4 × 60". Cathedral, Castelfranco Veneto, Italy. Fig. 264: Pieter de Hooch. *A Woman and Her Maid in a Courtyard.* c. 1672. Oil on canvas, 29 × 24 5/8". The National Gallery, London. Fig. 265: Michelangelo. *The Fall of Man and the Expulsion from the Garden of Eden.* 1508–12. Fresco. Sistine Chapel, The Vatican, Rome. Fig. 266: Quentin Metsys. *The Money Changer and His Wife.* 1514. Oil on panel, 28 × 26 3/4". The Louvre, Paris. Fig. 267: Francisco de Zurbarán. *Funeral of St. Bonaventure.* 1629. Oil on canvas, 98 3/4 × 86 5/8". The Louvre, Paris. Fig. 268: Albrecht Dürer. *Self-Portrait.* 1500. Oil on panel, 26 1/4 × 19 1/4". Alte Pinakothek, Munich. Fig. 269: Jan Steen.

The Lovesick Maiden. c. 1665. Oil on canvas, 34 × 39". The Metropolitan Museum of Art, New York. Bequest of Helen B. Neilson, 1945.

9. Modern Art, its Variety and Unities

1. The Seven Years' War (1756–63) was a conflict between France, Austria, Russia, Saxony, Sweden, and Spain on the one side and Prussia, England, and Hanover on the other. There were two issues: (1) French-English colonial rivalry in America and India and (2) the struggle between Austria and Prussia for supremacy in Germany. The war proved Prussia's rank as a leading power and made England the world's chief colonial power at France's expense.

2. See Jacques Barzun, *Classic, Romantic, and Modern* (Boston: Atlantic Monthly Press, 1961), pp. 155–68.

3. No one agrees on who appropriated the word *dada* as a trademark for the group, but it is supposed to have been discovered by accident in a German-French dictionary. Hugo Ball wrote: "In Rumanian, *dada* means yes, yes, in French a rocking horse or hobby horse. To Germans it is an indication of idiot naivety and of a preoccupation with procreation and the baby-carriage." Quoted in Hans Richter, *Dada: Art and Anti-Art* (New York: Abrams, 1970), p. 32.

4. Max Ernst is really *the* Surrealist painter. He invented most of the mannerisms commonly identified with a Surrealist style in sculpture, in painting, and in both "literalist" and "abstract" Surrealism.

5. The example of music might well have warned the zealots of the reality of their situation. After all, a symphony is the perfect example of an art form one cannot own. That is, one cannot possess Arnold Schoenberg's Second String Quartet, Opus 10, in the same, exclusive sense that one can own a portrait by Rembrandt.

That is because the quartet exists as a musical piece only when it is performed; the score is not the art work and a recording is only of a given performance. This ephemeral property of music has not prevented business interests throughout the world from making use of masterworks for commercial ends. The principal difference between symphony orchestras and groups of conceptual artists is that the musicians exert vastly wider influence and enjoy the support of serious-minded people from all parts of the political spectrum.

10. Media and Methods

1. Some writers differentiate between the *medium* and the *vehicle,* with the vehicle in oil paint being the binder (oil) and the medium being whatever is used to thin it (turpentine). Such a distinction is useful in technical discussions with studio craftsmen but would serve only to complicate a text intended for laymen.

2. Leonardo's *The Last Supper* was done in a version of *fresco secco.* The *buon fresco* method was too restrictive for his restless, inquisitive temperament. Always an experimenter, he decided to try out a mixture of tempera and varnish on a dry plaster wall sealed with a varnish. The paint began to flake away as soon as the work was completed. Before World War II, the method of repair had been a piecemeal one, with restorers replacing the missing pigments fleck by fleck. After the war, however, deterioration was arrested by fixing the pigment to the wall with synthetic resins.

3. Those original oil paintings sold in furniture departments are indeed "original" in the sense that they are handmade. But buyers should beware of what they are getting. The people who turn out this stuff paint the same pictures over and over, sending similar ones to different outlets in different locations. Every once in a long while something of quality sneaks in. But it's rare.

4. I have imitated the crayon texture the same way political cartoonists imitate it today: by use of a black lithographic crayon on a pebble-grained paper called *coquille board.*

5. It is possible, of course, to make any number of identical plates from the same negative. Since these would be expensive to ship through the mails to all the thousands of newspapers using syndicated comic strips, national advertising, and the like, another method is used. Asbestos molds, or *matrices* (plural of matrix), taken from the zinc plate are mailed to the newspapers, which then cast their own plates with molten metal.

6. The new taste for such notions—which earlier in the Middle Ages would have been considered "profane"—was surely lent impetus by the doctrines of St. Francis (1182–1226), whose pious heterodoxy held that the things of the world were not inevitably evil but might be considered gifts to humanity from a loving God. Wholesome pleasures, the taste of fruits, the song of birds, and so on, would be examples. During the course of the fourteenth century the Franciscan Order disseminated this view. Eventually, it gained ascendancy over the older, Benedictine conception which had laid such stress on otherworldliness.

7. Ada Louise Huxtable, "The Most Influential Architect in History," *New York Times Magazine,* July 17, 1977, p. 22.

8. It is important to note that the French word *hôtel* does not, in this connection, denote a hostelry for travelers. It corresponds, rather, to *townhouse.*

9. Frederick Hartt, *Art: A History of Painting, Sculpture, and Architecture* (Englewood Cliffs, N.J.: Prentice-Hall, 1976; New York: Abrams, 1976), II, p. 331.

10. Nikolaus Pevsner, *A History of Building Types* (Princeton, N.J.: Princeton University Press, 1976), p. 84.

Glossary

The following list contains many terms not used elsewhere in this book. Although one may expect to encounter these terms in connection with art, I have not always had occasion or space to touch upon them. Cross references are indicated by words in small capitals.

ABACUS. In architecture, a flat block used as the uppermost part of the capital of a COLUMN.

ABSTRACT ART. Art dependent on the idea that artistic values reside in forms and colors independent of subject matter. An abstract work may resemble something else (apples, nude women, etc.), but the stress will be on form and color. Any work of art can be looked upon as an abstraction, but some styles (CUBISM, ABSTRACT EXPRESSIONISM, NEOPLASTICISM) intentionally emphasize the formal over any symbolic value.

ABSTRACT EXPRESSIONISM. A style of painting in which the artist expresses his feelings spontaneously and without reference to any representation of physical reality. Normally the term signifies a movement that originated in America during the late 1940s, but Wassily Kandinsky had pioneered the essentials of the manner before World War I.

ABSTRACTION. A work that is deliberately "abstract art," as in: "This painting by Picasso is an abstraction."

ACTION PAINTING. A type of ABSTRACT EXPRESSIONISM incorporating impulsive gestures.

AESTHETIC. Having to do with art and beauty. Often used synonymously with a theory of art or to refer to the characteristics of a given style, as, for example, "the IMPRESSIONIST aesthetic." (Sometimes spelled ESTHETIC.)

AMPHORA. A jar with two handles used by the ancient Greeks and Romans for storing grain, oil, condiments, etc.

APSE. The exedra, normally semicircular, at the end of a Christian church. It occurs also in the Roman public buildings known as BASILICAS.

AQUEDUCT. A watercourse, often supported in places by an ARCADE.

ARCADE. A series of ARCHES carried by pillars.

ARCH. An engineering device used to span an open area. Arches are curved and made of wedge-shaped blocks called voussoirs. The central voussoir is known as the keystone. In arch construction no mortar is required; gravity operates to pull the blocks together in such a way that they lean on one another.

ARCHAIC ART. A term having various meanings depending on its context. (1) In reference to the field of art, generally, it suggests the very beginnings of art and is applied to all prehistoric art and, by extension, (2) to the artifacts of tribal cultures of later eras. (3) When applied to the art of ancient Greece, it refers specifically to objects created prior to 600 B.C.

ARCHAEOLOGY. The scientific investigation of ancient cultures and civilizations by means of their artifacts.

ARCHITRAVE, see ENTABLATURE.

ARMORY SHOW. The first large, public exhibition of modern art in the United States. Organized by THE EIGHT and some sympathizers, it was held in the 69th Regiment Armory building in New York City in 1913. The show outraged the average viewer and the press, but it was the most influential ever presented in America, for the European works in it opened a vast range of possibilities to domestic artists.

ART NOUVEAU. A decorative style of the 1890s which attempted to break with past traditions. It is characterized by interlacing plant forms and similar organic elements along with relatively flat color treatments.

ASH CAN SCHOOL, see THE EIGHT.

ATMOSPHERIC PERSPECTIVE. The illusion of depth in painting created by reduction of contrast between lights and darks, cooling of colors, and blurring of outlines as things represented recede from the picture plane.

AVANT-GARDE. French word for vanguard. Artists who are unorthodox in their approach. The connotation is that such people are "ahead of their time," but it sometimes happens that they are merely eccentric. Still, REALISM, EXPRESSIONISM, DADAISM, CUBISM, and the others are all examples of avant-garde movements.

BAROQUE. Generally, the seventeenth century. The term connotes grandiose elaboration in architecture and decoration, since that is typical of the period. Dutch art of the period, however, is quite different and is distinguished by the name Protestant Baroque.

BARREL VAULT, see VAULT.

BASILICA. In ancient Rome, a public building used for various assemblies, particularly tribunals. It is rectangular in plan and is entered on the longer side. See also CHRISTIAN BASILICA.

BATIK. A process of dyeing cloth by painting designs on in wax so that only exposed areas are impregnated with the dye. The wax is removed after dyeing.

BAUHAUS. A school of industrial design founded in Weimar, Germany, in 1919 by architect Walter Gropius. Known for its attempts to integrate art and technology.

BENDAY PATTERN. In commercial printing, the technique invented by Benjamin Day (1838–1916) which adds tints to the line-cuts by means of dots, lines, and other regular patterns.

DER BLAUE REITER. "The Blue Rider." A branch of German EXPRESSIONISM centered in Munich. Tends to be far more abstract than DIE BRÜCKE.

BROKEN COLOR. The technique of applying paint in brief, rather heavy strokes on top of a background color. Typical of IMPRESSIONISM.

DIE BRÜCKE. "The Bridge." A branch of German EXPRESSIONISM centered in Dresden. Very similar in appearance to FAUVISM but more pessimistic about things in general.

BUON FRESCO, see FRESCO.

BUTTRESS. In masonry, a support to take up the THRUST of an ARCH or VAULT. A pier buttress is a solid mass of stone that rises above the outer wall of a Gothic or Romanesque church. A flying buttress is an arch or series of arches carrying the thrust of the nave vaults across open space to a pier buttress.

BYZANTINE. Pertaining to the BYZANTINE EMPIRE. Byzantine painting is characterized by a religious ICONOGRAPHY, rich use of color, highly formal design, and frontal, stylized presentation of figures. Byzantine architecture is characterized by domes, spires and minarets, and the widespread use of MOSAICS.

BYZANTINE EMPIRE. The Eastern Roman Empire. It lasted from A.D. 395 to 1453. Its capital was Constantinople, built on the site of the ancient Greek city of Byzantium by Constantine the Great.

CAMPANILE. A bell tower.

CANTILEVER. An engineering form which projects into space at one end and is firmly anchored at the other.

CAPITAL, see COLUMN.

CARTOON. A full-size preliminary DRAWING for a painting. Also, a frivolous or satirical drawing. (The former is the original meaning but is retained today only within art circles.)

CENTRIFUGAL CASTING. A process of metal casting commonplace in jewelry-making and other fields in which smallness of scale and precision of form are usual. Molten metal is forced into a mold by spinning the latter at extremely high speed on the end of a steel arm.

CERAMICS. Pottery making. More specifically, objects made of clay and fired at high temperatures to render them stronger and/or waterproof.

CHARCOAL. A drawing medium produced by charring organic substances (wood or bone) until they are reduced to carbon. A drawing made with charcoal.

CHASE. To ornament metal by indenting it with a hammer and tools that do not cut it. See also REPOUSSÉ.

CHIAROSCURO. Light-dark relationships in a work of art.

CHOIR. The space in a Christian church reserved for singers and clergy.

CHRISTIAN BASILICA. An early church form resembling a Roman BASILICA in plan, but entered from one end and having an APSE at the other.

CIRE-PERDUE PROCESS (or lost-wax process). A process of metal casting that consists of building up a refractory mold around a wax model, baking it until the wax melts and drains off through small holes in the mold, and then pouring metal into the empty space.

CLASSICAL. Narrowly, the term refers to the art of the ancient Greeks during the "Golden Age" of the fifth century B.C. By extension it is applied to all the works of antiquity from 600 B.C. through the fall of Rome. By still further extension Classical is used to describe any form thought to be derived from Greek and Roman examples; thus, the art of the Italian Renaissance is sometimes called Classical. It is, however, rather more common to refer to styles derived from the Antique as representing CLASSICISM. To be Classical implies perfection of form, emphasis on harmony and proportion, and restraint of emotion. Normally, the term is applied only to art that is idealistic and representational.

CLASSICISM, see CLASSICAL and NEOCLASSICISM.

CLERESTORY (or clearstory). In architecture, a part of a building raised above an adjoining roof and containing windows in its walls.

CLOISONNÉ. From the French word *cloison* (partition). A metalsmithing process in which strips of metal are soldered to a base, thus forming cells to contain enamel or other decorative materials.

CLOISTER. A covered walk on the side of a court. Common in MEDIEVAL monasteries in western Europe.

COLLAGE. A picture made up in whole or in part by gluing various materials (newspaper, wallpaper, cloth, photographs, bits of wood, etc.) to a piece of canvas or other GROUND.

COLLAGRAPHY. A relief-printing method which uses as the printing surface cardboard shapes and pieces of materials glued onto a base. It is often used in conjunction with INTAGLIO or LITHOGRAPHIC techniques.

COLLOTYPE. A photoreproduction method for making prints from photosensitive gelatin spread on sheets of glass or metal.

COLOR-FIELD PAINTING. A kind of painting emphasizing large, usually unbroken, zones of color. Normally the term is applied only to paintings done by artists active after 1950.

COLUMN. A vertical, cylindrical architectural member used to bear weight. Columns consist of a base at the bottom, a SHAFT, and a capital. Sometimes, as in DORIC columns, the base is nothing more than whatever the shaft rests on. The capital is the upper member of the column, and serves as a transitional unit from the vertical SHAFT to the horizontal LINTEL.

COMPLEMENTARY COLORS. Colors which are opposite each other on a color wheel. When mixed together in proper proportions, they form a neutral gray.

CONCEPTUAL ART. A form of art whose "product" is not a physical object but a mental conception of some sort. The work may entail the use of pictures, documents, recordings, and other data, but the work itself is a mental synthesis of the material. Similar to and related to HAPPENINGS.

CONNOISSEUR. Technically, an expert on art whose profession is identifying the specific artist who created a specific work. Generally, a person of highly developed artistic sensibilities.

CONSTRUCTIVISM. A twentieth-century movement in sculpture which emphasizes precision, technology, and NONREPRESENTATIONAL form.

CONVENTION. A practice established by custom and performance and widely recognized and understood.

COOL COLORS. Blue and such hues as approach blue.

CORBELED ARCH. A primitive sort of ARCH which spans an opening by means of masonry walls built progressively farther inward until they meet.

CORINTHIAN ORDER. The least consistent of the three principal ORDERS of Classical architecture. Frequently it resembles the IONIC except for the capital (*the* distinguishing feature of Corinthian), which is treated as a vase of acanthus leaves. Invented by the Greeks, it was never popular among them but found favor with the Romans, who admired its grandiose character.

CORNICE, see ENTABLATURE.

COUNTER REFORMATION. The reform of the Catholic Church during the sixteenth century. (The term is objected to by Catholics because, in fact, the reforms had begun before the rise of Protestantism.) The founding of the Society of Jesus (the Jesuit order), the convening of the Council of Trent, and the establishment of the papal Inquisition are among the notable consequences of Catholic reform.

CROSS-HATCHING. The production of relative VALUE relationships in drawing by placing sets of more or less parallel lines on top of one another at varying angles.

CROSSING. The space in a cruciform church where the NAVE and TRANSEPT cross.

DADAISM. A MOVEMENT begun in Zurich during World War I. It reacted to the war by expressing the absurdity of all CONVENTIONS and the futility of all acts. It soon became international in scope.

DIPTYCH. A two-panel altarpiece or devotional picture, normally hinged so that it can be closed like a book.

DISTEMPER. Any of a number of water-base paints using a simple glue or casein as the binder.

Calcimine, show-card, and poster colors are examples. (The "TEMPERA" of the primary grades is a distemper.) The term is more common in Great Britain than in the United States.

DORIC ORDER. The most consistent of the three major ORDERS of Classical architecture. It is characterized by a COLUMN resting directly on the floor and a shaft with continuous fluting. The capital has a round, bulging element called an ECHINUS and is topped by an ABACUS. The ENTABLATURE has a plain architrave and a FRIEZE made up of alternating TRIGLYPHS and METOPES.

DRAWING. The projection of an image on a surface by some instrument capable of making a mark. Drawings may be done with pencils, pens, brushes, PASTELS, crayons, CHARCOAL, ETCHING tools, and numerous other implements. Most often, drawings serve as studies or sketches for a work in some other medium, but they are frequently done as completed works in themselves.

DRYPOINT. The simplest form of metal ENGRAVING. Done by scratching a soft metal such as copper with a sharp steel needle.

EARTHWORKS. In art, a form of sculpture in which the artist designs a pattern that is carved, dug, or built into the landscape itself.

ECHINUS. In the DORIC ORDER, the bulging cushion-like member between the ABACUS and the NECKING.

THE EIGHT. A group of painters active in New York City at the beginning of the twentieth century. For the most part, they were REALISTS with strong social convictions, and they took as their subjects the streets and back alleys, the tenements and their immigrant inhabitants. Critics disturbed by the raw candor of their pictures called them the Ash Can School, and that name is now better known than The Eight.

EMBOSS. To raise up from a surface.

ENCAUSTIC. A painting MEDIUM using hot colored waxes. It is extremely permanent.

ENGAGED COLUMN. A COLUMN forming part of a wall and more or less projecting from it.

ENGRAVING. The process of cutting a design into a substance, usually metal, with a sharp tool. Also refers to a print made from an engraved plate.

ENTABLATURE. The horizontal portion of a building between the capitals of the COLUMNS and the roof or upper story. In Classical architecture the entablature consists of a horizontal beam called an architrave (which may be plain or banded), a FRIEZE (in the DORIC ORDER made up of TRIGLYPHS and METOPES and in the IONIC and CORINTHIAN either unadorned or covered with a continuous relief decoration), and a cornice. The latter is a projecting molding that runs along the top of the entablature.

ENTASIS. A slight, almost imperceptible curve in architectural elements, particularly in the shafts of Classical COLUMNS.

ESTHETIC, see AESTHETIC.

ETCHING. The process of producing a design on a metal plate by use of acid or similar mordants. Also refers to a print made from an etched metal plate.

EXPRESSIONISM. Strictly, German Expressionism. A MOVEMENT in the arts that originated in Germany just prior to World War I, emphasizing the subjective aspects of the artist and his subjects. By extension, any art of this type.

FAUVISM. A turn-of-the-century MOVEMENT in France characterized by bright, flat zones of color. Similar to German EXPRESSIONISM of the more representational sort (e.g., DIE BRÜCKE), except that it took a far more optimistic view of humanity and our circumstances.

FENESTRATION. The arrangement of windows in a building. Sometimes the term is applied to the arrangement of all the openings—windows, doors, and so on.

FERROCONCRETE. Steel-reinforced concrete. That is, concrete reinforced by embedding steel mesh, nets, rods, or bars in the cement while it is wet.

FLORENTINE RENAISSANCE. The period from the fourteenth to the sixteenth century in the city of Florence, the cradle and the jewel of the Italian RENAISSANCE.

FLYING BUTTRESS, see BUTTRESS.

FOLK ART. Art and craft objects produced by untrained people as an expression of community life. Usually the craftsmen are anonymous and the objects relatively utilitarian.

FRESCO. The term *fresco,* used alone, refers to what is known, strictly, as *buon fresco*—a painting made on wet plaster so that the pigments become incorporated into the plaster. *Fresco secco* is painting done on dry plaster so that the wall surface serves as a GROUND.

FRONTALITY. In sculpture and figurative painting the term refers to deemphasis of the lateral aspects of things. In painting, generally, it refers to the arrangement of planes parallel to the canvas surface. With respect to modern art it has a less precise meaning, but suggests that the tangible, two-dimensional surface of the picture is emphasized.

FRIEZE. The band between the cornice and the architrave in an ENTABLATURE. By extension, any richly ornamented band and, further, any arrangement suggesting such a frieze.

FUTURISM. An Italian MOVEMENT originating prior to World War I which hoped to glorify the dynamism of the machine age.

GENRE. Normally the word is used to refer to pictures in which the subject matter is drawn from everyday life. It is also used in a more general sense to describe whole categories of subject matter. Thus, one may speak of "the landscape genre," "the still-life genre," "the genre of figure painting," and so on. Sometimes it is applied to mediums: genre of painting, sculpture, etc.

GEODESIC DOME. A building form, constructed of small, triangular MODULES, devised by Buckminster Fuller.

GERMAN EXPRESSIONISM, see EXPRESSIONISM.

GESSO. A mixture of plaster of Paris and glue used as a GROUND for painting.

GLAZE. In painting, a PIGMENT (usually oil) applied in transparent layers. In CERAMICS, a vitreous coating applied before firing to seal the surface or used as decoration.

GOLDEN AGE. Any age of high culture in a civilization. Most commonly, the term is applied to Athens under Pericles (495–429 B.C.) and to the BYZANTINE EMPIRE under Justinian (A.D. 527–565).

GOLDEN SECTION or GOLDEN MEAN. A ratio between the two dimensions of a plane figure or the two divisions of a line such that the shorter element is to the longer as the longer is to the whole.

GOUACHE. Opaque rather than transparent WATERCOLOR. The medium is essentially the same as in transparent watercolor, except that the proportion of binder to PIGMENT is greater and an inert pigment such as precipitated chalk has been added to increase the opacity of the paint.

GRAPHIC. Literally, written, drawn, or engraved. In the arts the term refers, in a narrow sense, to drawing and printmaking. But it is also used in the more commonplace sense to describe something that is striking in its clarity.

GROIN VAULT, see VAULT.

GROUND. Usually, the surface to which paints are applied. In ETCHING the term refers to the waxy coating used to cover the plate and prevent mordants from acting upon it.

HAPPENING. A satiric act which takes place in a specially constructed or devised environment. Has both sculptural and theatrical aspects, but no permanent form is established. The "put-on" side of such an event is considered a vital part of its seriousness.

HARD-EDGE PAINTING. Any painting style employing very clean, sharp edges and flat areas of color. Normally restricted in application to work done by artists active after 1950.

HUE. The name of a color, such as red, blue, yellow (primaries); orange, green, violet (secondaries); and the intermediate (tertiary) colors.

ICON. Literally, an image. Specifically, an image of a sacred person regarded as an object of veneration in the Eastern Church.

ICONOCLAST. Image breaker. Originally the term was applied to the BYZANTINE ruler Leo III (680–740), who opposed the religious use of images. It has been extended to apply to anyone who actively questions generally accepted intellectual, ethical, or moral attitudes.

ICONOGRAPHY. The study of images primarily in terms of their symbolic intentions. (The study of the deeper significance of content and its general importance is sometimes referred to as iconology.)

ILLUMINATED MANUSCRIPT. A manuscript whose pages (and especially the initial letters) are decorated with silver, gold, and bright colors. Sometimes such manuscripts contain MINIATURES.

ILLUSTRATION. Imagery that relates explicitly to something else—that serves to clarify or adorn an anecdote, literary work, description, event, etc.

IMPASTO. The texture of paint applied in a thick, pasty form.

IMPRESSIONISM. Specifically, French Impressionism. A MOVEMENT in painting that originated during the last third of the nineteenth century. It attempted to attain a sort of ultimate NATURALISM by extending REALISM beyond value relationships to an exact analysis of color. A typical Impressionist work is painted with short, brightly colored dabs of paint. The subject matter tends to be unproblematical and undramatic.

INTAGLIO. A design sunk into a surface so that the impression it makes is in RELIEF. Signet rings are common examples, as are engraved plates.

INTENSITY. The dullness or brightness of a color. (Not to be confused with VALUE, meaning the color's darkness or lightness.) Often referred to as chroma.

INTERCOLUMNIATION. The space between COLUMNS in a row of them.

IONIC ORDER. The second major ORDER of Classical architecture. It is lighter than the DORIC and is distinguished by the scroll-like volute decoration of the capital. The shaft has separated flutes and a concave-convex molding at its base. With the exception of those in Athenian buildings, Ionic COLUMNS usually rest on PLINTHS. The ENTABLATURE contains a banded architrave and a FRIEZE that is either plain or ornamented with a continuous RELIEF decoration.

JUGENDSTIL. A German decorative style that parallels ART NOUVEAU.

KEYSTONE, see ARCH.

KINETIC ART. Works of art that are designed to move, either in response to human presence (because of touch, electric-eye beams, etc.) or because they are mechanized.

LITHOGRAPHY. A printing technique in which the image to be printed is drawn on a flat surface, as on Bavarian limestone or a sheet of zinc or aluminum. The process takes advantage of the antipathy of oil for water.

LOCAL COLOR. The natural color of an object as seen under normal daylight.

LINTEL. A horizontal beam spanning an opening.

MAGIC REALISM. A style of painting that often overlaps with SURREALISM but is distinctive in that it involves a sharp, precisely detailed rendering of real things. There are actually two types: (1) that which brings prosaic things into unusual and disturbing juxtaposition, (2) a variety that depicts ordinary things with such abnormal clarity as to lend them extraordinary overtones.

MANDORLA. An almond-shaped aureole or nimbus (sometimes called a glory) surrounding the figure of God, Christ, the Virgin Mary, or sometimes a saint.

MANNERISM. A style in Italian art that developed between about 1520 and 1600.

MEDIEVAL PERIOD, see MIDDLE AGES.

MEDIUM. The vehicle or liquid with which PIGMENT is mixed. In a more general sense, the material through which an artist expresses himself (e.g., paint, metal, wood, printmaking). In technical usage the term refers to the substance used to thin or otherwise modify the PIGMENT and its vehicle.

METAPHYSICAL PAINTING. An Italian MOVEMENT in painting during the earlier part of the twentieth century. The strangely evocative pictures by Giorgio de Chirico formed the basis of the movement; his paintings also had a profound influence on SURREALIST imagery.

METOPE. One of the panels between the TRI-GLYPHS in a DORIC FRIEZE. Often these are decorated with RELIEF sculpture.

MIDDLE AGES. The period in Western history between, generally, A.D. 400 and 1300.

MIMESIS. Literally, to imitate. Thus, the representation by illusion of the properties of the external world.

MINIATURE. Any small image, but particularly a little picture illustrating an ILLUMINATED MANUSCRIPT.

MINIMAL ART. Painting and sculpture that stresses the simplest color relationships and/or most clearly geometric forms.

MODELING. The forming of three-dimensional surfaces. Thus, the creation of the illusion of such surfaces within the two-dimensional confines of painting or drawing.

MODULE. A given magnitude or unit in the measurements of a work of art or building. Thus, if one used a sixteen-inch module in designing a house, all dimensions would be some multiple of sixteen inches.

MONOCHROMATIC. Consisting of variations of a single HUE.

MOSAIC. The decoration of a surface by setting small pieces of stone or glass (called *tesserae*) into cement.

MOVEMENT. A general cultural tendency, sometimes carried out by people known to one another but frequently a more diverse response to given stimuli. Thus, one can speak of "the IMPRESSIONIST movement," of a "Black Nationalist movement," or of a "youth movement."

MULLION. A vertical bar used to section off the panes of a window.

NABIS. A group of French painters active between 1889 and 1899. The most outstanding members were Pierre Bonnard and Edouard Vuillard.

NAIVE ART. Works of art created by those without professional training in which a lack of sophistication is preserved as a positive value.

NARTHEX. A porch adjacent to the front of a church and forming a vestibule. Usually it is colonnaded or ARCADED.

NATURALISM. In literature the term corresponds to French REALISM in painting. In art, however, it usually signifies accuracy of transcription of nature. Harnett, Courbet, Manet, and Norman Rockwell are all naturalistic to some degree.

NAVE. The major, central part of a church. It leads from the main entrance to the altar and is separated from the side aisles (if any) by piers and COLUMNS.

NECKING. An indentation between the ECHINUS and shaft of a COLUMN.

NEOCLASSICISM. The attempt in the eighteenth and nineteenth centuries to revive the ideals of the Greeks and Romans in French painting. By extension, any style based on the principles of Neoclassicism. The style attempts to attain perfection and harmony through prescribed limits.

NEOIMPRESSIONISM. The style of painting devised by French painter Georges Seurat at the end of the nineteenth century. It involved a quasi-scientific method of applying color and a highly controlled system of drawing and composition. Called Divisionism by its inventor. Other prominent Neoimpressionists were Charles Angrand, Henri Edmond Cross, and Paul Signac.

NEOPLASTICISM. A type of NONOBJECTIVE painting that reduced form to horizontal and vertical movements and used only black, white, and the primary colors. Its principal practitioner was Piet Mondrian.

NEOROMANTICISM. A painting style associated with and resembling the representational form of SURREALISM, but distinguished by its evocation of lyrical and nostalgic sentiment. The main artists are the brothers Eugene Berman and Leonid Berman (who signs his work "Leonid"), Christian Bérard, and Pavel Tchelitchew.

NEUE SACHLICHKEIT. "The New Objectivity." A reaction against EXPRESSIONISM which occurred in Germany during the post–World War I period. It is "objective" only in that it took a more realistic view of the physical world. Marked by a concern with social problems.

NEW OBJECTIVITY, see NEUE SACHLICHKEIT.

NONOBJECTIVE ART. NONREPRESENTATIONAL art.

NONREPRESENTATIONAL ART. Works of art that make no attempt to produce illusions of reality.

OGEE. A double or S-shaped curve. Also refers to the bulging form produced by two ogee curves that mirror one another and meet in a point (i.e., ogee arch).

OP ART. "Optical art"—that is, works of art which depend for their interest on optical illusion, fugitive sensations, and other subjective visual phenomena.

OPTICAL COLOR. The apparent color of an object as opposed to its LOCAL COLOR.

ORDER. Any of the characteristic styles of Classical architecture determined by the particular kinds of ENTABLATURES and COLUMNS used. The three major orders are DORIC, IONIC, and CORINTHIAN. There are also, however, other types and also blends of elements referred to as Composite orders. Applied in broad usage to any systematic treatment of architectural form employing standard components.

PALETTE. The surface on which a painter mixes his paints. More generally, the habitual set of colors used by a given artist or group.

PASTEL. PIGMENTS mixed with gum and compressed into stick form for use as crayons. A work of art done with such pigments.

PATINA. A greenish film that forms on copper or bronze through natural or artificial oxidation. Effects similar to this on other substances.

PEDIMENT. In Classical architecture, the triangular space formed by the end of a building with a pitched roof.

PERISTYLE. A continuous colonnade surrounding a building or a court.

PERSPECTIVE. The common name for central projection, a scheme for representing three-dimensional objects on a two-dimensional surface in terms of relative magnitude.

PIER BUTTRESS, see BUTTRESS.

PIGMENT. A substance that has been ground into a fine powder and is used to color paints or dyes.

PILASTER. A flat, rectangular projection which resembles an ENGAGED COLUMN.

PLINTH. A block serving as a pedestal for a column or statue.

POINTILLISM. The application of pigment in small dots rather than by means of the usual brushstroke. Employed by the NEO-IMPRESSIONISTS but also used by other artists.

POLYPTYCH. A many-paneled altarpiece or devotional picture, sometimes hinged so that it can be folded up.

POP ART. Serious painting using elements from commercial illustration, cartoons, signs, and ordinary mass-produced objects as subject matter.

POSTIMPRESSIONISM. A catchall term for the styles employed by painters influenced by IMPRESSIONISM who modified it into more personal modes of expression. The painters most frequently cited as examples of Post-impressionists are Cézanne, Renoir, Van Gogh, and Gauguin.

POTTERY. Objects of clay that have been hardened by firing.

PRECISIONISM. A MOVEMENT in American art that began in the 1920s, typified by the work of Charles Sheeler and Georgia O'Keeffe. It combines realistic subject matter with extreme formal control.

PRIMITIVE ART. A term becoming less common because of overuse and pejorative connotations. It has the following meanings, more or less in this order: (1) art produced by tribal cultures; (2) art created by amateur artists in which unsophisticated vision and lack of technical skill have, for one reason or another, come to be counted as virtues; (3) art produced by Netherlandish and Italian painters active before 1500.

PRINT. A work of art produced in multiple copies by hand methods and printed by the artist himself or under his direct supervision.

RAKING CORNICE. The molding edge on the slanting sides of a PEDIMENT.

REALISM. A nineteenth-century MOVEMENT in painting which stressed matter-of-fact descriptions of actual things. Frequently, as in Courbet (who coined the name of the style), Realism focused on the squalid and depressing. But Manet's work shows that ignoble themes are not fundamental to the manner. It is really a nonsentimental, rather broad version of NATURALISM.

REFORMATION. A religious revolution in western Europe during the sixteenth century. It began as a reform movement within the Roman Catholic Church but evolved into the doctrines of Protestantism. Its outstanding representatives are Martin Luther and John Calvin.

REFRACTION. The bending of a light ray or wave of energy as it passes through a substance.

REGIONALISM. The name given to the work of certain American painters prominent in the 1930s. Their works tended to represent specific regions and to portray common people in everyday activities. Notable among these are Thomas Hart Benton, Grant Wood, Edward Hopper, and John Steuart Curry.

RELIEF. In sculpture, the projection of a form from a background to which it is attached. In high relief the figures stand far out from the base. In bas-relief (or low relief) they are shallow.

RENAISSANCE. Usually signifies the rebirth of art and humane letters (as opposed to divine letters) during the fourteenth and fifteenth centuries, particularly in Italy. Early Renaissance covers the period from about 1420 to 1500 and High Renaissance from about 1500 to 1527 (the date of the sack of Rome by the Holy Roman Emperor Charles V).

REPOUSSÉ. The forming of a design in metal by working it from the back and leaving the impression on the face. See also CHASE.

REPRODUCTION. The production of multiple images of a work of art by photomechanical processes. (Compare PRINT.)

ROCOCO. Primarily a style of interior decoration in vogue in France from the death of Louis XIV (1715) to around 1745. It had some influence in Germany, Austria, Italy, and Spain, particularly in the northern countries. Tending toward prettiness and frivolity, its effects can be seen in paintings by Watteau, Boucher, Fragonard, and Tiepolo, but it reached its loftiest form in Catholic Germany and Austria, where it produced extraordinarily beautiful church interiors.

ROMANTICISM. A MOVEMENT in painting that first appeared in France during the early nineteenth century. It attempted to express the entirety of human experience, both real and imagined. By extension, applied to any work of art expressing interests thought similar to or characteristic of Romanticism.

ROSE WINDOWS. The large circular windows of stained glass found in Gothic cathedrals.

SARCOPHAGUS. A stone coffin.

SCHOOL. A word with a great variety of meanings, all of them based on the assumption of identifiable similarities among the works of various artists who (1) studied with the same master, (2) imitate the same master, (3) work together as a group, (4) express the same interests in their works, (5) lived in the same place and time, (6) have the same country of origin. Thus: the School of Raphael (1 and 2); the French Impressionist School (3); the Pop Art School (4); the School of Florence (5); the Italian School, as contrasted with the French School (6).

SCULPTURE IN THE ROUND. Freestanding statues, such as Michelangelo's *David,* as opposed to RELIEF sculpture.

SGRAFFITO. A design produced by scratching through one layer of material into another of a contrasting color. Frequently used in pottery decoration, but also employed by painters and sculptors.

SHAFT. The long part of a COLUMN between the base and capital.

SLIP. Clay which has been thinned to the consistency of cream. It can be poured into molds of plaster and thereby cast into pots or can be used as a paint to ornament CERAMIC pieces.

SOCIAL REALISM. A general term used to describe various styles in art (Courbet's, Daumier's, Grosz's, e.g.) which emphasize the contemporary scene, usually from a left-wing point of view and always with a strong thematic emphasis on the pressures of society on human beings.

SPANDREL. The triangular space between the

curves of two adjacent ARCHES.

STEEL-REINFORCED CONCRETE, see FERROCONCRETE.

STEREOTYPE. In common usage, a standardized mental picture that represents things in a false and oversimplified manner. (For example, the stereotype of women as poor drivers or of Negroes as lazy and superstitious.) In art the term refers to a form that is repeated mechanically, without real thought. In printing it refers to identical relief printing surfaces produced by taking a mold from a master surface and then casting copies. These copies are called stereotypes.

DE STIJL. A Dutch magazine of the early twentieth century devoted to NEOPLASTICISM. (In Dutch, the title means the Style.) The term is used to refer to the ideas advocated by the magazine; they had a marked influence on the BAUHAUS and on commercial design generally.

STUCCO. A finish for the exterior walls of a structure, usually composed of cement, sand, and lime.

SUPREMATISM. A NONREPRESENTATIONAL style devised by Kasimir Malevich in the early twentieth century. It amounts to a kind of Russian NEOPLASTICISM.

SURREALISM. The post–World War I MOVEMENT which drew inspiration from Freudian psychology and extended the arbitrary irrationality of DADAISM into a doctrinaire exploration of the unconscious.

TAPESTRY. A heavy, handmade textile in which the threads (usually the weft or horizontal threads) are woven to create a picture or abstract pattern.

TEMPERA. Paint using egg as the binder for the pigment. Technically called egg tempera.

TERRA-COTTA. A brownish-orange earthenware used for sculpture and pottery or as a building material. Sometimes it is GLAZED, sometimes not.

TEXTURE. The tangible quality of a surface—that is, its smoothness, roughness, slickness, softness. The simulation of such qualities by illusion in drawing and painting.

THRUST. The outward force exerted by the weight of an ARCH or VAULT.

TRACERY. Stone forms that decorate Gothic windows and hold the glass in place.

TRANSEPT. Either of the arms of a cruciform church that extend at right angles to the NAVE.

TRIFORIUM GALLERY. In a cathedral, the area above the aisle and between the NAVE ARCHES and the CLERESTORY.

TRIGLYPH. In the DORIC ORDER, a panel of three projecting members separating the METOPES in the FRIEZE.

TRIPTYCH. A three-panel altarpiece or devotional picture, usually so designed that the central panel is twice as wide as the other two, with the latter hinged so that they can be folded over to cover the central one.

TYMPANUM. The recessed face of a PEDIMENT or, in medieval cathedrals and other buildings, the space above a LINTEL and within an ARCH, often containing RELIEF sculpture.

VALUE. The relative lightness or darkness of a color.

VAULT. Any roof constructed on the ARCH principle. A barrel vault is a continuous row of arches joined to one another. A groin vault consists of two barrel vaults intersecting each other at right angles. A dome is a hemispherical vault—an arch turned on a central upright axis. Vaults may be of masonry, brick, or concrete.

VOUSSOIR, see ARCH.

WARM COLOR. Red and the hues that approach red, orange, and yellow. Sometimes yellow-green is considered a warm color.

WATERCOLOR. Strictly, any pigment mixed with water, but usually signifying transparent watercolor in which the binder is gum arabic.

WOODCUT. A relief printing surface carved from the plank grain of a piece of wood. The image printed from such a surface.

WOOD ENGRAVING. A relief printing surface carved from the end grain of a piece of wood. The image printed from such a surface.

Guide to the Pronunciation of Artists' Names

Correct pronunciation of foreign names has very little to do with artistic understanding per se, but knowing the sound of a name is often helpful in communication. Therefore, I have included the following guide, which contains all names of artists whose work is reproduced in this text with the exception of those pronounced in the customary American way.[1]

The guide entails a simplified approach, aiming at *acceptable* pronunciations rather than absolutely perfect ones. The subtleties of variation among tongues make it impossible to illustrate precise discriminations without the use of language records and specialized alphabets and markings. In using the guide, keep in mind the following:

Italicized syllables are to be stressed.

An *x* indicates a gutteral. (*H* pronounced while clearing the throat approximates this sound.)

The sounds *ö* and *ü* have no equivalent in English; to say them, shape your lips to say *e* as in "evil" and sound the *o* or *u*.

The French nasal sounds (*an, in, on, un*) can only be conveyed orally, but the general idea is to sound the letters through your nose.

Words appearing in parentheses repeat the sound just given.

Vowel sounds are indicated as follows:

a is as in *man*
ay is as in *lane*
ah is as in *dart*
e is as in *Ben*
ee and *ea* are as in *keen* or *lean*
i is as in *in*

eye is as in *mine*
oe is as in *oar*
oo is as in *boor*
o is as in *box*
uh is as in *mud*
u is as in *use*

ANGELICO, FRA Ahn-*djay*-li-coe, Frah

ANUSZKIEWICZ, RICHARD Ann-uh-*skay*-vitch (*Not* An-*noose*-kuh-vitz)

BOCCIONI, UMBERTO Baht (bought)-tshee-oe-nee, Oom-*bar* (bear)-toe

BOTTICELLI, SANDRO Baht (bought)-tea-*tshel*-ee, *Sand*-roe

BOUGUEREAU, WILLIAM Boo-guh-roe, Vill-yam

BRAQUE, GEORGES Brack, Zhor-zh (Often, by error, *brock*.)

BRONZINO, ANGELO Bron-*dzee*-no, *Ahn*-djay-loe

BRUEGEL, PIETER *Brü*-gl, *Pea*-tr (Often spelled *Brueghel*, as the artist did until 1559, when he dropped the *h*.)

CAMPIN, ROBERT Can (French nasal)-pin (French nasal), Rahb-air

CANALETTO, ANTONIO Ca-nal-*et*-toe, Ahn-*toe*-nee-oh

CARAVAGGIO Cahr-a-*vadj*-gee-oe

CARPI, UGO DA *Cahr*-pea, oo-goe da

CÉZANNE, PAUL Say-zann, Pol (doll)

CHARDIN, JEAN-BAPTISTE Shar-din (French nasal), Zhahn Bat-tea-st

CIMABUE Tshee-ma-*boo*-ay

CORBUSIER, LE Cor-boos-ee-ay, Le (Real name: Charles Edouard Jeanneret)

COROT, JEAN-BAPTISTE CAMILLE Cah-roe, Zhahn Bat-tea-st Ca-mee-y

COURBET, GUSTAVE Coor-bay, Güss-tav

DALI, SALVADOR *Dah*-lee, Sal-vah-*dor* (more)

DAUMIER, HONORÉ Doe-mee-ay, Oe-nah-ray

DAVID, JACQUES-LOUIS Da-vid, Zhahk Loo-ee

DEGAS, EDGAR Duhg-gah, Ed-gar

DELACROIX, EUGÈNE Duh-la-crwa, Oe-zhen

DUCHAMP, MARCEL Dü-chan (French nasal), Mar-sel

DÜRER, ALBRECHT *Dü*-rur, *Al*-bre×t

EYCK, JAN VAN *Ay*-ick, Yan van

GABO, NAUM *Ga*-boe, *Na*-oom

GÉRICAULT, THÉODORE Zhay-ree-coe, Tay-oe-dor (more)

GIORGIONE Djior-dji-*oe*-nay

GIOTTO Dji*ot*-toe

GOGH, VINCENT VAN *Xoh×*, *Vinn*-cent van (But in English, usually van *goe*)

GOYA, FRANCISCO *Go* (gosh)-ya, Fran-*this*-coe

GRECO, EL *Grek*-coe, Ell

GROSZ, GEORGE Groes (grow), Zhorzh

GRÜNEWALD, MATTHIAS *Grü*-nay-valt, *Mat*-tea-as

GUARDI, FRANCESCO Goo-*ahr*(are)-dee, Fran-*chess*-coe

HOLBEIN, HANS *Hoel* (hole)-beyen (mine), Hans

HOOCH, PIETER DE Hoe-×, Pea-tr duh

KANDINSKY, WASSILY Kan-*din*-skee, Vass-*see*-lee

KIENHOLZ, EDWARD *Keyen* (mine)-hoelts (bolts)

KIRCHNER, ERNST LUDWIG *Kir*-×nr, *Air*-nst *Lood*-vig

KLEE, PAUL Klay, Pol (doll)

LA TOUR, GEORGES DE La-toor, Zhorzh duh

LÉGER, FERNAND Lay-zhay, Fair-nan (French nasal)

LEONARDO DA VINCI Lay-oe-*nar*-doe da *Vinn*-tshee

LICHTENSTEIN, ROY *Licked*-en-steyen (wine)

LORRAIN, CLAUDE Loe-rin (French nasal), K-load (Real name: Claude Gellée)

MALEVICH, KASIMIR Mal-*ay*-vitch, *Kah*-si-mir

MANET, EDOUARD Ma-*ne* (like *net* without the *t*), *Ay*-dwar

MANTEGNA, ANDREA Man-*ten*-ya, Ahn-*dray*-ah

MARC, FRANZ Mahrk, Frahnts

MASACCIO MA-*zatsh* (watch)-shee-oe

MATISSE, HENRI Mah-tea-ss, An (French nasal)-ree

METSYS, QUENTIN *Met*-sees, Kwen-tn

MICHELANGELO Me-kell-*an*-djay-loe

MIES VAN DER ROHE, LUDWIG Mees (lease) van duhr *Roe*-heh, *Lood*-vig

MIRO, JOAN Mi (mist)-*roe*, *Xo*-ahn

MONET, CLAUDE Mo (motto)-ne (Like *net* without the *t*), K-load

MORISOT, BERTHE Mo (motto)-ree-zo, Ber (berry)-t

NOLDE, EMILE *Noel*-day, *Ay*-meal

PERUGINO Pay-roo-*gee*-noe

PICASSO, PABLO Pea-*cahs*-so, *Pah*-bloe

POUSSIN, NICOLAS Poohs-sin (French nasal), Nee-coel (coal)-ah

PRAXITELES Prak-*sit*-uhl-eez

PRUD'HON, PIERRE-PAUL Prü-don (French nasal), Pea-air Pol (doll)

RAPHAEL *Rah*-fa-ell (Not *Ray*-fay-ell)

REMBRANDT VAN RIJN *Rem*-brant van Rheyen (Rhine)

RENOIR, PIERRE-AUGUSTE Ren-*wahr* (very soft *r*), Pea-air Oe (oh)-güst

RODIN, AUGUSTE Rod (not *road*)-in (French nasal), Oe (oh)-güst

ROUSSEAU, HENRI Rooss-*ssoe* (so), *Ahn*-ree

RUBENS, PETER PAUL *Roo*-bns, Pay-tr Pah-ool

SEURAT, GEORGES Ssö-rah, Zhorzh

STEEN, JAN Stayn (stain), Yan

TINTORETTO Tin-toe-*ret*-toe

TITIAN *Ti*-shn

VELÁZQUEZ, DIEGO Vayl(veil)-*ath*-keth, Dee-*ay*-goe

VERMEER, JAN Ver (very)-*may*-r, Yan

WATTEAU, ANTOINE Vat-toe, An (French nasal)-twahn (But usually Anglicized to Waht-toe in the United States.)

ZURBARÁN, FRANCISCO DE Thoor-bah-*ran*, Fran-this (thistle)-coe day

1. For a comprehensive list see Gustave E. Kaltenbach, *Dictionary of Pronunciation of Artists' Names* (The Art Institute of Chicago, 1965), a book which I have found indispensable in compiling this brief list.

Bibliography

The following books have been selected because they are (1) of general interest and intelligible to the layman, (2) generally available in college, university, and public libraries, and (3) usually contain bibliographies directing readers to more specialized works.

I. General

ARNHEIM, RUDOLPH. *Art and Visual Perception.* Berkeley and Los Angeles: University of California Press, 1954. A classic among writings on the psychology of art.

ELSEN, ALBERT E. *The Purposes of Art: An Introduction to the History and Appreciation of Art.* 2nd ed. New York: Holt, Rinehart and Winston, 1967. An art appreciation text written from the point of view of an art historian. The stress is on ways in which different visual forms reveal select examples of thematic content.

FAULKNER, RAY, and ZIEGFELD, EDWIN. *Art Today: An Introduction to the Visual Arts.* 5th ed. rev. New York: Holt, Rinehart and Winston, 1969. A very readable and comprehensive treatment of the visual arts, emphasizing the ways in which they satisfy human needs both aesthetic and practical.

FELDMAN, EDMUND BURKE. *Varieties of Visual Experience: Art as Image and Idea*. 2nd ed. Englewood Cliffs, N.J.: Prentice-Hall, 1971. New York: Abrams, 1971. An extremely thorough and all-encompassing text. Examines art in terms of its various functions, styles, and media. Contains a very good section on art criticism in theory and practice.

FLEMING, WILLIAM. *Arts and Ideas*. Rev. ed. New York: Holt, Rinehart and Winston, 1968. Considers the histories of art, music, and literature in the light of the dominant ideas of the historical epochs by focusing on exemplary locales and works.

GILSON, ETIENNE HENRY. *Painting and Reality*. 2nd ed. Cleveland and New York: World, 1967. A prominent Christian philosopher and historian attempts to work out the relationship between painting and being. Interesting less for the author's theories than for all the other things he touches on during the course of his discussion.

GOMBRICH, ERNST H. *Art and Illusion*. New York: Pantheon, 1960. A masterful work on the psychology of representation in the visual arts. Erudite and entertaining.

HUYGHE, RENÉ. *Ideas and Images in World Art: Dialogue with the Visible*. Translated by Norbert Guterman. New York: Abrams, 1959. An incredibly suave presentation of the artistic expression of all ages and peoples by the former curator of painting in the Louvre.

PANOFSKY, ERWIN. *Meaning in the Visual Arts*. Garden City, N.Y.: Anchor Books, 1955. A collection of essays by a great iconographer, written over a period of more than thirty years and covering a wide variety of subjects.

II. Art History

I. GENERAL

CLARK, SIR KENNETH. *The Nude: A Study in Ideal Form*. New York: Pantheon, 1956. One of the world's foremost art historians explores the tradition of the nude in sculpture and painting from ancient to modern times. Beautifully written and comprehensible to the layman.

GARDNER, HELEN. *Art Throughout the Ages*. 5th ed., revised by Horst de la Croix and Richard G. Tansey. New York: Harcourt, Brace and Jovanovich, 1970. A superb revision of the most famous of all American art history texts (first published in 1926), far more scholarly than earlier editions of the work. However, the editors were forced to sacrifice the discussions of Asian, primitive, and Pre-Columbian art, which the 1936, 1948, and 1959 versions retained.

GOMBRICH, ERNST H. *The Story of Art*. 12th ed. rev. and enl. London: Phaidon, 1972. Written for English high school students, this is an incredibly good brief introduction to the history of art.

HARTT, FREDERICK. *Art: A History of Painting, Sculpture, and Architecture*. Englewood Cliffs, N.J.: Prentice-Hall, 1976. New York: Abrams, 1976.

HAUSER, ARNOLD. *The Social History of Art*. Translated in collaboration with the author by Stanley Godman. 2 vols. New York: Knopf, 1951. A synoptic history of art and literature from a sociological slant. Of amazing breadth, the work is rather heavy going for the unsophisticated, and one must be wary of the author's biases. But it is full of stimulating ideas.

JANSON, H. W. *The History of Art: A Survey of the Major Visual Arts from the Dawn of History to the Present Day*. Rev. and enl. ed. Englewood Cliffs, N.J.: Prentice-Hall, 1969. New York: Abrams, 1969. An excellent survey of the history of Western art. Highly informed, easy to read, and beautifully illustrated.

MALRAUX, ANDRÉ. *The Voices of Silence*. New York: Doubleday, 1953. A famous and highly effective work by the French novelist, scholar, and political thinker.

PEVSNER, NIKOLAUS. *An Outline of European Architecture*. 6th (Jubilee) ed. rev. Baltimore: Penguin Books, 1960. The best overview of the history of architecture in Europe.

SEWALL, JOHN IVES. *A History of Western Art*. Rev. ed. New York: Holt, Rinehart and Winston, 1961. A well-informed but rather dry text that does an especially good job with architecture—usually given rather short shrift in surveys of art history. The author is antagonistic to modern art, and in this revision John Canaday has been given the task of dealing with the late nineteenth and the twentieth century.

2. PREHISTORIC

GRAZIOSI, PAOLO. *Paleolithic Art*. New York: McGraw-Hill, 1960.

3. AFRICAN AND PRE-COLUMBIAN AMERICAN

KUBLER, GEORGE. *The Art and Architecture of Ancient America*. ("Pelican History of Art.") Baltimore: Penguin Books, 1962.

LOTHROP, S. K.; FOSHAG, W. E.; and MAHLER, J. *Pre-Columbian Art*. London: Phaidon, 1957.

WINGERT, PAUL S. *The Sculpture of Negro Africa*. New York: Columbia University Press, 1959.

4. EGYPTIAN

MICHALOWSKI, KAZIMIERZ. *Art of Ancient Egypt*. New York: Abrams, 1969.

5. ANCIENT NEAR EASTERN

LLOYD, SETON. *The Art of the Ancient Near East*. New York: Praeger, 1961.

6. AEGEAN

DEMARGNE, PIERRE. *Aegean Art: The Origins of Greek Art*. Translated by Stuart Gilbert and James Emmons. New York: Golden Press, 1964.

7. GREEK

ARIAS, PAOLO E., and HIRMER, MAX. *A History of 1000 Years of Greek Vase Painting*. New York: Abrams, 1963.

BOARDMAN, JOHN. *Greek Art*. New York: Praeger, 1964.

LAWRENCE, ARNOLD. *Greek Architecture*. ("Pelican History of Art.") Baltimore: Penguin Books, 1957.

LULLIES, REINHARD, and HIRMER, MAX. *Greek Sculpture*. New York: Abrams, 1960.

8. ETRUSCAN

RICHARDSON, EMELINE. *The Etruscans: Their Art and Civilization*. Chicago: University of Chicago Press, 1964.

9. ROMAN

WHEELER, SIR R. E. MORTIMER. *Roman Art and Architecture*. New York: Praeger, 1964.

10. EARLY CHRISTIAN AND BYZANTINE

GRABAR, ANDRÉ. *The Beginnings of Christian Art, 200–395*. Translated by Stuart Gilbert and James Emmons. London: Thames and Hudson, 1967.

MOREY, CHARLES RUFUS. *Christian Art*. New York: Longmans, Green, 1935.

VOLBACH, WOLFGANG F., and HIRMER, MAX. *Early Christian Art*. New York: Abrams, 1961.

11. MIDDLE AGES

BECKWITH, JOHN. *Early Medieval Art*. New York: Praeger, 1964.

FOCILLON, HENRI. *The Art of the West in the Middle Ages*. Edited by Jean Bony and translated by Donald King. 2 vols. New York: Phaidon, 1963.

FRANKL, PAUL. *The Gothic*. Princeton, N. J.: Princeton University Press, 1960.

——————. *Gothic Architecture*. Translated by

Dieter Pevsner. ("Pelican History of Art.") Baltimore: Penguin Books, 1962.

MÂLE, EMILE. *The Gothic Image: Religious Art in France of the Thirteenth Century.* Translated by Dora Nussey. New York: Harper, 1958.

12. RENAISSANCE (LATE GOTHIC)

PANOFSKY, ERWIN. *Early Netherlandish Painting.* 2 vols. Cambridge, Mass.: Harvard University Press, 1954.

WHITE, JOHN. *Art and Architecture in Italy, 1250–1400.* ("Pelican History of Art.") Baltimore: Penguin Books, 1966.

13. RENAISSANCE (GENERAL)

HARTT, FREDERICK. *History of Italian Renaissance Art: Painting, Sculpture, Architecture.* Englewood Cliffs, N.J.: Prentice-Hall, 1970. New York: Abrams, 1970.

14. RENAISSANCE (EARLY)

BURCKHARDT, JAKOB C. *The Civilization of the Renaissance in Italy.* Translated by S. G. Middlemore. 3rd rev. ed. London: Phaidon, 1963. A genuine classic in the history of art, first published in 1860.

DEWALD, ERNEST T. *Italian Painting, 1200–1600.* New York: Holt, Rinehart and Winston, 1961.

15. RENAISSANCE (HIGH)

FREEDBERG, SYDNEY J. *Painting of the High Renaissance in Rome and Florence.* 2 vols. Cambridge, Mass.: Harvard University Press, 1961.

16. RENAISSANCE (NORTHERN)

BENESCH, OTTO. *The Art of the Renaissance in Northern Europe.* Rev. ed. London: Phaidon, 1965.

STECHOW, WOLFGANG. *Northern Renaissance Art: Sources and Documents in the History of Art.* Englewood Cliffs, N.J.: Prentice-Hall, 1966.

17. MANNERIST

BOSQUET, JACQUES. *Mannerism, the Painting and Style of the Late Renaissance.* Translated by S. W. Taylor. New York: Braziller, 1964.

WÜRTENBERGER, FRANZSEPP. *Mannerism, the European Style of the Sixteenth Century.* Translated by Michael Heron. New York: Holt, Rinehart and Winston, 1963.

18. BAROQUE

BLUNT, SIR ANTHONY. *Art and Architecture in France, 1500–1700.* ("Pelican History of Art.") Baltimore: Penguin Books, 1957.

MILLON, HENRY A. *Baroque and Rococo Architecture.* New York: Braziller, 1961.

ROSENBERG, JAKOB; SLIVE, SEYMOUR; and TER KUILE, E. H. *Dutch Art and Architecture, 1600–1800.* ("Pelican History of Art.") Baltimore: Penguin Books, 1966.

STECHOW, WOLFGANG. *Rubens and the Classical Tradition.* Cambridge, Mass.: Oberlin College, Harvard University Press, 1968.

WATERHOUSE, ELLIS K. *Painting in Britain, 1530–1790.* 2nd ed. ("Pelican History of Art.") Baltimore: Penguin Books, 1962.

WITTKOWER, RUDOLF. *Art and Architecture in Italy, 1600–1750.* ("Pelican History of Art.") Baltimore: Penguin Books, 1958.

19. MODERN

ARNASON, H. H. *History of Modern Art: Painting, Sculpture, Architecture.* Englewood Cliffs, N.J.: Prentice-Hall, 1968. New York: Abrams, 1968.

CANADAY, JOHN. *Mainstreams of Modern Art.* New York: Holt, Rinehart and Winston, 1959. Unlike most texts on modern art, this one gives a good deal of attention to academic painting as the background for the development of modern styles.

HAMILTON, GEORGE HEARD. *19th and 20th Century Art: Painting, Sculpture, Architecture.* Englewood Cliffs, N.J.: Prentice-Hall, 1970. New York: Abrams, 1970.

20. AMERICAN

BROWN, MILTON; HUNTER, SAM; JACOBUS, JOHN; ROSENBLUM, NAOMI; and SOKOL, DAVID. *American Art.* Englewood Cliffs, N.J.: Prentice-Hall, 1979. New York: Abrams, 1979.

LARKIN, OLIVER W. *Art and Life in America.* New York: Holt, Rinehart and Winston, 1964.

MENDELOWITZ, DANIEL M. *A History of American Art.* New York: Holt, Rinehart and Winston, 1960.

21. ASIAN

ALEX, WILLIAM. *Japanese Architecture.* New York: Braziller, 1963.

LEE, SHERMAN. *A History of Far Eastern Art.* New York: Abrams, 1964.

ROWLAND, BENJAMIN. *The Art and Architecture of India: Buddhist, Hindu, Jain.* ("Pelican History of Art.") Baltimore: Penguin Books, 1953.

SICKMAN, LAURENCE and SOPER, ALEXANDER. *The Art and Architecture of China.* 2nd ed. ("Pelican History of Art.") Baltimore: Penguin Books, 1960.

YASHIRO, YUKIO. *2000 Years of Japanese Art.* New York: Abrams, 1958. A beautiful book, but almost exclusively devoted to painting.

III. Color Theory

BIRREN, FABER. *Color, Form, and Space.* New York: Reinhold, 1961.

ITTEN, JOHANNES. *The Art of Color.* New York: Reinhold, 1961.

MAERZ, A., and PAUL, M. REA. *A Dictionary of Color.* New York: McGraw-Hill, 1950.

IV. Ceramics

LAKOFSKY, CHARLES. *Pottery.* Dubuque, Iowa: William C. Brown, 1968.

NELSON, GLEN. *Ceramics.* 2nd ed. New York: Holt, Rinehart and Winston, 1966.

V. Commercial Art and Cartooning

BECKER, STEPHEN. *Comic Art in America.* New York: Simon and Schuster, 1959.

BRUNNER, FELIX. *A Handbook of Graphic Reproduction Processes.* New York: Hastings, 1962.

COUPERIE, PIERRE, and HORN, MAURICE C. *A History of the Comic Strip.* Translated by Eileen E. Hennessy. New York: Crown, 1968.

NELSON, ROY P., and FERRIS, BYRON. *Fell's Guide to Commercial Art.* New York: Frederick Fell, 1966. Contains an extensive bibliography.

RICHARDSON, JOHN ADKINS. *The Complete Book of Cartooning.* Englewood Cliffs, N.J.: Prentice-Hall, 1977.

VI. Drawing

BRIDGMAN, GEORGE. *Life Drawing.* New York: Dover, 1970. An old standby.

MENDELOWITZ, DANIEL M. *Drawing.* New York: Holt, Rinehart and Winston, 1966. Very complete, covering all media and techniques as well as the history of drawing.

NICOLAIDES, KIMON. *The Natural Way to Draw.* Boston: Houghton Mifflin, 1941. A complete drawing course from a rather Expressionistic point of departure.

WATSON, ERNEST W. *How to Use Creative Perspective.* New York: Reinhold, 1955.

VII. Film

SPOTTISWOODE, RAYMOND. *Film and Its Techniques.* Berkeley and Los Angeles: University of California Press, 1966.

WHITAKER, ROD. *The Language of Film.* Englewood Cliffs, N. J.: Prentice-Hall, 1970.

VIII. Jewelry

GRANSTROM, K. E. *Creating with Metal.* New York: Reinhold, 1968.

MORTON, PHILIP G. *Contemporary Jewelry: A Studio Handbook.* New York: Holt, Rinehart and Winston, 1970.

IX. Painting

DOERNER, MAX. *The Materials of the Artist and Their Use in Painting.* Translated by Eugen Neuhaus. Rev. ed. New York: Harcourt, Brace, 1949. The classic in the field. Very scholarly and extremely historical in its approach.

MAYER, RALPH. *The Artist's Handbook of Materials and Techniques.* 3rd ed. rev. New York: Viking, 1970. The most popular of the technical manuals. It contains an extensive bibliography.

MAROGER, JACQUES. *The Secret Formulas and Techniques of the Masters.* Translated by Eleanor Beckham. New York: Studio Publications, 1948.

X. Photography

GERNSHEIM, HELMUT, and GERNSHEIM, ALISON. *Concise History of Photography.* New York: Grosset and Dunlap, 1965.

NEWHALL, BEAUMONT, and NEWHALL, N. W. *Masters of Photography.* New York: Braziller, 1958.

ZIM, HERBERT S., and BURNETT, R. WILL. *Photography.* New York: Simon and Schuster, 1956.

XI. Printmaking

BIEGELEISEN, J. I. *Screen Printing.* New York: Watson-Guptill, 1971.

HELLER, JULES. *Printmaking Today.* New York: Holt, Rinehart and Winston, 1958.

PETERDI, GABOR. *Printmaking: Methods Old and New.* New York: Macmillan, 1959.

ROTHENSTEIN, MICHAEL. *Relief Printing.* New York: Watson-Guptill, 1970.

XII. Sculpture

MILLS, JOHN W. *The Technique of Sculpture.* New York: Reinhold, 1965.

SELZ, JEAN. *Modern Sculpture, Origins and Evolution.* Translated by Annette Michelson. New York: Braziller, 1963.

XIII. Textiles

ALBERS, ANNI. *On Weaving.* Middletown, Conn.: Wesleyan University Press, 1965.

JOHNSTON, MEDA PARKER, and KAUFMAN, GLEN. *Design on Fabrics.* New York: Reinhold, 1967.

KREVITSKY, NIK. *Batik: Art and Craft.* Rev. ed. New York: Reinhold, 1967.

XIV. Wood

ROTTGER, ERNST. *Creative Wood Design.* New York: Reinhold, 1961.

WILLCOX, DONALD. *Wood Design.* New York: Watson-Guptill, 1968.

Index

Page numbers are in roman type. Figure numbers of black-and-white illustrations are in *italics*. Colorplates are specifically so designated. Names of artists whose works are discussed are in CAPITALS. Titles of works of art are in *italics*.

Photo Credits

The author and publisher wish to thank the libraries, museums, galleries, and private collectors named in the picture captions for permitting the reproduction of works of art in their collections, and for supplying the necessary photographs. Photographs from other sources are gratefully acknowledged below.

A.C.L., Brussels: 262; Alinari, Florence: 37, 46, 47, 48, 49, 51, 52, 54, 78, 80, 82, 87, 90, 121, 131, 147, 150, 160, 167, 170, 188, 189, 190, 208, 209, 227, 229, 254, 255, 260, 263, 265, 322, 327, 357, 360, 372, 374, 375, 378; Anderson, Rome: 85, 251, 319, 377; Wayne Andrews, Grosse Pointe, Mich.: 381; T. & R. Annan, Glasgow: 386; Archives Photographiques, Paris: 11, 55, 271; E. Irving Blomstrann, New Britain, Conn.: 123, 279, 313; Brogi, Florence: 373; Geoffrey Clements, New York: 237, 240; Deutsche Fotothek, Dresden: 285; A. Dinghan, The Hague: 117; French Government Tourist Office, New York: 365, 368, 369, 371, 382, 383, 384; Giraudon, Paris: 140, 267, 281, 284, 286; Hedrich-Blessing, Chicago: 77, 373, 387; G. E. Kidder Smith, New York: 379; Marburg Art Reference Bureau: 376; Photo MAS, Barcelona: 44, 45, 137, 359; M.I.T. Press, Cambridge, Mass.: 393, from Paolo Soleri, *Arcology: The City in the Image of Man*; City of Montreal: 392; Museum of Modern Art, New York: 391; O.K. Harris Gallery, New York: 228; Ad Peterson, Amsterdam: 6; Philadelphia Museum of Art: 352; Eric Pollitzer, New York: 8, 239; Edouard Renner, Frankfort: 380; John A. Richardson, Edwardsville, Ill.: 7, 20, 21, 99, 100, 169; Jean Roubier, Paris: 366; Service Photographique, Paris: 9, 53, 68, 89, 91, 102, 129, 139, 151, 156, 232, 236, 248, 282, 283, 287, 291; Shunk-Kender, New York: 318; Soprintendenza alle Antichità, Rome: 84; Walter Steinkopf, Berlin (Dahlem): 206, 231, 258; Eric Sutherland, Minneapolis: 92; Cole Weston, Carmel, Calif.: 81; A.J. Wyatt, Philadelphia: 311, 326.